IRELAND AND THE THREAT OF NUCLEAR WAR

Ireland and the threat of nuclear war

THE QUESTION OF IRISH NEUTRALITY

Edited by **BILL McSWEENEY**

DOMINICAN PUBLICATIONS

First published (1985) by
Dominican Publications
St Saviour's, Dublin 1

in association with

The Department of Peace Studies
Irish School of Ecumenics
Bea House, 20 Pembroke Park, Dublin 4

ISBN 0-907271-52-9

Cover design by Design and Art Facilities Ltd

Typeset and printed by
The Leinster Leader Ltd
Naas, Co. Kildare

Contents

Contributors

Georgi A. Arbatov is one of the Soviet Union's foremost Western experts and a world authority on East-West relations. Academician and member of the Central Committee of the Communist party of the Soviet Union, he is Director of the Institute of the United States and Canada in the USSR.

Desmond Dinan lectures in Peace Studies at the Irish School of Ecumenics. He has studied modern history and political science at the National Institute of Higher Education, Limerick, University College Cork, and Georgetown University Washington.

Patrick Keatinge is Associate Professor of Political Science at Trinity College, Dublin. He is author of several books on Irish foreign policy, including *A place among the nations* (1978) and *A singular stance: Irish neutrality in the eighties*, IPA, Dublin, 1984

Alan Kreider is an American Church historian and a prominent Mennonite who has done much to promote Mennonite literature and values. He is currently engaged in research on nuclear disarmament at the London Mennonite Church.

Bill McSweeney is former Lecturer in the Department of Sociology at the University of York, now head of the Department of Peace Studies, Irish School of Ecumenics. He is author of *Roman Catholicism: the search for relevance*, Blackwell's, Oxford, 1982

Jurgen Moltmann is Professor of Systematic Theology in the University of Tubingen. He is author of several well-known books, among them *Theology of hope*, *The crucified God* and *The Trinity and the kingdom of God*.

Paul Oestreicher is a priest of the Church of England, and General Secretary of the Division of International Affairs in the British Council of Churches. He is author of several noted books and articles and co-author of *The Church and the bomb*, Hodder and Stoughton, London, 1982.

Adam Roberts is Reader in International Relations at Oxford University and Professorial Fellow of St Antony's College, Oxford. He is a world authority on civil and territorial defence and author of *Nations in arms: the theory and practice of territorial defence*, Chatto and Windus, London, 1976

Foreword

This book is intended as a contribution to public debate on an issue of
great political and moral importance to Irish people. Democracy is
never perfect, but there is a growing fear in many Western societies
that public participation in vital areas of policy is being unduly
limited and that the process of decision-making is being unjustifiably
hidden from public scrutiny until it is too late to correct it. Even in
Ireland, reasons of 'national security' are too readily invoked to
hinder the democratic process, with the likely consequence that
secrecy will become more pervasive and acceptable within our institutions and cynicism about leadership will spread more extensively
among our people.

   Most of the papers contained here were commissioned for
seminars and conferences organised by the Department of Peace
Studies, Irish School of Ecumenics, or were written specially for this
book by members of the School's academic staff. It is earnestly
hoped that their publication will stimulate informed debate within the
churches, political parties, trade-unions, media and wherever Irish
people have a voice to be heard on the central questions of their own
prosperity, security and conscience.

Austin Flannery, O.P.
CHAIRMAN OF THE BOARD
IRISH SCHOOL OF ECUMENICS

1   Introduction: Some Arguments against Irish Neutrality

Bill McSweeney

This book is a product of the work of the Department of Peace Studies, Irish School of Ecumenics, and its publication has a particular purpose. It seeks to analyze a process of government which could have enormous political and moral consequences for the people of Ireland, but the reality of which is not open to public scrutiny and accessible to public control. It seeks to educate and to convince, and it carries the hope that Irish people and their political leaders — many of whom are valued friends of the Irish School of Ecumenics — will reflect on the implications of Irish foreign policy and take action to bring it in line with the principles they avow.

The Irish School of Ecumenics is a research and teaching institute, founded in Dublin in 1970. Like all academic institutes, its aim is to promote the growth of knowledge and learning through the application of logic and conceptual analysis on a body of factual and literary evidence. And like all academic disciplines, it starts from certain moral assumptions which function to direct the progress of work and the selection of relevant evidence. In the Department of Peace Studies, set up to extend the School's interest in the reconciliation of divided communities into the wider area of human and political conflict in general, the aim is similarly to study the evidence objectively and to construct arguments and opinions methodically into a body of knowledge. But not just any evidence, by any method which comes to hand. Like the disciplines of medicine, politics, anthropology, war studies, we start from a certain purpose and preconception which organize the work and move it towards a particular end. Just as medical researchers do not study disease simply to marvel at it, but to cure and prevent it; just as war students study organized violence in order to resolve it by the most efficient application of force, so we are concerned with the general problem of conflict in order to understand its source and to devise methods of peacemaking, conflict tolerance and the resolution of violence by the minimum application of force. We are not disinterested academics, nor are we pacifists, but students of the politics of peacemaking.

Within these limits, more apparent in some disciplines than in others, a respect for evidence — for what Max Weber called 'inconvenient facts' — is a virtue inseparable from any academic enterprise. This virtue is not just a qualification for acceptance within the academic community; it is also an essential component in the quality control of teaching and research. It is not very difficult to practice it in the area of ecumenism, since this work of the School is largely defined by the imbalance institutionalized in the divided communities of christendom and religious belief. But in Peace Studies, as in sociology and politics generally, the temptation of fashion and the pressure from interest groups places a constant strain on virtue. At best, we have no truths to impart, only a case to advance respectfully, if vigorously, inviting response and debate from all who are willing to keep their own prejudices in check. We are not aiming at balance, in the sense tediously exemplified in some media programmes, but at the presentation of a cogent argument, deriving from basic assumptions, which takes account of the inconvenient facts so that it may convince, but which is open to correction by a better case.

On the subject of Irish neutrality, different arguments are offered in this book which, taken together, tend broadly to support it. It may be useful, therefore, to recall for readers and to discuss some of the objections to this position which are not specifically addressed elsewhere. Obviously there are other arguments and other ways of expressing those which follow. They are not presented as a gesture towards balance. They are intended, rather, as a stimulus to discussion, in the conviction that the case for neutrality as an instrument of peacemaking is more compelling when set against the contrary arguments — only the sixth and last of which here causes some difficulty, at least to the author.

OBJECTIONS TO NEUTRALITY

1. *The gut reaction.* This refers, for want of a better title, to a sizeable body of feeling, innuendo and unargued comment in the writings of some politicians, journalists and historians, who are clearly unhappy with Ireland's ambiguous position and want it resolved once and for all. As far as one can determine it, the case rests on the fact of this ambiguity, not on any serious examination of the implications of NATO or some NATO-equivalent. Because we're the odd-man-out in the EEC, we had better join a military alliance; because we were never *really* neutral, we cannot be so now; because we're Christian, because we're Western, because we're small, because we're poor, because we're in Europe, because neutrality won't save

us in a nuclear war . . . because the whole thing is a sham and a shibboleth . . . The argument is often left to speak for itself. The reader has already got the message between the lines of the discussion of neutrality or the EEC which led up to it, and the writer does not have the still-embarrassing job of concluding the case for NATO.

This gut response to the problem is not by any means the monopoly of charlatans and opportunists, or even of simple ideologues. It is sometimes the inference drawn by honest and talented politicians and writers whose casual conclusion contrasts sharply with the detail and quality of their writing or speeches. There is an amazing blandness about this support for a defence alliance, as if it were simply a harmless arrangement like a trade pact or a friendship treaty which any decent person would advocate if it helped things along. It is something of the same tone used to whip up support in Europe for the arms procurement programme — tanks for efficiency, guns for butter, weapons for jobs . . . no problem! The absence of sustained debate and informed discussion of what a military alliance would mean for Ireland in the nuclear age, the absence of any attempt to investigate NATO strategy and its claims about Soviet intentions, above all the absence of any sign of genuine moral concern about NATO's share in the arms-race — what Thomas Merton described as 'the greatest moral evil since the crucifixion' — these gaps in the consciousness of otherwise widely-read and intelligent people point to a disturbing level of apathy and unawareness in the country as a whole. It is like reading a perceptive analysis of the Second World War which gives a footnote to the massacre of the Jews.

Consider the logic. Ireland's neutrality was not consistent, nor was it principled. It does not follow from this that it is a sham; but even if that is allowed, by what reasoning are we therefore invited to join a military alliance? There are other possibilities which are not presented and there is the moral dimension which is ignored. The mere fact that the rest of the EEC is in NATO does not mean that we have to join too, rather than fighting our case to be different. The rest of the EEC has fairly permissive laws on abortion. Should the Irish join them in that too? Even if Strasbourg tries to make it a condition of membership?

My reason for combining these objections to neutrality under the same heading, 'gut reaction', is not that a case cannot be made for the reasons they hint at, but because this kind of nudge-into-NATO discourages debate and is becoming more prevalent. It alludes to reasons of common-sense and decency and appeals to a rational, no-nonsense mentality, by presenting neutrality as many politicians saw it in the past and as some economists see it today, ignoring the other aspects which might make NATO appear indecent and neutrality sensible. And this is precisely what civil servants and governments have been doing with neutrality since 1962 — gradually weakening its public image, reassuring us that nothing much was happening, hinting at global threats and tensions which could justify setting up the compromising links with NATO, preparing for the day when this gentle persuasion has done its work and the people can be asked to choose between a now-discredited neutrality and a virtually established military alliance. It is not open government which is at issue here but an elementary right to choose on a matter of great consequence and to have the facts to enable us to make that choice before governments create the conditions which will make these facts irrelevant.

2. *The political objection to neutrality.* This and other objections which follow have the merit of being arguments rather than insinuations and, I think, of being a comprehensive, if brief, account of the main obstacles to neutrality which need to be considered in the Irish context. The political question refers to a number of related arguments, principally the fact that the division of the world into power blocs — whatever its evil or justification — is a fact we must live with. Though we cannot prove that deterrence works — only a war can prove that it does not — nonetheless the absence of a major war in Europe for forty years is an incalculable benefit which cannot be thrown away in favour of the unknowable alliances which would inevitably follow it, with a redistribution of nuclear weapons that no one could predict. Since we cannot get rid of the weapons, we are better off trying to stabilize the alliance. If this means risk and blood on our hands by theologians' criteria, it is a better gamble and morally preferable to the risk and blood that might follow a break-up of the existing powerblocs.

This is the kind of sober, realist argument favoured by policy analysts in Britain over the more shrill, moralist versions of it common in the United States.[1] From an Irish perspective, it faces us with the fact that we cannot avoid living in a world of nuclear weapons and we must choose between evils. It encourages the acceptability of NATO, not as a preferable alliance in itself, but simply as a balance to the Soviet bloc. And since it is politically impossible to join the Warsaw Treaty Organization, it opens the door to NATO by removing any moral inhibitions — above all for those who are already persuaded that our interests would be better served there. The argument makes a strong case against utopianism and moralism of a

1. See, for example, Laurence Freedman: *The Evolution of Nuclear Strategy*, Macmillan, 1981; Michael Howard: *Causes of War*, Temple Smith, 1982.

more pacifist kind and, if it paints a dismal picture for the indefinite future, it would be foolish not to recognise that nuclear weapons can only be controlled now, they cannot be abolished.

But how do we move from this realism, which seeks to preserve the precarious balance of power as it presently exists in the world between NATO and the Soviet bloc, to the position that Ireland should join NATO? For what it's worth, realism supports the opposite view, that Ireland should *not* join NATO but should remain neutral. Respect for the balance of power as it exists — quite apart for any moral judgment of the matter — should encourage existing members of the blocs to remain where they are and existing neutrals to remain neutral and avoid upsetting the balance. This is precisely the argument of British analysts against those who say Britain should leave NATO and it will certainly be the Soviet argument against Ireland abandoning neutrality.[2]

The shift from stark realism at the global level to justification of Ireland's membership of NATO in some form is equally question-able in some other versions of the argument. Political isolation, the loss of Ireland's opportunity to contribute to disarmament within NATO and the corollary that neutrality has had its day and is now politically useless for achieving either national or international goals — these are fallacious arguments which cannot be tagged on to the realistic acceptance of competition between the superpowers.

Political isolation may reasonably suggest itself as a consequence of some proposals for neutrality in Ireland, which emphasise the negative, military tradition in the context of total rejection of the EEC and of any alliance which requires Ireland to sacrifice some of its independence and autonomy. Isolation is further suggested by the image of neutrality popularized by all the major military powers — on this point, at least, prestigious Western opinion agrees fully with Soviet, for obvious reasons. This tacit, multilateral agreement to downgrade neutrality has undoubtedly succeeded in lowering its status and making it difficult for an aspiring neutral to win public support at home and international recognition abroad for a policy often seen as 'indifferent', 'self-centered', 'opportunist', 'short-sighted'. The United Nations, being itself the creation and, partly, the instrument of the major powers, has been a party to this process of definition in the way its Charter and machinery were construed — if not to exclude neutrality, at least to demonstrate its deviance within a community of collective security.[3]

---

2. In fact the point has already been made in the official Soviet newspaper *Izvestia*, which appealed to Ireland during the Haughey-Thatcher stage of the Anglo-Irish talks, not to be drawn into NATO. See *The Irish Times* 20.3.81. For the British argument mentioned see Lawrence Freedman: *ADIU Report*, Vol. 2, no. 4, 1980.

3. Nils Orvik: *The Decline of Neutrality 1914-1941*, Cass, 1971, p. 257ff.

But this pejorative idea of neutrality reflects a now-outdated version of the consensus view in the decade after World War II and it is based on a distorted picture of the role of neutrality drawn by the victorious Allies, who were by then intoxicated with the sense of righteousness and humanitarian concern which they discovered to be their motives for joining the fight against Hitler. The British opinion of Irish neutrality during the war, the common opinion of Swiss neutrality and the fear that others would refuse the sacrifices deemed necessary for averting another war contributed to the pejorative view. It was a distortion even in the mid-forties, before modern conceptions of neutrality made it clear that self-interested isolation in time of war was only one model among many which neutral states could aspire to. In the 1930s, Sweden and the Scandinavian countries tried to establish a form of collective security which would modify their individual neutrality, but would be based on the neutrality of Scandinavia. Later, in 1949, the Karlstad Plan envisaged a similar collective neutrality and security outside NATO.[4] So it is not the case that neutrality and collective security are entirely incompatible, though it is increasingly difficult, in a two-power world, to see the possibilities. And the reason for this is the unwillingness of the superpowers to restrict themselves to clearly-defined collective security, but rather to use the term as a gloss for mutual provocation and the arms-race. A neutral country willing to join in a military alliance set up to defend others against an aggressor — provided the aggression was not triggered by bloc membership in peacetime — this is certainly not the standard view of indifference and isolationism. On the contrary, it is a conception of neutrality wholly in line with the spirit and aspirations, if not the actuality, of the United Nations, given that the UN saw collective security as a mechanism of peace*making* — requiring a standing UN army to enforce it — but had to be content with a symbolic version of collective security and the capacity, in times of conflict, to recruit military forces for peace*keeping*.

During the formation of the United Nations, the Swedish government officially declared:

> We are willing to join a collective organization for security, and in case of a future conflict abstain from neutrality to the extent that the organization may want us. However, if there should appear within this organization, a tendency among the great powers toward a partition into two groups, then it must be our policy not to be driven into such group-making or formation of blocs.[5]

4. *Ibid.*, p. 259.
5. *Ibid.*, p. 260.

This was Sweden's position in 1945. By the 1960s, this determination to avoid war, but not at the expense of others, had developed into a policy of active peacemaking in a world gradually becoming aware of the instability of deterrence and the possibility of neutrality, non-alignment and nuclear-free zones as a counter to the brinkmanship of the superpowers and as a possible basis of a new role for neutrality in peacetime. As Adam Roberts says, 'it makes it possible for Sweden to occupy a position of moral strength rather than weakness and to create a situation in which the neutral Swedes could lecture to the Americans on the subject of immorality'.[6]

Political isolation, therefore, is not a necessary consequence of neutrality. The conditions today are not those of the early fifties. The possibility is there for an initiative to capitalise on the changing awareness of power blocs and neutrality and to raise the status and diplomatic effectiveness of neutrality — if the will is there. As for the idea of joining a military alliance like NATO in order to use bloc membership responsibly to promote disarmament, it is scarcely necessary to expose this gullible view of NATO's role and the role of smaller nations within it. It is comparable to the notion that common arms procurement will limit the effects of the arms-trade; similar to the bizarre view that retaining an independent nuclear deterrent gives Britain an effective voice in disarmament negotiations and a positive function in the vital process of peacemaking.

3.   *The ideological objection to neutrality.* Since the foundation of the state, Ireland has declared its ideological partiality to the West and to the Christian world. And increasingly since 1962, the fact that 'we are not ideologically neutral' has been repeated by several leading politicians as if it had grave political implications for national security. Our officials today do not often admit to being plainly anti-Communist and ready to fight for Christianity and freedom at whatever cost to neutrality.[7] They repeat the required phrase from their briefing manual in order to impress the conditional nature of Irish neutrality and emphasize the historical continuity which will facilitate a future alliance with NATO in some form. There are three arguments related to this emphasis on ideology. Firstly, that we must take sides in the Cold War, not only morally against Communism which is alien to our culture, but politically for NATO, since it is the Soviet bloc which threatens aggression and the destruction of Western civilization and ourselves with it. This argument is addressed in Chapter Four.

A second related argument is that our security is being gained on

6. Adam Roberts: *Nations in Arms*, Chatto & Windus, London, 1976, p. 79.
7. Jack Lynch was probably the last of the prime-ministerial warrior Christians: see Dáil debates, 241:631ff.

the cheap. We are free-riders on the NATO train, sheltering under the NATO umbrella but refusing to make even the minimal sacrifice of membership. Whether we like it or not, NATO protects us from the greatest — and, indeed, only — threat to our survival. This is not only immoral, but it is also politically unwise, since it gives us no opportunity to cooperate in our own defence and to modify in our own interests those aspects of it which relate to NATO strategy for Ireland.

This is a complex argument, somewhat similar to Churchill's simpler view that 'small nations must not tie our hands when we are fighting for their rights and freedom'.[8] The frequent assertion today by critics of neutrality that we ought to pay for the shelter given us is taken to be self-evident, though it rests on unstated assumptions: that the West is, in fact, threatened by the Soviet Union, and Ireland with it as part of the West; that NATO is not threatening Ireland but protecting her, rather as Churchill did in the Second World War; that Ireland desires NATO's protection and, logically, could do something to escape from it if she wished.[9]

Obviously, no one can prove that there is no Soviet threat. Those who like to believe there is, will find enough evidence to satisfy them in the extracts from the writings of Marx and Lenin compiled in the standard texts which are required reading for ideologues in the West. Those who are willing to question it will find a growing volume of literature from the United States and the UK which analyses Soviet foreign policy with the same fairness and rigour applied to American. The second and third assumptions can be taken together: what is the protection of NATO for which Ireland should be grateful? Here again, Churchill is a guide to the interpretation of the moral sentiments of a military power. Preparing the infringement of Norwegian neutrality which triggered the German invasion of Norway in April 1940, he wrote that the war might have been very short if all the neutrals had joined with the Allies:

> We have the greatest sympathy for those forlorn countries, and we understand their dangers and their point of view; but it would not be right, or in the general interest, that their weakness should feed the aggressor's strength and fill to overflowing the cup of human woe. There can be no justice if in a mortal struggle the aggressor tramples down every sentiment of humanity and if those who resist him remain entangled in the tatters of legal conventions.[10]

8. Winston S. Churchill: *Into Battle: War Speeches*, London, 1942, p. 432.
9. This argument was made, less explicitly, by the highly-respected Deputy Director of the Institute of Strategic Studies, Colonel Jonathan Alford, at the ICEM Seminar 29 April 1983.
10. Churchill, *op. cit.*, p. 181/2.

There is not the slightest doubt that NATO, too, has no intention of filling to overflowing the cup of human woe. Ireland is targeted as a contingency by NATO as surely as Sweden.[11] And if that is not quite the threat that should frighten us, we should at least remember that Norway's neutrality would certainly have survived — since it was in Germany's interest to respect it — if Britain had not first infringed it.

Provided we assume there is a Soviet threat to Ireland, there is some sense in which NATO protects us. But who protects us from NATO? Perhaps there is a reason for joining the alliance, but it is certainly not gratitude for NATO's 'protection'. That kind of logic should urge us to contribute to the British Health Service on the grounds that it provides our entire abortion service without cost to our government and makes it possible for us to keep our hands clean.

A third argument, drawn from the fact that we are not ideologically neutral, rests on a mistaken view of the status of neutrality. It claims that we cannot be neutral unless we are ideologically impartial with respect to the Eastern and Western blocs. This argument rests on the idea that neutrality is simply the legal status determining its possibility. It misunderstands the law and it confuses peacetime and wartime behaviour in their relation to the rules of war. There is nothing in international law bearing on neutrality which determines the relations of a neutral state during peacetime. Legal neutrality is a wartime policy. The law, for what it is worth, places no barrier to neutrality for a nation which is ideologically close to one of the belligerents. Nor does it demand ideological impartiality even during a war. The emphasis of the Hague Conventions and London Declarations of 1907-9 is on impartiality, not with respect to ideology or culture, but to some of the likely consequences of ideology, such as trade, communication links, ease of physical access, possibility of recruitment, propaganda and suchlike. It concerns all the factors De Valera was concerned to be officially impartial about during World War II and there is no doubt that De Valera fulfilled the requirements of the law, just as the other neutrals did.[12] From a strictly legal point of view, neutrality does not require a change in normal trade patterns, nor any change in an existing cultural or religious affinity with either of the parties in conflict.

The fact is that international law is only a minor factor determining the possibility of neutrality. It has been clear from the First World War — and all the more so from the second — that the successful

11. Michael Howard: 'NATO and the year of Europe' in *Survival*, February 1974, p. 23.
12. Ireland attended a meeting of European neutrals to co-ordinate policy and establish rules of neutrality in May 1938. See Orvik *op. cit.*, p. 217.

declaration of neutrality depends almost entirely on the political will expressing the consensus of the people and, secondly, on the capacity of a nation to accomplish its neutrality. Neutrality is an accomplishment, not a fact, and it depends on a multitude of factors outside the control of the neutral state — such as geography, resources, belligerent needs and strategies — and on many within its control which can be used to manipulate the external factors. Even in World War II, it was becoming clear that successful neutrality required careful peacetime planning and preparation — as Norway found out to her cost. Today, this is all the more true — it would be foolish to expect Ireland, pursuing present policies, to be able to accomplish neutrality in the event of war simply by declaring it. Furthermore, the conditions obtaining today make a declaration of military neutrality in the event of war absurd unless it is understood as the declaratory basis of a policy of neutrality in peacetime.[13] For it is only an involved, active, peacetime neutrality which will contribute to a reduction of the tensions leading to war and to the creation of the conditions at home which may mitigate its effects.

Is not peacetime neutrality even more at odds with not being ideologically neutral? This depends on what our government leaders mean by the phrase. If they mean that we are ideologically anti-Soviet then they should say so and put the logical implication to the test by requiring us to join NATO. If they mean that we are culturally and religiously oriented to the West, not to the East, this is certainly true. And it is true also of Switzerland, Sweden, Finland, Austria, Yugoslavia and to a lesser extent of East Germany, Poland — none of which countries find it a compelling argument to join NATO, or even a significant point to make in respect of their foreign policy.

4. *The economic objection to neutrality.* This refers primarily, of course, to the EEC benefits which are commonly assumed to be threatened by Ireland's reluctance to abandon neutrality. As the argument will be discussed at length in Chapter Eight, it is only useful here to make a general point. As with the supposed threat of Soviet invasion, so with the threat of economic loss, we have yet to read a coherent case for either. The former is highly contentious, yet it is asserted — or, more often, taken for granted — as if it were self-evident; the latter has acquired the credibility of a political fact. It would be of great interest to establish it, if it were true. It is a sad reflection on the provincialism of Irish life that the hearsay of NATO ideologues and European bureaucrats should become the dogmas of Irish politics without apparently any independent effort to establish

13. Military neutrality today stands in relation to active neutrality rather as chastity to traditional religious life; in itself it is negative and, at best, pointless. Its only function is to provide the opportunity for a richer involvement with others.

the facts. Even if it were true that our economic welfare in Europe is being made conditional on joining a military alliance, political leadership requires that we examine strategies of resistance to that pressure instead of doffing the nation's cap to the Genschers and Thorns of Europe. Ireland needs a strong European involvement; it does not need to fall into line with every policy adopted by its European partners.

The other main economic problem will be considered in the following section.

5.   *The military objection to neutrality.* We have neither the money nor the equipment to defend our neutrality. This objection was given publicity following the statements of the former Chief of Staff, General Carl O'Sullivan, in his address to a seminar on 'The Future of Neutrality' at the Irish School of Ecumenics. Though O'Sullivan's point was that we should not glibly talk of being neutral if we are not prepared to pay the cost, it was widely understood as an authoritative recommendation that Ireland should join NATO.

Adam Roberts is an international authority on territorial defence and it would be presumptuous to add to what he writes in Chapter Two. But some general points in relation to cost can be made. The fact that Sweden and Switzerland spend vast sums on weapons and equipment and military forces to protect their neutral status does not mean than an adequate defence of Ireland is not possible within our existing resources. Any smaller nation can only hope to deter the infringement of neutrality. Paradoxically, this minimum deterrence is cheaper with respect to nuclear war than conventional, particularly for a country whose geographic situation gives it minor strategic significance only to one side of the conflict — it would be unthinkable that the Soviet bloc would attempt to occupy Ireland as a base for war-fighting as it might consider it in relation to any of the other European neutrals. Even in the Second World War, Ireland's potential to Germany was not a factor seriously considered by the British. And De Valera succeeded in making a small prize too costly for the British to take with negligible territorial defence preparations.

While, theoretically, defence needs must be assessed in relation to the actual forces capable of infringing neutrality, all neutrals must accept that there is no defence of a military kind against the will of the superpowers. Neutrality can only be protected by a combination of symbolic and political strategies based on organized resistance and spoiling tactics — and, ultimately, on the well-publicized will of government and people to resist and to spoil.

International law is a poor guide to the accomplishment of neutrality strategy. What matters is the diplomatic and military planning, based on careful independent assessment of international interests and changing strategies, to create the public image of a determination to resist, to neutralize possible strategic utilities and to avoid in peacetime any suspicion of military or quasi-military co-operation with either party which might be a prize or target in the event of conflict. It is consistent with the provincialism of our political life and an indicator of the drift of thought on the subject that, on the military question as on the EEC, we have apparently given little thought to the independent assessment of these problems, content instead to rest our future on the clichés of dominant British and European opinion. To use Swiss or Swedish military expenditure as the standard for dismissing the possibility of territorial defence in Ireland is inappropriate. We do not have their problems, their geography, their military traditions. And the essence of the defence of a smaller nation, in the long run, is not military hardware put peace-time planning, negotiation and commitment. While any neutral will use whatever financial resources it has to build a strong symbolic and military structure to make an invasion uncomfortable, the fact that such deterrence must now be directed towards nuclear powers and towards the possibility of nuclear war minimizes the advantages of wealth. The technological nature of nuclear war makes neutral terri-tories less significant to belligerents but impossible to defend at whatever cost against a belligerent superpower.

Above all, the impossibility of an extended period of war between the superpowers makes for two important consequences: the strategic invasion and occupation of a small, marginal country like Ireland, far into enemy territory and surrounded by enemy forces is unlikely in a protracted conventional war; it is unthinkable in a nuclear war. Secondly, even if it succeeded, the war-time cost of infringed neutrality in a nuclear war will be no worse and, probably, far less than the suffering in war which would follow our military coopera-tion with NATO. As far as Ireland's suffering in a nuclear war is con-cerned, it would be foolish or mischievous to suggest that our interests would be better served within, rather than outside a military alliance. At worst, a neutral Ireland would suffer a very short occupation in no way comparable to the infringement of neutrality suffered by Norway in the Second World War and Belgium in the First, though, of course, the fact of now being a target of nuclear weapons like the NATO countries could make brevity irrelevant. At best, a neutral Ireland might avoid the worst effect of war and also avoid active complicity in the massacre of millions of Soviet people in the name of freedom.

Between these extremes lies the fallout factor. There is a peculiar coincidence in effect, as regards the wartime significance of neutrality, between the government tactic of downgrading its value and certain views prominent in the peace movement negating the wartime usefulness of neutrality. Neutrality can only save us if it is used actively to promote détente and the reduction of risk – it cannot save us in a nuclear war, it is said.

Since we have not yet had a nuclear war it is impossible to be certain how the neutrals will fare. What is certain is that all the evidence points (a) to the extensiveness of explosive damage; (b) to the greater extensiveness and relative unpredictability of radioactive fallout; and (c) to the fact that a neutral Ireland, by virtue of its geographic and climatic conditions, is in the most privileged position of all the neutrals in Europe. A merely military neutrality which looked only to saving Irish skins during a nuclear war would be an immoral and senseless policy, fundamentally because it couldn't work. It would lack the elements of international involvement and moral conviction which are essential to create the will and the consensus to make it work.

But without the realistic component of hard-nosed self-interest it wouldn't work either. It is short-sighted to focus a neutrality campaign – which must confront the carrots of economic self-interest and ideological prejudice being dangled by the government – on lofty ideals of service to mankind and to ignore the basic appeal to self-preservation which neutrality offers in Ireland more than anywhere else in Europe. If an all-Ireland neutral territory can avoid attracting direct explosive damage, the fallout problem, for all its severity, is incomparably easier to deal with from a distance, principally because – whatever the wind direction – warning times for Ireland are in the order of five to ten hours, as distinct from the minutes to react from the launching of missiles to their direct hits and the immediate spread of fire and fallout in the five- to thirty-mile area surrounding. A professional and volunteer army, backed by a government committed to neutrality, is already well within our capacity to train and organize as an effective means of saving the lives of most of the Irish people and of coping with the social consequences of a nuclear war outside Irish territory.

This is not to make light of the consequences of nuclear war. It is simply to make a realistic assessment of the risks involved. There is a sense in which we can truthfully speak of the end of civilization in the event of war between the superpowers – all the more if the war is of such a scale as to cause a nuclear winter in its wake. We are certainly talking of deaths in the hundreds of millions, disease, disorder and corruption for several generations. But it is absurd to take that literally to mean the destruction of humanity. It is fashionable to say death is preferable to life in such an environment. But that sentiment will not survive the first stirrings of a Minuteman missile in its silo, and the populations of the NATO and Warsaw Treaty countries will envy the prospects of the peoples in parts of Australia, New Zealand,

Latin America, Africa whose deaths will be less predictable. The odds against a neutral Ireland are undoubtedly greater than in those parts of the world even more distant from the obvious targets of attack, but they are considerably less, by virtue of neutrality, than if we join NATO and become larger red dots on the maps of Soviet military strategists.

As in the Second World War, the real military threat to Irish neutrality is closer than Moscow, Vladivostock or Berlin. It comes from our fellow-Westerners, our colleagues in the defence of freedom, towards whom we are not ideologically neutral. Since their threat is largely contingent on the belief in a Soviet threat, and since, if they have a positive interest in Irish communications and other facilities, it will be defined by them as the belief in a Soviet threat, after the example of Churchill, it is obvious that Irish neutrality can only be defended by careful and intelligent planning to create the most favourable perceptions of this country consistent with our neutral commitment. This is not something that can be accomplished after the launch of missiles. But it is well within our capability, at moderate cost, to minimize, if not eliminate the threat to infringe our neutrality both from NATO and the Soviet Union.

A word finally on Civil Defence. It only makes sense to prepare for the protection of our people from the fallout of a distant nuclear explosion if we are at the same time preparing our foreign policy to increase the chances that the explosion will be distant. A Civil Defence exercise — such as that conducted by the government in February 1984 — directed to the fallout problem only and carried out by volunteer labour is admirable. It is exactly what a responsible government should do, given meagre resources — to gamble on a dangerous, but not intolerable situation arising from radioactive fallout drifting from a direct hit on the nearest targets in NATO territory. To anticipate a direct hit on a neutral Ireland would be a worst-case prediction. *Not* to expect direct hits on NATO territory in a nuclear war would be clearly stupid — where else would the war take place? What then is the point of exercising against fallout from a distance when we are at the same time conducting other exercises which will ensure fallout from direct hits? What is the sense of having an impoverished section of the Department of Defence carry out a massive training programme to cope with those effects of nuclear war which are only likely to occur if Ireland is neutral, while at the same time the rest of the government is engaged in an even bigger operation to abandon neutrality and to make Civil Defence a laughing-stock?

That is not the government's intention. This major exercise, costing next to nothing and attracting enormous publicity, was not what it seemed to a population kept in ignorance about the process of government. It was an exercise in gradual persuasion, a kite being

floated by our political leadership to ensure an acceptable picture as
Ireland moves inexorably into a military alliance. It was an expression of official concern about the threat of nuclear war; it was a
government spokesman saying — as Margaret Thatcher said of her
National Health Service — 'neutrality is safe with us'.

6. *The Northern Ireland objection.* As I argue in Chapter Eight, it is
becoming increasingly a tacit assumption of government that British
agreement to bring about the unification of Ireland, and thereby end
the twin evils of violence and partition, is conditional upon Ireland's
abandonment of neutrality. The argument has a moral force which,
taken together with the belief that neutrality must go anyway if our
EEC benefits are to survive, gives it the character of a fact of life.
Either we join NATO — in some shape or form — or violence continues, partition continues, and the economic recession deepens with
unforeseeable consequences for the future. An additional minor
factor in the Northern Ireland objection, not without foundation, is
the belief that neutrality has particular cultural and political connotations for the Northern Ireland majority which make it an unattractive
element in an electoral campaign to win their support for some form
of unification.

To take the last point first, the association of neutrality with anti-
British feeling in Ireland derives from the cultural connotations given
to it during the Second World War and probably owes a great deal to
Churchill's ability later to make real for Northern Unionists a
definition of neutrality as cowardice, moral indifference and an
implacable resentment of Britain. But this is not significantly
different from the definition of neutrality privately accepted by the
Irish government. It is little wonder that there is continuing evidence
of a misunderstanding of one of the more attractive attributes which
Southern Ireland could offer the North when the Dublin government
itself has taken Churchill at his word and made no effort to present
the positive advantages of neutrality over the other option for the
Northern Community — of being a NATO outpost which will cost
the Soviet Union little more than two SS-18s to eliminate. When the
Dublin government presents the positive case for Irish neutrality, it
will be time to rebut this objection. Until then, it would be very surprising if the Northern majority does not hear the echoes of Church-
hill in any talk about neutrality which reaches them from Dublin.

It can be taken as probable that a Conservative government in
Britain is likely to view Northern Ireland as a strategic foothold in
Ireland which is valuable, if not crucial, given Tory attitudes to the
question of defence, NATO and the Soviet threat. Its value, moreover, makes the neutrality of the rest of Ireland strategically unimportant. As mentioned in Chapter Eight, this is also likely to be the

American and NATO view. So the dilemma for Southern Ireland is that no one seriously threatens our neutrality or cares much about what we might have to offer in time of war. But, without the North, the value of neutrality to us is diminished.

It is easy to appreciate the pressure on any Irish Taoiseach, aware of this fact and burdened by the responsibility to end violence and end partition, to try to slip neutrality under the table to his opposite number in the hope that the people will not notice. If the tit for tat is not too embarrassing — like requiring him to join NATO, which is already defined in Ireland in stark opposition to neutrality — then the chances are it can be well wrapped, carefully labelled and sold to a grateful people.

It is easy to imagine this scene since, according to all the clues and hints and circumstantial evidence available, this is what happened in December 1980 and the trade-off is still on the agenda of Anglo-Irish discussions. The wrapping and labelling of Ireland's commitment has been an ingenious one. Thatcher might have settled for a European defence involvement, since that would have guaranteed Ireland to NATO. But a bilateral defence pact with Britain is cleverer. Since the foundation of the State and throughout the De Valera era in particular, Ireland has acknowledged the need for close alliance with Britain, our nearest neighbour, and defined partition as the only obstacle. Now that the dreams of history are within grasp, making the IRA and anti-British sentiments redundant, what better way to disguise involvement with NATO and to deflect criticism of cynics than to offer a mutual defence treaty which will do for these islands what countless other regional and apparently harmless defence pacts do for close, interdependent neighbours? It lends itself to the needs of anti-terrorist security in the new Ireland and to the definition of the role of bilateral *defence* (NATO) as bilateral *security* (peace and reconciliation in Ireland). The Dublin proposal on common security for the whole of Ireland, currently under consideration by Westminster, makes sense against the IRA. But it will be used as the institutional precedent for further development — the first stage of the Anglo-Irish arrangement, a security pact publicly debated and accepted as necessary and worthy, to smuggle in the second stage of the defence pact which was under the table since 1980.[14]

It is, of course, membership of NATO which is at issue. We are not likely to be planning a defence pact to defend the British Isles against a surprise attack from Argentina or the North Sea against marauding cod warriors from Iceland. The military alliance with Britain will be irresistible in a united Ireland and, at the same time, it

14. Whoever first conceived of 'security' as code for defence in the EEC context cannot have imagined how useful it would be to Irish diplomacy and government.

will give the EEC all they seem to be asking for. To those who know the score the label doesn't matter.

One is tempted to despair at the convergence of circumstances which lend this argument such force and make it potentially the most dangerous of all. A Tory government in power, a NATO idealogue in Downing Street, the desperate need to end violence in the North, unstable government in Dublin making the dash for glory tempting — all this and a lack of public awareness throughout Ireland of the shabbiness of the bargain being struck.If the Northern problem were not the main factor driving Ireland into a military alliance with NATO, one would be tempted to feel that the conspiracy was a conscious and cynical one. But all the signs are that our politicians, with only a few exceptions, are as oblivious of the moral implications and the physical dangers of the drift into NATO as are most of the population. Their minds are dominated by problems of economics and public order. Like all politicians, they have had to come to terms with the inescapable dirtiness of politics — at least by lay standards of ethics. And like all Irish people, they are accustomed, since childhood, to having the moral issues defined for them by the Church. While ministers, priests and lay Christians throughout the rest of the world have helped to push the disarmament question to the forefront of conscience and in most cases have gone beyond empty approvals of disarmament or denunciations of nuclear war, the Irish Church still struggles with that cautious piety and conservatism which fails to recognize tomorrow's problems unless they look like yesterday's. The lonely episcopal statement on nuclear weapons, which came later but was as far-sighted as most on the general problem, hardly registered on public consciousness. Not surprisingly, it failed to alert politicians, who are as sensitive to the signals of the hierarchy as the most traditional and devout Catholics. It included a surprisingly radical approval of controlled unilateralism — the first episcopal body in the world to do so — but this does not make great demands on a country which has no nuclear weapons to be unilateral about. It said nothing about the main issue which connects Ireland to the problem of war in the nuclear age: neutrality. And it singled out for praise the 'continuing efforts of Irish government over the past two decades in favour of disarmament' — this is precisely the period when Ireland began to abandon neutrality, as Chapter Eight will show.[15]

A Labour government in Westminster will be more likely to want a quick solution to the North, but is not likely, without intelligent diplomatic pressure from the Irish government, to let go a piece of NATO. One can only hope that the people and their politicians will become

15. *The Storm That Threatens*, Catholic Press and Information Office, Dublin, July 1983, p. 11/12. This is clearly an unfortunate error of judgment and oversight in a document which is otherwise open and searching.

aware of what their government is doing on their behalf and will have the sense, the vision and the courage to reject it, even if it means turning down the false promise of peace and unity which will be offered in return.

The papers which follow attempt to explain some of the background to be considered in making such a decision — in Chapters 2 to 4, the political and military factors, in Chapters 5 to 7 the ethical, and in Chapters 8 to 10 some specialized considerations of the viability of Irish neutrality. Finally, in a postscript, the possibility of a new form of active neutrality is discussed, going beyond the isolation of the war years and the symbolism of the 'fifties. Whether it is politically realistic, morally imperative and economically possible are questions which each of us must decide in the interests of peace and of Ireland's capacity to make some contribution to it.

One final point must be made and emphasized in this Introduction. The advocacy of Irish neutrality and the recognition of the difficulties posed by membership of the European Community commonly give rise to an anti-Europeanism based on an alleged incompatibility between neutrality and the EEC. Nothing could be more damaging to the cause of neutrality and to the economic and moral welfare of Ireland than this simplistic and isolationist view. If neutrality is worth having, it is so because of its internationalist potential, and Ireland's internationalism must begin with the neighbours with whom its destiny has been forged by history and geography and culture and with whom its future will be inevitably interlocked. It may be that other alliances with other neutrals and members of the Eastern bloc will play a key role in the peacemaking process which active neutrality entails. But without a close and mutually beneficial relationship with the United Kingdom, above all, and with our other neighbours in Western Europe, from whom we have already received far more than we have given, such alliances will be nothing more than foolish pipedreams and ideological fantasies.

2 Can Neutrality Be Defended?*

Adam Roberts

The question in the title is as deliberately ambiguous as it is genuinely interrogative. It is not easy for anyone, least of all for someone who is in formal terms a foreigner, to assess how seriously a state should take its security problems; or even to identify properly what those problems are. One is necessarily dealing with imponderables, and emotionally charged ones at that. This paper seeks merely to raise a few questions, both about Ireland's security situation and about possible alternative policies; and it examines briefly the position of some other, possibly comparable countries.

The most striking feature of Ireland's present defence system is revealed by the figures. With the exception of a few micro-states (such as Andorra and the Vatican City), and very small states (such as Malta and Luxembourg), Ireland spends less on defence, and has fewer men in arms, than any other European state. Even when expressed in percentage terms, Ireland's defence effort is relatively modest: the 1980 defence expenditure of £144 million was less than two per cent of the country's Gross National Product (GNP).[1] Moreover, because of the professional character of the Irish Defence Forces, Ireland does not have the large concealed cost of conscription. In short, Ireland's defence policy, although it has increased in cost in recent years, is still quite cheap by international standards, and does not place great burdens on the economy and society. Defence does not seem to be too serious a business.

THE SPECIAL CHARACTER OF IRISH NEUTRALITY

Ireland couples this modest military outlay with a policy commonly described as one of neutrality. Thus, at least legally speaking,

*This is a revised (1982) version of a paper given at a conference on 'The Defence of Neutrality in the Nuclear Age' at the Irish School of Ecumenics, Dublin, 6 February 1982.

1. Figures from International Institute for Strategic Studies, *The Military Balance, 1981-82,* London, 1981, pp. 42 and 112.

Ireland's lack of military potential is not compensated by any alliance with larger powers. Ireland is not a member of the North Atlantic Treaty Organization (NATO);[2] and indeed it seems likely to remain the only full member of the European Economic Community (EEC) which is not in NATO. Occasionally, suggestions that Ireland should join NATO are heard, and a although little seems to come of them, the matter is mentioned again below.

Ireland may indeed be a neutral state, but it is certainly not easy to describe in a few words the exact character and purpose of its neutrality. It is clearly still very different from such European paradigms of neutrality as Switzerland and Sweden — both of which put great emphasis on strong national military defence systems, and both of which have a tradition of internal stability and independent statehood going back to 1815 or beyond. Such traditional neutrals are occasionally referred to in Irish discussions on security, but they are not studied very closely, nor are they emulated.

Indeed, perhaps an Englishman can be forgiven for saying that Irish neutrality has always in the past been a function almost exclusively of the tragic relations between Britain and Ireland. When, in 1938, De Valera agreed with Chamberlin a settlement which ended the 'economic war' with Britain and abrogated the defence arrangements of the 1921 Anglo-Irish Treaty, Ireland embarked on neutrality not so much for its own sake, but rather as the only available policy once the unequal liaison with Britain was ended. It was a symbol of independence of the Irish state from Britain. This was a perfectly reasonable approach, and the continued existence of partition was used — and even today is used — as a justification for the policy of neutrality.

Ireland's lack of identification with traditional models of neutrality is also indicated by its apparent neglectful attitude *vis-à-vis* some parts of the laws of war. Ireland has never formally acceded to the two main international agreements regulating the position of neutral states in international war — namely 1907 Hague Convention V, on neutrality in land war, and 1907 Hague Convention XIII, on neutrality in naval war. Since Great Britain had never ratified either of these agreements, there could be no question of Ireland having simply become bound by succession at the time of independence. This does not appear to have caused any special problems during the Second World War. Nevertheless, the failure to accede formally to these agreements has been, and remains, an odd and idiosyncratic

2. A few years ago, *The Irish Times* had a long article on NATO activities in the Republic; which baffled me, until I realized that it referred to the National Association of Tenants' Organizations.

feature of Ireland's brand of neutrality.[3] On 19 December 1968 the UN General Assembly adopted resolution 2444 (XXIII), which *inter alia* called 'upon all states which have not yet done so to become parties to the Hague Conventions of 1899 and 1907 . . .' But although this resolution was adopted unanimously, without a roll-call being taken, Ireland is one of the many states which has taken no action in regard to it.

Events after the Second World War confirmed the extent to which Irish eyes were focused on the UK. Although in 1949 the Republic of Ireland, outside the framework of the Commonwealth, was proclaimed — so that Ireland was at last a fully independent state — the content of its policy was still very largely influenced by relations with the UK. Thus, at around the time when the NATO organization was coming into being (after the signature of the Washington Treaty in 1949), Irish leaders frequently reiterated the proposition that Ireland would not join NATO as long as the island of Ireland was partitioned.

In the decades after NATO was formed, Irish neutrality — essentially a sensible and undemanding policy — never acquired much in the way of exotic or cosmopolitan trappings. It was different from UK policy in the way that green letter boxes are different from red, but there was surprisingly little by way of identification with continental — let alone tri-continental or global — models. Ireland did not seem particularly influenced by any of the leading European neutral states. It had little to do with the emergence of the non-aligned movement, which was launched at the 1961 Belgrade Conference. Ireland appears to have played a rather quiet role in the negotiations at the Conference on Security and Co-operation in Europe, which led to the conclusion of the 1975 Helsinki Final Act; and at the subsequent review conferences in Belgrade and, now, Madrid. In so far as it sought to assert an independent role abroad, this was largely through the relatively safe vehicle of the United Nations: Ireland has taken an important part in many UN peace-keeping operations.

It is an issue for discussion whether Ireland could, or should, adopt a more thorough-going and articulated policy of non-alignment or neutrality; and whether it could, by such means, add a bit more ideological content to its neutrality than the mere hangovers of anti-British or anti-partition sentiment, or the cautious identification with the UN. Certainly a case can be made for such a policy, even though it would go against the grain of Irish thought. Ireland has almost no intellectual tradition in relation to international relations.

But the reasons for the present rather quiet approach to foreign

3. For texts of these agreements and lists of states parties to them, see Adam Roberts and Richard Guelff (eds.), *Documents on the Laws of War,* Oxford University Press, 1982.

policy need to be understood and respected. They can be put under three rather arbitrary headings: associations, history and geography.

There have been powerful associations with Western countries, and these have provided good enough reasons for not adopting any strident or shrill stance of neutrality. Despite unhappy past and even present relations, Ireland has continuing close ties with the leading NATO state, the USA. The coolness towards the USSR and Eastern Europe has been striking. The Church in Ireland has been traditionally anti-communist. Even if neutral, Ireland has been firmly anchored to the West. In the economic sphere, particularly, Ireland's links are with Western states: a fact which Irish accession to the EEC simply confirmed.

The facts of Irish political history perhaps reinforced the case for a certain quietism in foreign policy. The bitter memories of past troubles at home may have led to a desire to avoid unnecessary adventures abroad, and the awareness that any major change in foreign policy might be internally divisive reinforced such a conclusion. Here there is some analogy with Spain, another country which kept out of the Second World War, and whose own experience of internal violence before the war was a prime cause for the adoption of a neutral stance. After the experience of a civil war, involvement in international war could simply be too much — especially if that involvement is likely to be internally divisive.

Finally, geography helps to explain the special character of Irish neutrality. As an offshore island of an offshore island, stuck off the edge of Western Europe, Ireland has been up to now in a rather secure position. It is probably fair to say that its security has derived from being well away from the major *foci* of conflict — a crucially important fact when one bears in mind that those unfortunate neutrals which have been invaded in this century have usually been invaded because they were on major communications routes between antagonists: Belgium, between France and Germany; Norway, between Germany and Great Britain; and so on. Ireland has not been is such a position. It might possibly be so in the future (a matter to which I return below), but Ireland's lack of experience of being a bone of international contention has had its effect. As Patrick Keatinge has written: '. . . because of the country's fortunate strategic position, Irishmen have rarely been compelled to think at all about security from external threats . . . The Irishman talks about neutrality, not about security; moreover, he does not talk about it much and thinks about it even less.'[4]

During the Second World War Ireland's security may have owed something not just to a firm application of a policy of neutrality, but

4. Patrick Keatinge, 'Odd Man Out? Irish Neutrality and European Security', *International Affairs*, London, July 1972, p. 438.

also to a perception that Ireland was still in some vague sense within a British sphere of concern. And today Ireland may again be in a position of combining a certain legal neutrality with a factual location in a British, EEC and NATO framework. To be neutral in such a position — where geography saves one from being a bone of contention between the super-powers — is quite an enviable fate in a troubled world.

The events surrounding Ireland's accession to the EEC reinforce the contention that Ireland's neutrality has a rather special character. When, around 1969-71, many European neutrals were considering their future relations with the EEC, the Soviet Union sent notes to several of them (including Finland, Sweden, Austria and Switzerland) indicating that full membership of the EEC would be incompatible with neutrality. So far as I am aware, Ireland received no such note. Its position was thus recognized as unique even before it formally became the only neutral member of an otherwise wholly NATO-aligned EEC.

Ireland's whole security situation seems to have strong elements of similarity with two (in other respects very different) countries: Spain and Japan. Spain too is in a geographically quite secure position and it has long devoted just under two per cent of GNP to defence — the same figure as Ireland. Japan is clearly within the sphere of US security interests, and has kept its defence spending to just under one per cent of its rapidly rising GNP. Of course, both Spain and Japan have long been formally linked to the USA by security treaties and liaison agreements, and Spain is currently in the process of joining NATO, so the analogy with Ireland should not be pushed too far. These cases simply confirm that states which fall rather clearly within the area of security concern of one super-power may be particularly able to get by with a comparatively modest defence system and budget. Japan is sometimes accused of being a 'free rider' in the international system. Similarly Patrick Keatinge has said of Ireland that it has 'been enjoying the benefits of whatever security NATO has had to offer for over twenty years without paying a penny.'[5]

Even if this is a rather strong verdict, it focuses attention on the peculiar and idiosyncratic elements in Irish neutrality policy. These historical factors need to be borne in mind in considering Ireland's present foreign and security problems.

IRISH SECURITY IN THE 1980s

One might expect Ireland's security policy to be very widely questioned as the world enters the 1980s. Is it really possible for a state nowadays to keep out of alliances, and simultaneously to take

5. Keatinge, *loc. cit.*, p. 446.

such a low-key attitude to defence? But in fact Ireland's policy does not seem to be widely questioned today. As far as I am aware, no foreign governments have in recent years been alarmed by the country's vulnerability and urged on it a new approach to defence. It would thus appear that Ireland's defence policy is not seen as posing a major problem.

The simple explanation for all this is that at the moment Ireland does not face a classic military threat — of conquest, subjugation, or occupation. Ireland's traditional adversary is England. But Britain seems to be definitely in a post-imperial phase. Moreover, the British are sick enough of Northern Ireland, and the last thing they want is control of the rest of the island as well.

The one serious security problem that Ireland faces is Northern Ireland. It is not so much the existence of Ulster as such: to have one and a quarter states on one island is geographically untidy, but not necessarily immoral or impossible. Rather it is the unhappy population-mix and history of Ulster, the upsurge of conflict within Ulster in the past twelve years, and the Republic's proximity to that conflict, which pose special dangers. These dangers are of cross-border incidents; of gun-running becoming big business; of splits on basic policy issues within the Republic; of possible influxes of embittered refugees; and of the millennarian political visions of a minority being allowed to take over from the democratic management of affairs in the Republic. These dangers are all real, but the extent to which they may be solved by buying bigger and better weapons, or putting more men in uniform, is questionable. For Ireland, therefore, the main security problem seems to have an idiosyncratic and very largely political aspect.

The problems of Ireland *vis-à-vis* the North may not be totally unique: many other countries have had on their doorsteps similar crises involving equally intractable problems of the relationship between nation and state. But Ireland's problems certainly need to be considered in their own right. Although other countries' security policies are mentioned here, Ireland could hardly copy any of them mechanically.

The problem of the North is not the only possible security concern. The Soviet Union certainly has the capacity to hurt Ireland, but there is little evidence of any great Soviet interest in the Republic, and certainly there is no great bone of contention between it and the USSR. However, it is not to be excluded that the Soviet Union could develop an increased interest in Ireland. The vastly increased Soviet naval capacity in the North Atlantic brings the Societ Union closer than it was; fishing rights provide a possible source of disputes; and the role of Ireland in the West European economy might give the Soviet Union a special interest in being able to threaten certain facilities.

For their part, the Western powers might see in Ireland a certain strategic utility. In the past, after all, the British have often referred to the strategic value of Northern Ireland;[6] and while Ulster's strategic value must be pretty minimal today, principally because of its endless internal problems, this does not mean that Ireland, as a whole, is considered to be without strategic value. Ireland, with its large land area and sparse population, might be considered militarity useful for nuclear bases, for communications facilities, and as a staging post for re-supplying forces in Europe.[7] U.S. interest in all these matters might well increase, but at present the evidence of U.S. pressure on Ireland to change its stance away from neutrality is scanty.[8] Such pressure might well be unpopular in Ireland, especially if the presence of U.S. bases was conceived as making Irish involvement in a nuclear war more likely. There would have to be some very tangible gain if the ditching of Ireland's position as non-nuclear haven was even to be contemplated.

Perhaps the biggest challenge to Irish neutrality would come if the EEC moves towards a more co-ordinated foreign policy should gather momentum — as seems entirely possible. In the past decade, the EEC has increasingly become a vehicle by which the states of Western Europe have articulated a view on the Middle East and other issues which is not just in some vague sense a collective view, but is also in some respects a view distinct from that of the United States. This process is gradually coming to incorporate certain security matters and this could have serious implications for Irish neutrality.

Finally, one may speculate as to how long the issue of partition can be seen as providing a logical basis for neutrality policy. The link seems always to have been more psychological than diplomatically functional. It is hard to accept it as a sufficient argument for neutrality, not least because it contains (if it is taken seriously) a self-destruct mechanism. If Irish unification was to be achieved, would the case for neutrality cease to exist? Irish neutrality needs a more enduring intellectual basis than that of a temporary staging-post.

6. See the references to strategic factors in Ronan Fanning, 'London and Belfast's Response to the Declaration of the Republic of Ireland, 1948-49', *International Affairs*, London, Winter 1981-82.
7. For a claim that Ireland is already involved in the U.K. Air Defence Ground Environment radar and microwave network, see the article by Brendan Munnelly in *Dawn: An Irish Journal of Nonviolence*, issue of December 1981/January 1982.
8. However, one definite if uncorroborated complaint was made on 22 March 1982 by Mr. James Molyneaux, M.P. for South Antrim and the leader of the Official Unionist Party in Northern Ireland. Speaking in Belfast, he suggested that paramilitary groups in Ireland, including the I.R.A., were being manipulated in a complicated international conspiracy to bring the Republic of Ireland into the NATO defence structure. He claimed that documents would be published shortly to confirm this. — *The Guardian*, London, 23 March 1982.

The above factors do not all point in unison in any one clear direction, and one should not expect Irish foreign policy to change suddenly and completely in the 1980s. But some of the factors outlined above do suggest that the purposes and character of Irish neutrality may need to be defined more clearly if Ireland's present idiosyncratic status is not to be whittled away. They also suggest that Irish defence policy may need some re-thinking.

A STRONGER CONVENTIONAL DEFENCE?

The arguments for muddling through on the basis, very approximately, of existing defence policy are bound to be strong. But they are challenged. Perhaps the clearest challenge to present policies has come from the former Chief of Staff, Lieutenant-General Carl O'Sullivan. In an interview published in *The Irish Times* on 2 February 1982 he said that Ireland would need to spend about £500 million — i.e. more than twice its existing defence budget — if it was to have the capacity to handle an attack from the outside and to back up the claim that Ireland is militarily neutral. He suggested that Ireland's geographical position had become more exposed and critical than it had been in previous times:

> We are in a crucial position in the north Atlantic. The threat in the last war came from Europe and the UK. Now the Soviets have a strategic fleet sited in Murmansk. They have airborne divisions in the Kola peninsula which poses a threat to the north Atlantic and Ireland is in a crucial position there. So morally we owe it to Europe to consolidate our defences either on our own, or in consort with other people.

O'Sullivan went on to recommend talks with other European countries about some sort of defence pact. He hinted that such a pact might have a purely European rather than a NATO character, and he referred to the possible emergence of Europe as an area of armed neutrality. He also suggested that in any defence arrangement with other countries, Ireland's particular contribution might be to give facilities of various kinds, possibly including bases. He said: 'We are politically and economically a part of Europe. If it is so beneficial, why don't we take steps to defend what we are going to unite?'

O'Sullivan's proposals undoubtedly carry weight, and it is excellent that some fundamental questions have been asked about the future of Irish neutrality and Irish security. However, his remarks do not seem likely on their own to bring about any major change in public mood, let alone government policy. That is partly because of a tradition in Ireland of not thinking very hard about these matters; but partly also for the more solid reason that any major attack on Irish neutrality by a foreign power is seen as being simultaneously hard to imagine and hard to deal with: powerful arguments indeed for turning the mind to other more rewarding matters.

OTHER APPROACHES TO DEFENCE

Perhaps the debate about Irish defence policy need not be limited to the existing policy on the one hand, and the O'Sullivan proposals on the other. In particular, it may be worth looking briefly at three possible options. They are presented below in a deliberately brief and simplified form, and in considering them one must bear in mind that in matters of defence, as in other areas of life, the perfect paradigm or ideal type which one may visualise in theory is, in fact, seldom implemented in practice without substantial compromises and modifications.

The three possible options are:

1. *Territorial defence*, which would involve preparations for a guerrilla-type defence in depth of Irish territory against possible foreign military attack and occupation.

2. *Defence by civil resistance*, relying on the use of non-violent methods (such as strikes, non-cooperation, etc.) against possible foreign military attack and occupation.

3. *A non-nuclear military collaboration with other Western European states*, on the basis of a new, primarily conventional, military strategy.

Before looking at each of these options in turn, a few general points should be noted. In every case it is taken as axiomatic that, other things being equal, the aim of a security policy must be to deter foreign states from attacking in the first place, as well as to provide some means of defence if they do nevertheless attack. Further, it is accepted that no policy offers anything even approaching absolute security, and that decisions about these and other approaches to defence involve a balancing of risks. It is also accepted that there are significant advantages in having a *manifestly defensive* defence policy, based round the idea, not of threatening adversaries with airborne genocide, but of making the society being defended inherently hard to conquer.

Underlying all this is the idea that it is useless and even counterproductive simply to follow the traditional approach of calling on states to disarm (whether unilaterally or multilaterally) without saying what alternative security arrangements are to take the place of those which are removed. This traditional approach has traditionally failed, for good reasons: in a dangerous and uncertain international environment, states and their inhabitants are likely to cling to existing military policies unless and until something more satisfactory is produced.

In the United Kingdom, considerations such as these contributed to the setting up, in 1980, of an unofficial body (of which I am a member) called the Alternative Defence Commission. Its membership is small, and the whole enterprise is on a modest scale. It is grappling with extremely difficult problems, to which there do not appear to be any easy and simple solutions. Since it is a totally new and pioneering venture, it would probably be unwise to expect too much of it, or of the report which it hopes to complete later this year. But it is considering, in a U.K. context, defence options similar to the three listed above. This paper offers a chance to say something about how such ideas might relate to Ireland.

Option 1: Territorial Defence

Superficially, the idea of territorial defence is an obvious one for a neutral state such as Ireland. It can be defined as follows:

> *Territorial defence* is a system of defence in depth; it is the governmentally-organized defence of a state's own territory, conducted on its own territory. It is aimed at creating a situation in which an invader, even though he may at least for a time gain geographical possession of part or all of the territory, is constantly harassed and attacked from all sides. It is a form of defence strategy which has important organizational implications, being liable to involve substantial reliance on a citizen army, including local units of a militia type. Characteristically, a territorial defence system is based on weapons systems, strategies and methods of military organization which are better suited to their defensive role than to engagement in major military actions abroad.[9]

Territorial defence has been included as a major element in the defence systems of three of the most significant European neutral states: Sweden, Switzerland and Yugoslavia. It has helped to keep the first two of these states out of war for over 165 years, which is something of a world record; and it has helped keep Yugoslavia independent and non-aligned, despite very intense pressure in 1948-53 and subsequently to make concessions to the Soviet Union. If territorial defence has thus proved to be a basis for maintaining the independence of neutral states, and to be compatible with the goal of peace,

9. Adam Roberts, *Nations in Arms: The Theory and Practice of Territorial Defence*, Chatto & Windus, London, for International Institute for Strategic Studies, 1976, p. 34.

there would seem to be a strong case for Ireland adopting such an approach.

The question of territorial defence certainly deserves careful consideration in Ireland. This is especially so because Ireland faces a security problem which is fairly typical of European neutrals: that is to say, with limited resources it has to plan for a possible foreign attack which is very unlikely to materialize, but is also very hard to deal with if it does materialize. Keeping small standing conventional forces is really no answer to such a problem: but having an 'inflatable army', capable of resisting attack throughout the country, might be as persuasive an answer in Ireland as in the other countries mentioned.

However, the disadvantages of a territorial defence approach for Ireland must be honestly faced. In Ireland the following four arguments would be likely to loom large: (a) the option would inevitably involve conscription, which would be politically unpopular; (b) it may be questioned whether a society which is urbanizing as rapidly as Ireland can quickly develop, or re-discover, a capacity for guerrilla resistance throughout the territory against foreign military attack; (c) Ireland, as an offshore island, has very different defence problems from those faced by Switzerland, Sweden, or Yugoslavia, and is bound, if it takes its own defence seriously, to put relatively more emphasis on maritime and air defence rather than on territorial defence strictly defined; and (d) any Irish defence system which involved training a large part of the population in the use of weapons would be seen as deeply threatening by the Ulster Protestants, and might actually make the principal security problem on the island of Ireland worse, not better.

These four arguments do not necessarily end the debate about territorial defence; and indeed they might suggest to some, not that territorial defence is wholly inapplicable, but rather that it needs to be modified substantially to meet the particular circumstances of Ireland. If the proposal is discussed further, one hopes that it will be done free of the enticing but misleading vision so frequently conjured up of the guerrilla as a free actor and a late twentieth-century hero. Guerrilla warfare is exceedingly cruel, tends to involve foreign entanglements, easily degenerates into civil war and intercommunal terrorism, and is exceptionally hard to stop. If it is to be a basis of a state's defence policy, there has to be some general agreement within the state about when it is to be used — and when not used.

Option 2: Defence by Civil Resistance

In several European states, whether in NATO like Britain, or neutral like Sweden, a quite distinct approach to the problem of defence has sometimes been proposed: defence by civil resistance. It can be defined as follows:

> *Defence by civil resistance* is a policy of national defence
> against possible internal threats (e.g. *coup de'état*) and external
> threats (e.g. invasion) by advance preparations to resist such
> threats by means of civil resistance applied by the population.
> The aim is to deter or to defeat such attempts not simply by
> altering the will of the usurper but by making successful
> usurpations impossible through massive and selective non-
> cooperation and defiance by the citizens. Defence by civil resist-
> ance thus involves the use of a wide variety of methods of non-
> violent action, including economic resistance, political non-
> cooperation, various types of intervention, and methods of
> undermining the attackers' morale and loyalty.
> The term 'defence by civil resistance' is broadly synonymous
> with such other terms as 'civilian defence', 'civilian-based
> defence', 'non-military defence', 'non-violent defence, and
> 'social defence'. These other terms may have some slightly dif-
> ferent connotations, but their broad meaning is the same.[10]

Defence by civil resistance is not a wholly abstract proposal. In
numerous cases of foreign military occupations in the nineteenth and
twentieth centuries, the population of the occupied territory has
reacted by using strikes and other non-violent methods. Sometimes
such resistance has led to a greater degree of independence or the
withdrawal of occupying forces; sometimes it has done no more than
modify the terms of occupation; and sometimes, as in
Czechoslovakia after the 1968 Soviet-led occupation, it has been
followed by massive concessions to the demands of the occupying
powers. The very widespread use of this technique in past cases needs
to be studied, because it is far richer and more interesting than any
pure theorizings about civil resistance.

However, there are obvious difficulties which are so considerable
that no state has yet adopted this policy in any substantial way. The
most commonly feared difficulty is that of facing extremes of repression: could civil resistance stand up to bombing, torture, mass
deportations? There are also great problems in maintaining any non-
violent discipline, not only because the adversary may provoke
counter-violence by his own use of repression, but also because within
the state being defended there may well be individuals or groups who
quite genuinely believe in the need to use violence. Further, defence

10. For an introduction to defence by civil resistance, see Adam Roberts (ed.), *The
Strategy of Civilian Defence: Non-violent Resistance to Aggression*, Faber, London,
1967. For a much more detailed survey of civil resistance generally, see Gene Sharp,
The Politics of Nonviolent Action, Porter Sargent, Boston, 1973.

by civil resistance may be a particularly limited method when it comes to defending maritime interests, or sparsely-inhabited and remote areas, or combatting internal terrorism.

As far as Ireland is concerned, the idea of defence by civil resistance is certainly not completely unknown or unthinkable. Indeed, a classic early work advocating such an approach was Arthur Griffith's *The Resurrection of Hungary: A Parallel for Ireland.*[11] But defence by civil resistance, while it might indeed have relevance in the future in the unlikely event of a foreign occupation of Ireland, does seem less relevant to the actual problems being faced today, or likely to be faced in the next decade or so, by the Irish Republic.

Option 3: A Non-Nuclear Military Collaboration with Other Western European States

This option is based on certain assumptions, which may or may not be correct, about the direction in which the European members of NATO may move in the next decade. The question posed here is essentially: If NATO were to revise its military strategy and dispositions in such a way as to put more emphasis on conventional defence, and less on nuclear weaponry, might there be a strengthened case for Ireland forging some formal links with the organization? What is being discussed here is in some respects similar to the O'Sullivan proposals mentioned above, but it is predicated much more explicitly on a non-nuclear approach.

The case for NATO itself considering such an approach is this: (1) from the distant past, when NATO states had a clear nuclear superiority over the Soviet Union, NATO has retained a doctrine of possible first use of nuclear weapons — a doctrine which is now, in view of increased Soviet nuclear power, so patently incredible that it is a source of weakness; (2) the cause of stability might be well served by NATO states adopting a military strategy based on no-first-use of nuclear weapons; (3) there might also be a case for a no-first-use agreement or treaty between the nuclear powers;[12] (4) many of the new conventional weapons developed in the past ten or twenty years,

11. Originally published in Dublin in 1904, Griffith's book went through many editions.
12. Up to now, NATO powers have generally opposed moves towards no-first-use of nuclear weapons, and they did not support, for example, the resolution adopted by the U.N. General Assembly on 9 December 1981 which solemnly proclaimed, *inter alia*, '1. States and statesmen that resort first to the use of nuclear weapons will be committing the gravest crime against humanity. 2. There will never be any justification or pardon for statesmen who would take the decision to be the first to use nuclear weapons ...'
In the U.N. General Assembly, Ireland has usually aligned itself with the NATO states in opposing such resolutions.

particularly that group of weapons known as Precision Guided Munitions, are widely believed to add particularly to current defence capacity and may thus open up the possibility that NATO could at last create a credible conventional deterrent defence; and (5) such an approach by NATO, while by no means solving all defence or nuclear problems, might provide some intellectual and moral coherence to defence policy, might alleviate some of the most unstable aspects of the East-West nuclear competition, and might provide a basis (signally lacking of late) for some popular consensus in the NATO states on the defence question.

Such an approach by NATO might not assume a purely 'conventional' form. It might also involve some degree of reliance on unconventional methods, such as defence in depth on territorial lines, to make invasion and occupation much more hazardous for a potential adversary. This is not just a matter of an Englishman being prepared to die to the last German: there is some West German advocacy of such a course, and it is noteworthy that the anti-nuclear movement in West Germany does not appear to be opposed to defence as such.

If NATO adopted such an approach, it might accentuate some of the those tendencies, already evident in the alliance, for NATO states to be in a certain limited sense independent of, and even non-aligned towards, certain global policies of the United States. This is not the place to discuss so large an issue, but the emergence of a distinctively European view of the world, containing some elements of a neutral approach, might well affect the way in which Ireland viewed the question of its relations with NATO's European members.

What could all this mean for Ireland? It seems likely that if NATO were to adopt a more conventional strategy along these lines as a solution to its current crisis, it might well want more, not fewer, facilities for resupply; and more, not fewer, links with such conventional forces as exist in the 'NATO area'. Thus NATO would have an enhanced interest in Ireland, but would Ireland have an enhanced interest in NATO? It is possible that it might do so, if NATO came to be seen as having a military policy which was less provocative, and more intellectually defensible, than its present doctrine of 'flexible response'. Ireland might be particularly attracted to such a course if it also seemed to offer improved possibilities of maritime or air defence; or if it opened up better prospects for relations with the North.

My own prognosis, already hinted at in this paper, is that inertia is likely to rule supreme, as it often does in security matters, and not only in Ireland. It might only be in the event of some sudden new threat that Ireland would make any definitive change in its defence or foreign policy. But there is sometimes merit in thinking these problems out even in periods of comparative peace, and asking whether some changes may not be desirable or even necessary.

3 The Urgency of Nuclear Disarmament*

Georgi Arbatov

During the war I heard many stories, from eyewitnesses, of pilots who, having been shot down, were unable to open their parachutes in time, and yet survived their fall. In one case the fall was broken by the air wave caused by the aircraft's explosion seconds earlier. In another case the pilot hit the slope of a snow-covered hill on impact and slid down tens or even hundreds of metres, just rolling in the soft snow. These are true stories, but it would take a madman to conclude from them that one can always survive such a fall without serious injury or even death.

I think it would take the same insanity to believe that, under the conditions of the present dangerous arms race, one could live on with total immunity just because this has been the case for the past thirty years. To begin with, these years have hardly seen global peace. Hundreds of military conflicts have arisen, causing great loss of life, and very often the strategic nuclear forces have been placed on alert. Not once, but many times in these past thirty years, the world has approached the brink of the abyss and has even come close enough to see its horrors. Many times it has been rescued, not so much by wisdom, as by chance. But, tragically, humanity will not always have such good fortune.

Every year, and especially every decade, sees the arms race increase in pace. In thirty-seven years the number of nuclear warheads has increased from one to fifty thousand and this trend continues.

There can be no weapons without the human will to create and use them. But the huge accumulated arsenals of weapons of mass destruction foreshadow great danger in themselves. They hang over humanity like the Sword of Damocles, poisoning the political atmosphere and undermining the stability of the entire international

*This is an edited version of an address given to the 'World Conference of Religious Workers for Saving the Sacred Gift of Life from Nuclear Catastrophe', in Moscow, May 1982. It is published here with permission of the author.

scene. There is a widely held conviction that the arms race has its origin in bad international relations. Today we can see a 'feed-back' phenomenon — the arms race causes distrust and suspicion, causes international relations to deteriorate and creates a general background against which any friction, disputes and differences of opinion can grow into dangerous conflicts.

Take, for example, Soviet-American relations. The Soviet Union does not have any pretensions to the territories of the United States of America. We have no pretensions to American riches. We see no cause for discord and conflict between our countries which would be founded on the present U.S. Constitution, their state laws or its criminal code and emigration law. But since 1945, our concern and suspicion have grown owing to the huge nuclear arsenal which the U.S. has directed against us. This build-up has caused us to take counter measures which are displeasing to the U.S. Recently, the tempo of this build-up has increased. This results in still greater suspicion on our side. I shall not go into greater details for, from what I have already said, I think one may conclude that nothing causes such dramatic deterioration in Soviet-American relations as the nuclear arms race. The quantity of these arms also causes grave concern. When one has over-armed one wonders what to do with the excess. With regard to nuclear weapons, this means the search for a possible "victory" in a nuclear war or the possibility of a "limited" war, i.e. one which is free of danger for oneself. All these illusions are extremely dangerous.

The new height of the nuclear arms spiral increases the danger of a catastrophe not only because of the increase in the number of war-heads; of greater importance is the problem of qualitative modifications. New weapons-systems are on the way multiplying fears of a first-strike capacity which undermines international stability. These new weapons will be extremely difficult if not impossible to control, either by national or by international means. If international control fails, the entire diplomatic process of negotiations will also inevitably fail as will the possibility of reaching an agreement on arms reduction. Thus suspicion, fear and uncertainty are sure to grow also.

Here I must mention another obvious danger generated by the nuclear arms race, namely the proliferation of nuclear weapons. This may become inevitable, thus increasing the danger of Armageddon. There are unfortunately many flash points in the world. Examples of this are to be found in the Middle East, in the Southern Atlantic, in South Africa, and in the Iran-Iraq war. In the climate of the proliferation of nuclear weapons, every such conflict could easily develop into a catastrophe and make inevitable what now seems unthinkable.

Of course, behind the arms race there are evil people, but they hardly present the major danger. The most dangerous fact is that the arms race is tolerated and supported and, what is more, it is tolerated and supported by people who are either oblivious of what they are doing or who accept the accumulation of these deadly weapons as if they were supporting some noble cause. I have never come across any claims suggesting the necessity of accumulating nuclear weapons in order to unleash a nuclear war.

I have read many statements urging the need to prevent war as justification of these weapons. This was true on occasions in the past; one must not attempt to re-write history, and the world would have been in a much worse state than it is now if one country had a monopoly of these horrible weapons. But in many other cases such statements were either erroneous or blatantly untruthful. All this, however, belongs to history. Thinking about tomorrow rather than yesterday, it becomes obvious that further accumulation and modi- fication of nuclear weapons are leading us straight down the road to universal catastrophe. As far as peace is concerned, there is no other way to achieve it but through nuclear disarmament. On the agenda of countless representative forums, this task is presented as a matter of urgency. I would call it 'super-urgent' as no one knows how much time we have to stave off this disaster. No one knows when we shall pass the point of no return. An increased number of weapons, nuclear powers and increased international tension with less dialogue and understanding would be enough to make humanity's destiny depend upon computer error, political misjudgment, mental instability of a key military official; or — even worse — it can force mankind forward to its doom in an escalating conflict in full realization of catastrophe, and powerless to prevent it.

To set out on the road of nuclear disarmament is a task which is not only extremely urgent but also extremely complex. There are many reasons for this. Powerful political and industrial interests are, as a rule, linked to the arms race. Highly advanced economic and political mechanisms are created to advance it. Whole branches of science, technology and industry are involved in aggravating military rivalry and exacerbating it.

This rivalry, coupled with economic interests, has also a spiritual and psychological inertia of its own. Throughout history, man has been drawn to the sphere of politics as well as to other spheres of social life, not only by virtue but also by vice. Our opinions of their origin may differ. But we know only too well what these vices are: profit, greed, egoism, unrestrained arrogant nationalism and pre- judice. Very often, such vices, which include utter disregard for the lives of others, were encouraged. Thus a militaristic culture developed with the cult of violence and war. In many parts of the world such has become the lifestyle, polluting the political and moral atmosphere, public conscience, psychology and morality. This is a powerful ally to the arms race and contributes greatly to its momentum.

I would go so far as to name one more 'ally' and that is mythology, in which the whole subject of war, national security, and arms is cloaked. Such myths, standing in the way of nuclear disarmament, as they do, should be removed. I refer here particularly to the myth which suggests that security can be ensured by the accumulation of arms. This myth has proved a viable one, although it is becoming increasingly clear to all that with each new decade, arms increase but security decreases. The road to disarmament and true security is also impeded by the myth that this concern for military build-up stems from patriotism and realism whereas negotiations, detente and international cooperation are nothing but a mere illusion, or, even worse, an appeasement of the enemy. Very much in tune with this is the myth that it is necessary, first of all, to accumulate weapons before embarking on disarmament and for the negotiations to succeed it is necessary to produce a 'trump card', in other words, new weapons of mass destruction. In present day conditions, anxiety for military superiority is both groundless and dangerous. All these myths contribute to the arms race. They are being presented today in the most complicated form, unintelligible to the outsider. It is most probable that the plan behind this is to keep the general public ignorant of the true facts.

It is said that to give the public access to these matters, to theories of war and peace would be dangerous and detrimental to national security. In my opinion, this is the most dangerous myth of all.

There is a wise saying that war is too serious a matter to be left to the generals. This holds even more true of the problems of war and peace in a nuclear age, and of the problem of the survival of civilization. Even the greatest experts must not be allowed to monopolize this field, nor even the best trained military and political elite. This problem must be solved in active cooperation with those whose vital interests and destiny are at stake, the countless millions throughout the world. And, of course, this cooperation should involve all people of good will, no matter whether secular or religious, state or public figures, scientists, admirals and generals, if they wish to promote the preservation of civilization and not its destruction.

We know that negotiations, which should be open and candid, are the way to nuclear disarmament. But how can we make stubborn people sit down and negotiate? It is no easy matter to give a laconic and explicit answer to this question. However, it does not seem possible unless all in society show by their political and moral will that they will not accept politicians whose policies prepare for the destruction of mankind.

There is valid proof available to us today to testify that the courageous 'interference' by the 'non-professionals', 'the voice from the streets' did not impede but rather promoted the cause of peace as it pressed many politicians to re-think very seriously their statements and their policies.

I do not lose hope that under public pressure they will, in the long run, change not only their stated policies but their deeds also.

I am not so egotistic as to try to suggest to religious workers what should be the best path for them to follow which would lead to nuclear disarmament. I have no wish to enter into a theological discussion in this regard.

But I would like to admit that, having heard the esteemed Dr Billy Graham, whose speech made a great impression on me, I was at first somewhat puzzled by one of his interpretations of the Bible i.e. that the salvation from the final all-destructive war will be brought to sinful mankind by the Second Coming of Christ. It is not that I do not believe in the very idea of the salvation of mankind. Nor would I challenge the idea of man's sinfulness, or, to be frank, the sinfulness of governments. But I had a doubt: might not people understand this interpretation as permission to remain sinful and do nothing for the sake of their own salvation but just to wait.

But perhaps my understanding of what Dr Graham said might be primitive. Maybe, the very role of the deliverer was being interpreted in a broader sense — as an enlightenment of millions of people with the truth, the truth which inspires them to action. If this is so, it is probable that we do not basically disagree so very much. Perhaps we would agree that it is only the actions of people themselves that can save humanity. Some of us see the road to such actions in rational awareness of the current threats to survival and in working towards ways to overcome them; while for others, their way is in the enlightenment mission of Christ, or Allah, or Buddha or Krishna but the main thing is that humanity should save itself.

At the same time as sharing the bright hopes that were expressed here, I would like to remind you of some of the unpleasant facts. One of them is that today it is not necessary to commit any evil act to help the continuing arms race and the slide towards confrontation and catastrophe. This is taken care of by the already established and highly active interests, the enormous power of inertia, the nuclear arms race. In order to stop this dangerous slide, in order to overcome inertia and draw humanity away from the edge of the abyss, continued efforts are needed, actions are needed and, if you like, heroic conduct is needed.

I can assure the assembly that the government and people of the Soviet Union are participating most actively and in every possible way in these efforts and will continue to do so. Our nation knows better than others the meaning of war. This nation is still mourning the loss of twenty million of its sons and daughters who fell in the struggle against Nazism. This is a nation which cherishes peace first and foremost, as the dearest and most valuable thing on earth. The Soviet government has put forward many important proposals for nuclear disarmament and has repeatedly emphasized its willingness to discuss, in the most serious way, all realistic proposals put forward by others.

Naturally, we expect that these proposals will result in fruitful agreements which serve to advance the cause of peace and not political manoeuvres. If there is a zero choice, then it should be a real zero choice for both sides. If there is to be a radical reduction in strategic armaments, then it should not be one which might radically disturb the balance and change the correlation of forces to the benefit of one side.

I would like to stress again, there is nothing our nation is not prepared to do to strengthen peace. We, in the Soviet Union, even though we are a secular people, are humble enough to realize that the great goal of disarmament can be attained only together with other nations which cherish life on earth, only in the great coalition of peacemakers, which unites everybody irrespective of their religious and national background, political and ideological convictions. Whatever the differences the members of this coalition may have, they are united in one great ideal — their concern for the preservation of the human race. This goal justifies their active and passionate concern. No one can stand aside.

I would like to conclude my presentation with the words which a Soviet author of the 1930s put an epigraph to one of his books:

Do not be afraid of enemies — at worst they may kill you.
Do not be afraid of friends — at worst they may betray you.
Fear the indifferent ones for they do not kill and they do not betray, but it is only with their silent consent that murders and treason are at work on our earth.

4 Evaluating U.S. and Soviet Foreign Policy

Bill McSweeney

At an Oxford Union debate in February 1984, the question was posed that 'There is No Moral Difference Between the Foreign Policies of the United States and the Soviet Union'. Supporting the motion was the man who has become the leading British and European intellectual of the peace movement, Edward Thompson. His opponent was the US Defence Secretary, Caspar Weinberger. The motion was defeated, not because Thompson fell below his normal standard of elegant, reasoned passion, but because Weinberger, despite occasional heckling, gave a polished and controlled performance which won special applause for the clinching argument at the end. 'You are free to have a debate like this in the West,' he told the assembled students. 'You can vote yes or no and nothing will happen you, no secret police will detain you or question you when you walk out of this hall. I'm asking you to reject this motion so that you can be free to do that again.'

The argument has echoes of British Defence Secretary Michael Heseltine telling CND that they should camp outside the Berlin Wall, or Mrs Thatcher telling the Greenham Common women to try linking hands around the Kremlin. There is no doubt that peace activists are not evenhanded in their criticism of West and East. They mount protests, sign petitions, write pamphlets and books attacking the policies of Western governments without even a pretence at balancing it, in force or quantity, with similar criticism of the East. Much more important than symmetry, they do it all in their own and other Western societies which protect their freedom to do so, not in the East where such dissent is not tolerated. And they do it, moreover, without adequately acknowledging that fact of political and moral imbalance between the two sides of the Cold War.

Measured by the dominant values of Western society — and probably of some Eastern countries also — and by standards of freedom and religious liberty enshrined in the Christian churches, there is no disputing the moral superiority of the West, however much one may be cynical of the weight given to it, or admiring of the compassion embodied in the welfare systems of the Communist countries. The capacity to tolerate dissent, to reward initiative, to make leadership accountable, information accessible, human rights defendable — these do not exhaust the range or monopolize the highest level of human virtue, nor are they practised in the West as they are preached by our governments and ideologues. But we can hardly question their importance for the quality of life of the individual, or dispute the fact that they are not practised at all in the Soviet Union and scarcely in any of the other nations which make up the Soviet bloc. What is more, if the Western countries of Europe have a poorer record than their governments acknowledge, on this score, it is the United States which leads the world and provides a model of openness and accountability which we in Europe should envy. If freedom and democracy are restricted to these virtues — and there is no implication intended that they are not central and indispensable elements — then the Soviet Union stands in sharpest contrast in that respect to the country of which Caspar Weinberger is Defence Secretary, and the United States can justly claim to embody in its Constitution, laws, practices, style and attitudes the values which have become the standard under which the West has formed an alliance against the Communist world. Why, then, does the peace movement appear to take sides against the West and to unite its considerable political force against their own governments and, above all, against the government of the United States which enshrines freedom and democracy in its social and political structure to a degree not realized in the other countries of the West?

We are not ideologically neutral, even in the neutral countries of Europe. And such is our easy identification of West European moral attitudes with human morality *in se*, and our ignorance of the Soviet system, that most of us in Europe find it unproblematic to attribute our cultural or ideological preference for the West over the East to a virtuous preference for the moral over the immoral, rather than the familiar over the unfamiliar. The moral case against the Soviet system may not be what it seems, but it is substantial. Translated into support for NATO, it encourages the aggressive stance of virtue against evil, of superior strength protecting home territory against the incursion of a feared enemy. It is probably true that most supporters of the NATO alliance view the Cold War as the confrontation between a familiar and powerful friend and a dangerous enemy of unknown but malevolent potential. If a cat corners a rat in our back-yard, we know where our sympathies and allegiance lie, we cannot afford the luxury of moral vegetarianism and we move indoors quickly to avoid the fallout. Commonsense tells us that the rodent is not only dangerous because it is vicious and agressive, but it is dangerous also because it harbours undesirable elements with which we cannot afford to be contaminated.

Supporting NATO, like keeping a cat, makes sense if it prevents the fallout of collateral damage from a violent confrontation with the enemy. As with the rodent in our backyard, we fear the aggression of Soviet foreign policy and the disease of the Communist system, and these political and moral motives mingle into a general fear which makes the enormous cost of the Western deterrent seem justifiable.

We have good reason to dislike the Soviet system and to judge it unfavourably by contrast with our own. When the question is posed, as it is frequently in Europe today, that we take sides between West and East, between the policies of the United States and those of the Soviet Union, most of us opt for virtue against wickedness, for freedom and democracy against totalitarianism and oppression. But the character of the two superpower systems alone cannot account for NATO. Many Americans dislike the British system, and, probably, the majority of the British dislike the South African system but there are no plans yet to target Minuteman missiles on Surrey or Trident on Johannesburg. We must, therefore, attribute to the Soviet Union an aggressive foreign policy which threatens to destroy the West. And if we cannot directly counter that threat by military force, we must assume that the moral and political bankruptcy of the Communist system will lead to its own disintegration — but not before the Kremlin's 'act of desperation, the dying giant lashing out across the central front'.[1] Whether the Soviet Union is strong enough to dominate the world, or weak and corrupt enough to disintegrate, we assume that its policy is still that which was formulated over sixty years ago in the Communist ideology of Marxist-Leninism. Whichever way the rat turns, it is heading for us. We can dismiss the determinism of Marx and smile at the future of capitalism which it predicts, but we are serious when we make similar predictions of the Soviet Union. Those who are still not convinced must be shown the alarming evidence of militarization in the USSR, which can hardly indicate the pacific intent of foreign policy.

These three perceptions of the Soviet Union which condition American foreign policy — the level of armaments, Soviet ideology, internal corruption and instability — are publicly affirmed by Western leaders and their representatives in order to strengthen popular support for NATO and popular resistance to the growing dissent of the peace movement, which minimizes the moral case and either rejects the foreign policy argument or tars the West with the same brush. The case rests, therefore, on the objective validity of Western

1. Thus British Defence Minister John Nott in the House of Commons 7 July 1981, echoing the theory of Laurence Eagleburger expounded three weeks earlier in London, which, in turn, repeated similar views given by President Reagan and Alexander Haig some days before.

views of the USSR. If we cannot be sure of Soviet aggressiveness then there can be no justification for a NATO posture predicated on that extreme and highly likely therefore to destabilize relations and to trigger the conflict which it claims to deter. There is a growing number of sober, clear-headed Europeans, with a profound repugnance towards the Soviet system, who are beginning to feel that the United States, for all its genuine support of freedom and democracy within its own borders, is the most dangerous country on earth at present for those who are its enemies and even for some of its friends abroad. And that danger is most visible in the foreign policy of Reaganism which, for its crude moralism, its incoherence, its adventurousness and its vulgar manipulation of public opinion in the United States leaves many Europeans aghast at its irresponsibility. This is still undoubtedly a minority view which has its own political axe to grind, but it is one which is not restricted to pro-Soviet sympathisers.[2] No one expects America to keep producing great leadership. But they do expect statesmanship in a country which has willingly shouldered the burden of protecting peace and democracy in the world. They have a right to complain if foreign policy seems to be communicated in one-liners and the man on whom the security of the world most depends seems to direct his available energy to the task of public comic and cheerleader.

Were Reagan less affable, less personable, less representative of all that is friendly, dynamic and optimistic about the American character, it is hardly likely that his stock would be high enough for him to contemplate a second term of office. Were it a Nixon or a Ford who was carrying nuclear brinkmanship to such wild excess, the opinion polls would long since have ushered in a new Republican candidate. But American foreign policy is not just a stage prop for Europeans; it is the only script that matters, and whether it is uttered by a laid-back Californian, an East-coast intellectual or a Chicago gangster matters a great deal less to Europeans than whether it is a coherent, trustworthy, realistic response to international affairs.

Reagan's foreign policy is rooted in certain key assumptions reflecting the perceptions of the Soviet Union mentioned above. But where Reagan differs dangerously from his right-wing policy-advisers and friends in Washington and Europe is that he genuinely believes in them. This is not to make a cheap point about his intellectual ability. Reagan is well known to have been a life-long anti-Communist whose vision of the world never extended beyond the coasts of America.

2. Nor is it by any means restricted to Europeans. Former US Ambassador Averell Harriman is the latest in a long line of respected establishment figures in the US who have been driven to public denunciation of Reaganist foreign policy and its betrayal of American hopes for peace. See his *New York Times* article, reprinted in *Bulletin of the Atomic Scientists*, vol. 40, no. 3, 1984.

And he has always himself been profoundly convinced of the moral righteousness of the American way of life — perhaps because he has never allowed himself to experience any other. Communism in Hollywood and Trotskyism in Kansas City was as much as he experienced of a system which he has always believed to ·be evil. His innocence about the outside world springs from the boredom with international affairs which has made life difficult for his aides in the White House since coming to office. For Reagan, the evil of Communism is like the Harlot of Rome for bible-belt Protestants in the deep South, who have little opportunity and less desire to test their theories against the reality. Reagan, in sum, is no cynic. That is an unusual attribute in any world statesman today. For a US President with Reagan's vision it is a tragedy.

It is not so with his European friends and security advisers in Washington. They belong to a long tradition of cooking the books and fiddling with the texts in order to satisfy domestic needs without irreparably damaging international interests. They belong to the school of realism which has always dominated in Europe and which, until recently, held moralism at bay in the United States. Thus, while Reagan and Thatcher screamed abuse at the Kremlin, Alexander Haig and Henry Kissinger were wondering if the Soviet Union ever had aggressive intentions towards the West and were recognizing the gross miscalculations of nuclear balance which allowed previous Administrations to accelerate weapons production with the same public support that Reagan now demanded. And the British Foreign Office, while Thatcher was attributing demonic motives to the Soviet leadership, was coolly describing its foreign policy in terms no different from that of the United States or the United Kingdom: the main aim was 'to accumulate power and influence in the world as a means of preserving the security of the Soviet State'.[3] These are the professional policy-advisers, career diplomats and civil servants whose experience and expertise in international affairs have taught them the limits of virtue in the conduct of foreign policy, imbued in them a keen sense of the political function of moral ideals and made them indispensable defenders of stability and consistency against the moral excesses of politicians and their political parties. They have a reputation, particularly in the United States, for being anti-Soviet on political principle, but not for being crusading anti-Communists. They want to regulate Soviet conduct in their country's interests, to achieve a working relationship which protects the balance of power in their country's favour, and if Cold War rhetoric helps to this end they are ready to use it. But they see it as rhetoric and dis-

3. Kenneth Myers ed: *NATO: The Next Thirty Years*, Croom Helm, London, 1980, p. 4, 436; British Foreign Affairs Committee Report 1980, quoted in Noam Chomsky *et al*: *Superpowers in Collision*, Penguin, London, 1982, p. 18.

tinguish it from the cold analysis of self-interest which is the essential intellectual tool of their trade. They are not deluded into believing that the destruction of Communism and of the Soviet system is realistic or even desirable as a principle of policy.

Thatcher's antipathy towards her own Foreign Office and her desire to neutralize their input into British foreign policy by surrounding herself with advisers who believe in her cause is not a state secret. Her capacity to do this within the British system of government, however, is severely limited. Less well-known, but more successful, is Reagan's systematic exclusion of non-believers from his inner circle of security advisers, in a manner which not only excluded the input of the State Department into policy but applied the test of doctrinal orthodoxy even to the validating of statistical information and intelligence reports.

I shall discuss the three perceptions of the Soviet Union which comprise the Reagan perspective and which condition current US foreign policy and, in the course of criticizing them, outline a more objective view of Soviet intentions. Then I shall examine what appear to be the principal assumptions of Reaganism which colour these perceptions. Finally, I shall return to the question of choosing which side we are on in the confrontation between the superpowers.

U.S. PERCEPTIONS OF THE SOVIET UNION

1. *Level of armaments*
As stated, a moral repugnance for the Soviet Union is not sufficient for mobilizing Western support for a powerful military alliance against the USSR. An important factor is the level of armaments believed to give the Soviet Union a capacity to gain political control over parts of the West by attacking or threatening to attack Western territory. There is no question about Soviet military capacity to inflict enormous damage on the West or on any part of the global territory outside the Communist bloc. What is in question is its past and current capacity to expand its zone of control relative to NATO's ability to deter it. Here, I shall not attempt to enter the complex and highly technical dispute about the military balance, other than to accept the minimal case upon which the present and past US Administrations have rested their claim for continuing support for a strong, nuclear and conventional defence under NATO and US control. That there has been a rough parity in all that is significant for the security of the Soviet and NATO blocs since around 1974 is stated by the Soviet Union and not consistently denied by the United States or by any independent research body competent to judge these matters. What is more important here is to judge the claims of the traditionally superior rival — the United States — that its military

capacity was dangerously inferior in critical areas and to judge the manner in which these claims were made acceptable to American — and later European — public opinion and were translated into intensified production and deployment of new weapons and weapon systems.

In April 1950, a report was submitted to the National Security Council on the consequences for security of the explosion of the atomic bomb by the Soviet Union the previous August. Known since as NSC-68, its principal author was Paul Nitze, now chief US negotiator on arms control. Nitze was then director of the State Department policy planning staff, appointed by Dean Acheson as more likely to take a hawkish line on the Soviet Union than Nitze's predecessor, George Kennan.[4] Nitze wrote of the Kremlin's fundamental design to achieve world domination which only the integrity and vitality of the United States — and a substantially increased air, ground and sea capability — could subvert. That design arose because the Soviet Union 'possesses and is possessed by a world-wide revolutionary movement, because it is the inheritor of Russian imperialism and because it is a totalitarian dictatorship'. The exaggeration of NSC-68 was quite deliberate, as Acheson made clear in his memoirs. He had got his own man in place of Kennan to 'bludgeon the mind of top government'. As he saw it, the job of policy adviser 'is not that of the writer of a doctoral thesis. Qualification must give way to simplicity of statement, nicety and nuance to bluntness, almost brutality'. 'If we made our points clearer than truth, we did not differ from most other educators and could hardly do otherwise'.[5] While educators may have disputed the role allotted to them, no one could dispute the educational success of NSC-68. It postulated maximum danger for the United States in 1954, when the Soviets could have two hundred atomic bombs to destroy the US unless . . . The US Defence Budget was almost quadrupled in the year following Nitze's report.

The thinking behind NSC-68 was: if something is possible, then it is better described as likely. Since almost anything is possible, the job of the National Security 'educator' comes close to that of the creative writer, not too far from science fiction. The fact that such worst-case predictions can stimulate a perception-race, analagous to the arms-race, and that the social cost — whatever about the money — of escalating perceptions and fears far beyond a level determined by objective evidence can be so high as to destroy the value of the security intended, was not generally seen as problematic in 1950.

Another period of peril was discovered in 1955. The bomber gap

---

4. For a fuller account of this and the following military scares in the US, see Robert H. Johnson: 'Periods of Peril' in *Foreign Affairs*, Spring 1983: and 'Fred Kaplan: *The Wizards of Armageddon*, Simon and Schuster, New York, 1983.
5. Dean Acheson: *Present at the Creation*, Norton, New York, 1969, p. 374ff.

of the Killian Report postulated a series of increasingly dangerous imbalances, beginning in mid-fifties and continuing for a decade. The main danger came from the inadequate strategic airpower and air defences against a huge Soviet bomber force which was dramatically displayed on USSR Aviation Day, 1955. Once again, the right educators had the job of counting the hardware which threatened US survival. US Air Force Intelligence estimated Soviet bomber capability by 1960 at a level which would make urban and strategic targets within the US vulnerable. But CIA Intelligence placed a much lower figure on the Soviet threat. The bomber gap was never established, but the factor which made it drift from public awareness was the emergence of a third and more dangerous gap, which the Killian Report also predicted, and which seemed even more promising to the US Air Force as a means of gaining in prestige and defence budget over its Army and Navy competitors.

Paul Nitze, once again, was given the task of drafting the Gaither Report, which President Eisenhower had requested in order to test claims for a forty-billion dollar civil defence shelter programme. This Report also, submitted in November 1957, had none of the niceties of a doctoral thesis, as befitted Nitze. It warned of the rapid expansion of Soviet military capability, of spectacular progress in cruise and intercontinental ballistic missiles in which they had probably surpassed the US. But Eisenhower was unimpressed by the Report and reluctant to spend even one of the forty-four billion dollars now called for in the Report. With Nitze's help, the substance of the Gaither Report was leaked to the Washington Post and a lurid story told of a country exposed to an almost immediate threat from the missile-bristling Soviet Union.[6] The already existing fears in Congress over the launching of the Russian Sputnik now made the missile gap a terrifying matter of fact for the American people, though no American had ever set eyes on a Soviet missile, and presented a golden opportunity to the US Air Force, which now had the support of public opinion against the more modest intelligence reports of the other Armed Services. John F. Kennedy used the scare to good advantage, seeing the Russian missile superiority as 'the shield from behind which they will slowly but surely advance' . . . 'The periphery of the free world will slowly be nibbled away'.[7] But then, in 1960, the United States launched its first spy satellite and the missile gap closed dramatically to move in the opposite direction. (In 1979, NATO Chief Alexander Haig was speaking nostalgically of the ten-to-one strategic superiority of the United States in 1962.)[8]

The fourth gap to be considered is probably the most dangerous of

6. Kaplan: *op. cit.*, p. 153/4.
7. Quoted in *ibid.*, p. 249.
8. Myers: *loc. cit.*

all in terms of the extensive fears, massive defence programme and escalation of Cold War tension which it has generated. This is the 'window of vulnerability' argument which helped Ronald Reagan to power in 1980, the main ideas of which were formulated by the reports of the Committee on the Present Danger, created in 1976 by opponents of détente.[9] Paul Nitze founded the Committee (with Eugene Rostow) and the writings and political influence of that group of experts forced President Carter to respond with a new targeting directive — Presidential Directive 59 — which, in effect, planned for winning a limited nuclear war. The Committee — and the new Reagan Administration — argued that the Soviet Union's military spending in the previous decade had opened up a wide gap with the United States; the Soviets, they said, planned for fighting and winning a nuclear war and were undertaking 'programmes of expansion far beyond Stalin's dreams'. Thirty-two members of the new Reagan Administration in 1980 — including Reagan himself — had been members of the Committee on the Present Danger. Nitze became Reagan's chief negotiator on arms control and Eugene Rostow the Director of the Arms Control and Disarmament Agency. They stressed the superiority of Soviet nuclear capability and the particular danger of the vulnerability of US strategic forces, because of the accuracy and explosive potential of Russian missiles. And this danger would last through the 1980s and perhaps beyond. The MX missile programme, being advanced by Reagan, would counter the threat. (As Robert Johnson notes, the Reagan Administration decided, three years later, window of vulnerability does not begin until the mid-1980s.)[10] The talk about a winnable nuclear war, which was attributed to the Soviet Union, thereby became legitimated on the part of the present US Administration. The founding members of the Committee included members of the famous Team B, which George Bush created in order to counter what he saw as the insufficiently pessimistic intelligence report of the CIA. George Bush had long been a believer in the idea of a winnable nuclear war; President Reagan himself has alluded to limited nuclear war in terms not removed from Caspar Weinberger's frequent references to 'prevailing' in a nuclear exchange with the Soviet Union."[11]

Then, in January 1984, a NATO study of 'Military Expenditures

9. Johnson: *op. cit.*, p. 951ff.
10. *Ibid.*, p. 967. The near-octogenarian Nitze has, more recently, shown some Kennan-like concern at the intransigence of the US Administration in its conduct of arms control negotiations. The fact that he is now under attack for his 'dovishness' says much about the stranglehold of ideology over reason in the foreign policy of the Reagan Administration.
11. By 'prevailing', Weinberger does not mean 'winning', he claims, but he does mean 'not losing'. *New York Times*, 10/8/1982.

of the Soviet Union and prospects for the Future' was leaked in which it was acknowledged that Russia's defence spending over the past seven years had been increasing at less than half the rate previously thought.[12] This should come as no surprise to observers of the military gaps which opened and closed, with significant military and industrial results, since the Second World War, But it was a confidential report, not requiring a television appearance of the President or a leak to the Washington Post, though such publicity would certainly have had a remarkably positive effect on the sense of security in the NATO nations. Only two years ago, Defence Secretary Weinberger defended the size and urgency of his current military build-up: 'we are trying to recover enough strength in time and nobody knows how much time we have'. As Johnson comments, the same sense of urgency does not seem to inspire his disarmament efforts — or, one might add, his need to tell the world about the latest intelligence figures on Soviet defence spending. It is certainly true that we would never know anything about the Soviet military strength if we relied on the Soviet Union. It is because the United States is an open society and because it has the capacity for revealing its past errors — if also for repeating them — that we know something of the situation in both camps. But a little less information and more knowledge of the truth might make that openness more significant.

2. The threat of Soviet ideology

Judging the foreign policy of any nation is not a matter which can be decided by reference to a single indicator. 'Foreign Policy' suggests a blueprint of plans and strategies rationally formulated and consistent with each other and with domestic policy, which is there to be examined or interpreted by other states and measured against performance by observers at home and abroad. But the reality is more confusing, and it is never clear, even to policy-makers, how the conflicting motives, actions and internal inconsistencies are to be presented with the coherence implied by the term 'policy'. The major factors which enter into the determination of foreign policy as it relates to the Cold War confrontation between the superpowers are ideology, military strategy and political posture, the latter being understood as the real intentions of political decision-makers, expressed in concrete actions, statements and the general management of international relations. The ideological element in the policies of Western democracies is vague, diffuse and difficult to identify by contrast with the Soviet Union. There is an obvious case for distinguishing between the political and the ideological elements in any foreign policy, and only rarely in history do the two converge to a point where doctrinal ideals and practical policy are closely inter-

12. Reported in the *Observer*, 19/2/1984.

woven. The distinction between policy and military strategy is, similarly, critical. Only in wartime can they be assumed to converge, and then only confusingly. In peacetime, strategic planning does not necessarily indicate policy; all armies plan to fight and win with maximum efficiency, whatever the present intentions reflected in the foreign policy of the nations they represent.

The consistency with which Soviet foreign policy is seen in the West as ideology and is interpreted mechanically according to the *military* literature of the Soviet armed forces is so clearly a distortion of the evidence that one must conclude that it springs from ideological assumptions in the West. The evidence that the Soviets are planning to fight and win a nuclear war is almost entirely drawn from the military literature and contradicted by repeated statements of policy from the Soviet leadership. On the other hand, the West's own war-fighting plans in Western military literature is, correctly, placed in context — what else would responsible soldiers do in peacetime but plan for every military contingency? — but there are disturbing indications that nuclear war-fighting is being considered in the United States also at the political level. It is simply propaganda, therefore, to conclude from an assessment of Soviet military power that the USSR 'doctrine, structure and offensive posture combine to constitute a threat of direct military action that is of unprecedented proportions' and to describe the matching military posture of the West which, in some respects — like first-use option — appears to be even more adventurous as our 'capabilities needed to prevent war'.[13]

The more plausible case which can be made is that which identifies Soviet ideology with Soviet foreign policy. No nation on earth parades its dogmas and fundamental beliefs as openly and militantly as the Soviet Union. Khrushchev's famous 'We will bury you' was no more than a cheeky use of a line from a literature of revolutionary tracts which begin with the 1848 *Communist Manifesto*:

> The Communists everywhere support every revolutionary movement against the existing social and political order . . . The Communists disdain to conceal their views and aims. They openly declare that their ends can only be attained by the overthrow of all existing social conditions . . . .

Regularly, in this October and May Day celebrations and many other ritual events of the year, the speeches and writings of Marx and Lenin are displayed to the world as proof of the identity and solidarity of the nation, and the cult of Lenin, expressed in the mystical acclaim 'Lenin lives!' pervades Soviet culture like the advertising in the capitalist West. How can we be sure that their advertising is not their

13. Caspar Weinberger: *Soviet Military Power*, US Dept of Defence, 1983, p. 106.

policy? Stalin . . . Hungary . . . Afghanistan . . . Poland — these are
not indicators of a benign policy attitude which permits us con-
fidently to bracket their military deployments and strategy as a purely
technical operation. An obsession with security arising from a history
of war and siege may be a factor in *explaining* Soviet aggression but
it is hardly an explanation that permits Westerners to sleep soundly in
their beds. These actions are too close for comfort to Lenin's explanation: 'We stand on the threshold of a world-wide proletarian
revolution'.

The fashion today among the new right of sneering at Soviet
history as an account of Russia's paranoia with the security of border
territories is helped by the fact that such an account can easily be
interpreted by sympathizers as an excuse. But the issue is not the
justification of Soviet actions but the interpretation of foreign policy
vis-a-vis the West. The right-wing sneer is helped also by the fact that
no other country seems to behave quite as abominably as the Soviet
Union. Afghanistan may have been a border territory but it was not
Soviet bloc territory.

However, we must ask what is the significant fact for the West,
about Soviet intervention outside its own territory, which makes it
unique? It is certainly not the *fact* of intervention. With respect to the
Communist bloc, Soviet stability, caution and predictability in foreign
involvement since the Second World constitutes, for the West, as
clear a sign as we are likely to get that the boundaries of Potsdam and
Yalta will be respected. This is not very pleasant for the East
Europeans under Communist control, we may feel, but that is not the
issue — unless, of course, we insist in the West that we ourselves
stand on the threshold of a world-wide anti-Communist revolution. If
it is the security of Western Europe from Soviet invasion we are concerned with, then no great military power has given more stable
grounds for confidence in its policies — as distinct from its ideology —
than the Soviet Union.

The USSR is a nation trapped within its own dogmas. They
legitimate the system, control the consensus, but, in countless
respects, hinder the efficient functioning of the economy which is
central to the pragmatic policies of its leadership. Certainly, there are
many areas of significance in which Soviet influence is sought around
the world and far beyond the borders of the Communist bloc. But
that is the way of any great military power and such involvement is
particularly significant for a country for which prestige as a superpower in relation to the United States has long been a declared
ambition. All the evidence of internal and external dynamism, such as
there is, points to the irrelevance of ideology and the primacy of
security and status in foreign policy. Afghanistan is never publicly
regretted, though it is so privately — on the grounds that it over-

extended Soviet capacity and damaged relations with Western Europe which are vital to Soviet interests, whatever the propaganda hoardings say. To characterize the Soviet Union as a crafty giant watching for the opportunity to pounce on an unguarded piece of Western territory is simply crude. There is no unguarded piece of Western territory or Eastern territory, since both superpowers have long ago stamped their ownership and protection throughout the continent. If little Ireland today seems like 'little Belgium' in the First World War, that is because the blinkers of ignorance or ideology blind us to the fact that, whether Ireland likes it or not, her neutrality is as fiercely protected by NATO from the Soviet Union as it was by Britain from Germany in World War II. Soviet foreign policy was never characterized by the adventurism and risk possible for the United States because of America's political system, its different mode of foreign intervention and its vast wealth and military potential. Today, more than ever, the Soviet Union exercises extreme caution in foreign affairs by every indicator including Afghanistan — which is not to say, once again, that its policies are pleasant or moral. It is cautious, because of Reaganism and the difficulty of interpreting US signals, because of a traditional conservatism, because of the value of détente which still operates with Europe and because of its own uncertainty about leadership after succession.[14]

The Soviet preoccupation with the security of its borders is extraordinary, given the military force at its command. There is a long tradition of such concern, as there is also about secrecy and authoritarianism, and that tradition is powerfully reinforced by the continuing hostile relations with the Western world. Because no other military power has been similarly burdened by history, it is impossible to draw a clear parallel with other nations. The United States has no such history, yet one hundred and fifty years of Monroe Doctrine have tuned its antennae to the hint of danger in Central and South America. While some US citizens may be proud of the behaviour of their marines in El Salvador, Honduras and Guatemala, the fact of intervention should help them appreciate a little better the Soviet point of view.

Another country which, for its size, has considerable military capacity and which also has a history of insecurity arising from hostile neighbours is Israel. Israel is a nation with non-Communist traditions, and it does not have the capacity of a superpower to dominate it neighbouring territories. But tradition has given it military status, made it fear for its security, encouraged it to engage in strategic take-over of areas of foreign territory as a buffer against a hostile Arab world. Yet only the Arabs regard it as an expansionist power and only the

14. Seweryn Bialer and Joan Afferica: 'Reagan and Russia' in *Foreign Affairs*, Fall, 1982.

bordering Arab peoples live in fear of Israeli aggression. Why do we refuse to see the Soviet point of view, insist on defining it as hostile, engage in reciprocal hostility in a manner which is guaranteed to damage our own security and produce the worst in the Soviet Union? Perhaps we, too, suffer from the burden of history and the weight of our tradition. Perhaps, in addition, we want to destroy the Communist system because it rejects our culture and we believe that current US policy is designed to that end.

3. *Internal weakness and instability*

While the ideology of Marxism-Leninism is a rich store of quotes to justify Western fears of Soviet aggression, Marxist theory rests the case for the destruction of the West on the internal tensions of capitalism. The mechanism of history will expand the proletarian revolution, leaving Communist leaders to preside over the obsequies of a capitalist system stricken by its own contradictions, destroyed by its own incapacity to adjust to the historical process in which it is essentially only a stage. 'We will bury you' may have been intended as the worst-case interpretation has it, but it did have another meaning more consistent with Soviet military capacities in the 1960s.

The Western obverse of Marxist theory holds that the political, social and economic bankruptcy of Communism, working through ethnic discontent and dissident opposition, will gradually strain the social system and bring about its collapse, with unknowable but ultimately beneficial consequences for the Soviet people. The Western version, however, is less determinist than later Marxism would hold; it requires a hefty push from the non-Communist world to stimulate the collapse desired, and this cooperative pressure needs to be applied at the diplomatic, economic and military levels. If the Soviet Union does not collapse entirely, Western manipulation of its domestic base should certainly force a radical modification of its foreign policy and thereby create more stable conditions for world peace. The race is on between the superpowers to see who will bury whom.

European scepticism about this Reaganist justification of American foreign policy is understandable on theoretical grounds alone. But, as Bialer and Afferica make clear in their comprehensive critique of this delusion, it is not merely a greater familiarity with Communism and the Soviet system which fosters scepticism but an awareness that the principal elements of this strategy seem to place a far greater burden on Europeans to pay the cost than on the United States.[15] The military build-up which will stretch the Soviet economy,

15. *Ibid.* To this point one should add the much-ignored disparity of wealth between the superpowers and their respective back garden satellites. Compare, for instance, the higher standard of living enjoyed by East Germans and Hungarians over the Soviet Union with the enormous gap between the US and Europe — not to mention Central America.

the diplomacy which will alienate the Soviet Union from potential allies and the economic sanctions which will directly undermine the material base of the Communist system are all seen in Europe as threatening or damaging to the interests of the European nations involved. The economic sanctions feasible in US terms hit Europe harder than the United States; diplomatic moves to alienate the USSR directly damage the détente with Europe which still operates; and the escalation of the arms-race is seen as encouraging a more menacing Soviet presence and posture in Europe.

But even if one ignores Euorpean scepticism about the strategy, there are fundamental reasons to believe that it is a delusion born of ideology rather than a programme of action based on rational and objective consideration of the factors involved. There is no evidence, historical or political, to support the view that the Soviet system can be sufficiently damaged by the West to provoke an economic crisis of the order intended, or if it were possible, that this would cause a political collapse and profoundly change Soviet foreign policy. Undoubtedly, there is some truth in the popular view of the American Right that Russians understand and appreciate toughness, and there is some evidence to suggest that they preferred to see Reagan elected, with his belligerent anti-Soviet campaigning, to the re-election of Carter in 1980. But this because of a preference for clarity and predictability of policy towards the USSR, which Reagan promised, over the fuzziness and uncertainty of Carterism. Carter was as tough in other respects, but his Administration was also dangerous because of its indecisiveness in relation to a cautious and predictable Soviet leadership. Now the Soviet Union faces Reaganism with Carterism, a combination of belligerence and instability that is without precedent in US-Soviet relations.[16]

The West can undoubtedly damage the Soviet Union, which relies on trade with the non-Communist bloc to maintain even the present low level of economic development. But it is simplistic, dangerous and profoundly erroneous to infer from this that the effect of the damage would create conditions favourable to the West and to peace. The consequences would almost certainly be the reverse. For reasons which include the authoritarian and oppressive control of thought and expression in the Soviet Union, there is a consensus in the USSR on the legitimacy of security policy, and on the relation of military preparedness and foreign policy to the domestic economic and social conditions, which is unparallelled in the West. The attempt to damage

16. The point about the novelty and danger of Reaganism is emphatically made in Strobe Talbott's lengthy critique of US foreign policy in the highly conservative *Time* magazine 18 April 1983. Reagan's cherished self-image is characterized in a later piece (5 December 1983) which quotes Reagan to Nitze: 'Paul, you just tell the Soviets that you're working for one tough son of a bitch'.

the nation by economic sanctions and threatening military deployment will certainly concentrate the minds of the Soviet leadership on
domestic conditions, as Reagan intends. But it will have the opposite
effect on these conditions to that postulated by Reaganism. Since the
Second World War, we have the Politburo's repeated statements,
backed by actions, to prove their determination — at whatever
domestic cost — to attain military parity and equal security with the
United States. The Soviet perception of increased American threat
will be matched in the military field by the escalation of weapons production, not only to counter the perceived threat from the West but
also to legitimate the harsher economic and more repressive social
conditions which the military effort demands. While Reaganism
ignores the clearly untapped resources of the Soviet Union to bear the
costs of rising to any direct US challenge — precisely because it is perceived as directly aggressive and threatening — it is blind also to the
costs to the United States of sustaining such a challenge and to the
relatively weaker American resources (clearly demonstrated in the
last years of Vietnam) to pay for foreign policy through domestic
sacrifice. If the destruction of Communism is the goal of Reaganism,
as it appears to be, the present policy is as crude and counterproductive an instrument as one could imagine. If, on the other hand,
coexistence with global Communism were the policy aim, it would,
paradoxically, be more likely to achieve Reagan's present goal of
undermining the system without the huge risk of damaging aspects of
freedom and democracy in the United States itself, which are
essential for maintaining the consensus at home and the alliance with
Europe.

THE MORAL ROOTS OF REAGANISM

If these three perceptions of the Soviet Union which constitute the
objective rationale of Reaganism are fundamentally mistaken, and if
prima facie and other evidence suggests that they are not based on any
serious attempt to relate US foreign policy to the reality of the USSR,
we must look for an explanation of their origin to those beliefs and
assumptions which have historical roots and electoral appeal in the
United States and which can be seen to have played a significant part in
the philosophy of the Reagan Administration.

Of the four major attitudes which have had a key role in post-war
consciousness in the United States and which are clearly detectable as
unargued assumptions in the speeches and writings of the Reagan
school of conservatism, moralism is, probably, the oldest and most
profoundly rooted. Its origins go back beyond the Founding Fathers
to the theology of Calvin and the idea of a chosen people into whose
hand 'God has placed an afflicted mankind', in Reagan's view and in

the words of Pope Pius XII,[17] America as the redeemer of mankind was a recurring theme in the eighteenth and nineteenth centuries, during which period it inspired a revulsion towards the *realpolitik* which motivated the squabbling monarchs and princes of Europe and — strange as it now seems — a withdrawal from the world of power politics into a righteous isolationism. When President Reagan preached to evangelicals in his 'focus of evil' speech in March 1983, he quoted Tom Paine: 'We have it our power to begin the world all over again'. This idea of the messianic role which God has given the American people and which, in God's time, would recreate an afflicted universe, runs as a motif through American history as through no other nation's past. It is a little out of tune today after the post-war experience of American messianism and the embarrassing clarity with which Reagan expresses it, but it is nonetheless deeply fixed in popular consciousness that the United States holds a monopoly of the moral high ground in international affairs.

Since US involvement in the First World War, American presidents have put the national interest first and preached the messianic vocation loudest in order to legitimate it. It was as unthink-able that a president could win electoral support for a foreign policy of self-interest no different from that of the squabbling Europeans without dressing it up in the theological finery of Calvin, Calhoun, Wilson, or, at least, Kennedy, as it was that he could be elected as a militant atheist. Reagan's moralism succeeded where Carter's failed because it was militant, exaggerated, unambiguous and linked to the scaremongering of the 'window of vulnerability' in a way which gave every middle-American a personal stake in believing, like the president, that 'a divine plan placed this great continent here between the oceans to be found by people from every corner of the earth who had a special love of faith and freedom'.[18] US involvement in Central America shook that confidence and drew from one of Reagan's staunchest ideologues, Jeane Kirkpatrick, a televised confession that her country had as much right as anyone else to protect its interests abroad. But that concession to reality is unlikely to register on the national consciousness. If Kissinger, with his explicit and sustained realism, could not remove the blinkers of moralism — indeed his brand of realism was an important factor in Reagan's later success —

---

17. Robert Scheer: 'The Reagan Interview' in *With Enough Shovels*, Secker and Warburg, London, 1982, p. 260. For a fuller account of moralism in general and US moralism in particular, see Bill McSweeney: "Morality and Foreign Policy", in Dermot Keogh ed.: *Central America: Human Rights and US Foreign Policy*, Cork University Press 1985 (forthcoming).

18. Arthur Schlesinger Jr: 'Foreign Policy and the American Character' in *Foreign Affairs*, Fall, 1983, p.5.

it is unlikely that Kirkpatrick on Central America will be seen as anything more than a lapse of taste. This is because the real manifestation
of God's anointing lies, not in the unregenerate and machiavellian
character of politics in the old world in general, but in the 'evil empire'
which now directly threatens the new.

Anti-Communism is the second of the Reaganist perspectives and,
like the first, it has a longer history than its current hype would
suggest. In the 1920s, Soviet Bolshevism was identified by Secretary
of State Kellogg as the agent of takeover in Nicaragua on the grounds
that Mexican workers were approached for help by a deposed vice-
president.[19] Before the Second World War had ended, the variety of
international powers which required the vigilance of the State Department to counter any imbalance which might threaten US interests
had begun to narrow. With France, Britain and Germany crippled by
the war effort, with the rapid spread of Communist parties beyond
the territories of the USSR and its Eastern allies, only the Soviet
Union posed a challenge to the awesome military and industrial might
of the United States. The massive Marshall Aid programme, which
stiffened European resistance to Communism, was proof — if it were
needed — that global involvement was no less an element in
America's divine mission than the isolationism which it supplanted.

Anti-Communism had a potential for American foreign policy
which might have remained untapped had George Kennan not
unwittingly provided the key. His concept of containment, later translated into the domino theory, helped to narrow the range of potential
enemies even further, to a single moral and military evil of near-
Satanic proportion, which threatened freedom and democracy
wherever the United States was threatened and threatened the United
States wherever the interests of capitalism were threatened. Korea,
Vietnam, South America, Europe and now Central America — all
became theatres of the battle between good and evil, freedom and
oppression, whatever the real issues were. The irony is that several
countries in the American hemisphere today are forced to tolerate
cruel and oppressive military regimes of a kind not seen in the Soviet
Union since the Stalin era on the grounds that the only alternative is
godless Communism. Had Communism not been banned in the
United States — and also, therefore, in South and Central America —
its threat might have been better contained, and at far less cost to the
world, by the democratic process. If Americans had been permitted
the Europeans' experience of Euro-Communism, at least in their
neighbouring territories, they might never have allowed the hysteria

19. Walter LaFeber: *Inevitable Revolutions: The United States in Central America*,
Norton, New York, 1984.

of anti-Communism to distort their perceptions of the world and
corrupt their foreign policy.[20]

A third factor which conditions US involvement in global affairs is
the attitude of dominance. Two distinct and opposed attitudes have
marked the American approach to relations with the rest of the world
during this century: isolationism and dominance. They are connected
by the common moral purpose advanced to motivate and justify
them. If Woodrow Wilson's description of America as having the
'privilege of fulfilling her destiny and saving the world' became a
recruitment slogan for US *involvement* in the First World War, the
same lofty aim had already inspired the *withdrawal* from global
entanglements and would later be proposed to justify American
neutralism in the late 1930s. But it was with the emergence of US
technological and economic supremacy from 1945 that the
isolationist option was finally laid to rest and the redeemer nation
turned to foreign alliances and confrontations as the proper field of its
mission. The illusion of American omnipotence, wrote Reinhold
Niebuhr in 1953,

> is a natural mistake of a commercial community which knows
> that American hegemony is based upon our technical-economic
> power but does not understand the vast complexities of ethnic
> loyalties, of social forces in a decaying agrarian world, of the
> resentments which a mere display of military power creates
> among those who are not committed to us.[21]

In the post-war and, probably, permanent shift from isolationism to
global involvement, it has become impossible for American
politicians and people to conceive of a foreign relationship of friendship or enmity which was not dominated by the United States. The
impulse to dominate is not, of course, a peculiarity of Americans.
What is particular is the huge gap in resources between the US and
the rest of the world which gave rise to this habit of thought in the
first place, the emphasis on morality as its justification, the sense of
failure in the 1970s to maintain the gap as the basis of domination
and to exploit it to clear moral purpose, and, finally, the militarization of the idea of dominance, making it impossible to perceive of a
stable peace which is not guaranteed by overwhelming US superiority.

20. Containment, American style, is a crude instrument. The more effective
European approach to containing conflict, by contrast, was exemplified in the
control of heresy in the medieval church. By monasticizing heretics, rather than
excommunicating them, medieval Catholicism for long avoided the disaster — in
sociological terms — which befell the Church at the Reformation. The management
of Euro-Communism since World War II is in the same tradition.
21. Reinhold Niebuhr: *Christian Realism and Political Problems*, Scribner, New
York, 1953, p. 64.

The fourth assumption of US policy concerns its militarization and its faith in military solutions to problems of international conflict over economic, political or other options. With the natural and manufacturing resources of the US undamaged by World War II and a massive productive capacity created by it, with a huge arsenal of military equipment and weaponry at its disposal and a monopoly on the atom bomb, and with a political need for rapid demobilization of manpower, it is not surprising that faith in the future of America was placed, after God, in military strength. In the absence of other tolerable possibilities, the purpose of this awesome power was, and is, to dominate the Soviet Union.

> With Germany and Japan out of the way, there was need of a new prospective opponent with relation to whose military personality a new American military posture could be designed. The Soviet Union was the obvious, indeed the only plausible, candidate.[22]

The ideological urge to depict the USSR in the most menacing terms, facilitated by deducing its foreign policy from the rhetoric of its founding dogmas and from the literature of its military strategists, resulted in a definition of the enemy which perfectly suited the resources at hand to deal with it. If, in 1950, US policy-makers started at Stalin and saw Lenin, so today the ideologues of Reaganism remain 'forever in 1950', as Arthur Schlesinger says, 'with a crazed Stalin reigning in the Kremlin . . . a fanatic state carrying out with implacable zeal and cunning a master plan of world domination'.[23] The militarization of foreign policy is nowhere more clearly and tragically ineffective in securing its aims than in Central America. It is inconceivable to policy-makers that socialism or Marxism could exist independently of the Soviet Union, least of all in the tiny agrarian territories many thousands of miles from the USSR which are the backyard of the United States. And if Communism is the problem, military force must be the solution. Since the domino theory holds that every threat to US interests is a threat from Moscow then the El Salvador rebels and the Nicaraguan government are really the evil empire at work, against which the Kissinger Report claims that there must be a major victory or a major defeat. As President Reagan said to Congress in April 1983: 'If we cannot defend ourselves there, we cannot expect to prevail elsewhere'.

22. George F. Kennan: *The Nuclear Delusion*, Hamish Hamilton, London, 1984, p. 220.
23. Schlesinger: *op. cit.*, p. 6.

These four attitudes which colour present American perceptions of Soviet foreign policy are interrelated and self-reinforcing. Moralism — the most pervasive, unshakeable and traditional of the four — can be understood independently of the other three, in the sense that their historical emergence was not conditional upon their definition as moral imperatives. The compulsion to wrap foreign policy in an ethical package is a long tradition in the United States, which is only partly explained by a fairly universal modern practice of calculatedly disguising power politics in ethical terms. There is good reason to believe, as already stated, that President Reagan and many of his close advisers sincerely believe most of their claims to righteousness and are themselves victims, rather than merely manipulators, of the American illusion.

Communism, with its explicit reference to religious faith, freedom and democracy, matches so perfectly the enemy identikit of the believing American that it might have been invented in Washington had the Bolsheviks not got there first. No other country — except possibly the Soviet Union — has a common enemy so finely tuned to its domestic and global needs, so ready to respond to the promptings of its policy-makers like the switch on a radio or a megaphone, as the United States. Anti-Communism has become the prevailing expression of moralism, making the one inconceivable without the other. Dominance and militarism are similarly related to each other as two sides of a coin and similarly moralized to serve and to reflect the policy aim of anti-Communism.

The effect of these controlling assumptions is to generate a degree of hysteria about the Soviet Union in the United States which matches that of the Reagan Administration; to create the public support and demand for 'excommunicating' the Soviet Union from the kind of cultural, physical, economic and, to a degree, even diplomatic contact with the United States which is a precondition of reconciliation and peace; to make the alliance with Europe conditional, in effect, on the 'good behaviour' of Europeans in these respects without consideration of the very different problems, traditions and perceptions of Europe; and, finally, to encourage the agencies of religion, media and industry to increase the pressure of moralism, sensationalism and profit which have forced politicians to match foreign policy to the demands of American public opinion, not to the objective situation in the Soviet Union or the needs of the international community. At a time when the United States is still the greatest industrial and military power in the world, it is sobering to read the words of its former ambassador to Moscow and original architect of the policy of containment:

Never before has there been such utter confusion in the public mind with respect to US foreign policy. The President doesn't understand it; the Congress doesn't understand it; nor does the public, nor does the press. They all wander around in a labyrinth of ignorance and error and conjecture, in which truth is intermingled with fiction at a hundred points, in which unjustified assumptions have attained the validity of premises, and in which there is no recognised and authoritative theory to hold on to.[24]

This is not a quotation from Kennan's famous essay on the instability of Reaganism, 'America's Unstable Foreign Policy', published in 1982. It is taken from his diary of 1950 and it underlines the point that incoherence and instability of policy is not an accident of Reaganism but has become a traditional aspect of American postwar attitudes towards the Soviet Union which the Reagan Administration has raised to a new and perilous level. The obsession with Communism not only damages the European alliance and the friendship of Europeans towards the United States. It also damages the capacity of the US to utilize its enormous power and influence in the world effectively to protect its own national interests.

Repeatedly over the past five years and more, the militarized policy of the US towards Nicaragua and El Salvador has done nothing but exacerbate the problem it was intended to solve. The failure to understand the elementary human problem of poverty and suffering in these countries would be unremarkable had the United States been as indifferent to their fate as were most other countries at the time. But to regard Central America as vital to US interests, to delay economic aid until after a broken Nicaragua had established trade links with the Soviet bloc and then to pour in massive military help to the putative anti-Soviet forces of both countries in order to achieve the only goal which the Reagan Administration seems capable of conceiving — a major victory over Communism — this is stupefying in its crudeness. The Soviet Union is not responsible for the poverty and suffering of Central America. The United States has directly contributed to these conditions and, by the dogmatism of its approach to this and other global problems, it has effectively advanced the only condition it was concerned to avoid — Soviet involvement. The Communist factor so blinds American policymakers that they cannot see or find the energy to remedy the indigenous problems which may have nothing whatever to do with the Soviet Union. Finally, and perhaps most tragically, by not solving the problems which Americans are superbly equipped to solve, the

24. George F. Kennan: *Memoirs (1925-1950)*, Bantam, New York, 1969, p. 527.

United States is forced to tackle a problem which it cannot solve — the creation of global conditions which will destroy Communism and undermine the internal structure of the Soviet Union.

This obsessive drive to achieve the impossible is responsible for the remarkable tide of uneasiness, hostility and even crass anti-Americanism which has swept Europe since 1979. It cannot be accounted for by reference to the personalities of Reagan or Carter or their advisers alone. American foreign policy has not radically changed in the past five years. It has simply become more moralistic, more militaristic, less stable and more dangerous for Europeans. It is also, it appears, very popular with Americans. By looking briefly at the policy which preceded it, it may be possible to understand a little better the paranoid fear of Communism which Reagan articulates and to draw some conclusions which can help in choosing sides in the Cold War.

The policy of détente was the main target of attack by the Committee of the Present Danger, through whose writings and campaigning the road to the White House was cleared for Ronald Reagan. Apart from the impact of détente and the SALT II agreement on Soviet military spending and arms build-up, which have been discussed, there were other features of this policy which are relevant to an understanding of the popularity of Reaganism. The Nixon-Kissinger approach to the challenge of the Soviet Union was a calculated attempt to contain Communism in limited and specific spheres of US-Soviet global areas of interest and to avoid the total commitment which ideological anti-Communism required and which the United States could ill-afford.[25] It was a policy of classical power politics designed to conserve American resources during a period of internal weakness caused primarily by US involvement in Vietnam, later reinforced by Watergate and by the growing awareness of the relative decline of US dominance in the international sphere, indicated by the economic challenge of Japan and Europe and the crisis over American hostages in Iran. Détente, understood in traditional moralistic terms, became an appropriate scapegoat for America's ills — the desire for peace and coexistence had caused a US military decline relative to the Soviets. Understood more objectively and rationally as *realpolitik*, détente was an affront to the American sense of piety. Not only was power politics against the grain of the American self-image in foreign affairs, against the tradition of virtuous involvement, but it had failed to yield the benefits which that tradition demanded and to halt the decline in power which world events signalled. It was time to abandon the Nixon-Kissinger experi-

25. For an account of détente policy, see John L. Gaddis: *Strategies of Containment: A Critical Appraisal of Postwar National Security Policy*, OUP, New York, 1982.

ment and to reassert the old standards and the old dominance. It was time, too, to ignore the complexity of the balance of power with its varied and multitudinous challenges to different levels of American interests and to return to the simplicity of the common enemy, whose military might and moral turpitude were simpler to grasp and more comfortable to contemplate than Japanese electronics, Arab oil politics, European trade restrictions and Central American poverty and violence.

Since there is no justification in current or recent Soviet policy for the obsessive preoccupation with Communism which dominates American foreign policy, and since this policy cannot but fail anyway, one is driven to the conclusion that the explanation for it lies somewhere in the same perception of the world which encouraged the abandonment of détente. In other words, it is not the foreign policy of the Soviet Union which accounts for the policy of the United States, but the fact that, at a time when American dominance was apparently in decline, the USSR emerged as the only state capable of challenging the prestige of the United States as the moral and military superpower in the world. American status was founded on the unprecedented combination of unassailable military force and unrivalled goodness. Now, for the first time, the world is divided between two superpowers, each of which makes exaggerated moral claims for its legitimacy and for the subordination and allegiance of its existing and potential bloc allies, and each of which possesses unprecedented powers of destruction of the other and of the entire globe. Faced with a rival which claimed superiority of virtue and demanded equal rank in the military league and which, moreover, might well become an economic rival also if a policy of détente were to facilitate its expansion of trade, the United States understandably, if tragically, turned to Reaganism for a solution. It is, therefore, the fact of a rival *ethical* giant with comparable military capacity, rather than any reasonable assessment of Soviet foreign policy, which accounts for the all-or-nothing hysteria which inspires current US thinking on international affairs and the resort to moral denunciation and arms escalation, neither of which can be sustained for long enough to achieve their stated goal without damaging the political and economic structure of the United States itself.

Whose side are we on, as Europeans trapped between rival moral claims, rival military powers, rival foreign policies? To declare a plague on both houses solves nothing. To promote Europe as a third superpower could well be the most dangerous solution of all, even worse than uncritically continuing West European support for the United States through the Atlantic Alliance. In some measure, taking sides depends on judging the effectiveness of any action which follows from such a choice and which provides a reduction of international tension and a more lasting sense of security from the threat of nuclear war which hangs over Europe and European Russia more menacingly than it does over the United States.

It is clear, as already indicated, that most of us in Western Europe would have no difficulty in making a moral choice between the American and the Soviet social systems.[26] But that is not the vital question posed for Europeans today, nor was it the question facing Caspar Weinberger at the Oxford Union debate. Of course it is better to live in a Western democracy than in a Communist state, to be free to believe or disbelieve, to agree or dissent. It may not appear that clear from Leningrad or Prague but there is no doubt how the people would vote in Frankfurt, London or Dublin. But the question of taking sides amounts to making a different and twofold judgment — about the rival foreign policies and their implications for peace, and about the effectiveness of any action, consequent on that judgment, in ameliorating the dangerous political climate of the Cold War. Weinberger avoided the question he was asked by stating the obvious and seducing his student audience into believing he was addressing the motion under debate. It is no comfort to Europeans to know that life in New York or Los Angeles ranks higher on their ethical scale than in any town or city of the Soviet bloc if they also know that American foreign policy contributes to making nuclear war in Europe more likely. Neither will it give relief to the peoples of Central America to know that the violence endemic in their societies is, in part, occasioned by the intervention of a government in Washington which was democratically elected by an American citizenship free to choose otherwise. Even if Soviet policy is judged to be equally adventurous and dangerous, the political fact of importance for Europeans is which superpower can they influence in order to reduce the tension and avert the danger of nuclear war without at the same time destabilizing the overall balance of power.

If Europeans spend far more time and energy criticizing American foreign policy, it is because they have already judged the moral issue in terms favourable to the United States, though not as uncritically as Reagan and Weinberger would like. It is because they have also judged that American foreign policy is a totally inadequate response to the global problems which cry out for a solution and an excessively military and dangerous response to the problems posed by the USSR. In choosing their own governments, and ultimately Washington, as their targets of criticism, Europeans are realistically judging the uselessness of attempting to oppose the Kremlin and, at the same time,

26. The author was made particularly aware of this by the generosity and remarkable courtesy of the US Information Agency in facilitating the travel and contacts with policy officials of every persuasion in the United States which led to the writing of this paper.

affirming the validity of the case made in this paper that the United States under Reagan represents a threat to world peace which can be reduced by safe and graduated unilateral action. In so far as one can infer a common purpose in the large and multifaceted body of European dissenters or peace groups, it is probably true to say that they take the side of neither superpower, of neither bloc, but rather of sustained détente between West and East of a kind that Europe has continued to experience since the early seventies, which the Soviet Union claims to desire, but which the United States has unilaterally repudiated.

This unbalanced criticism of the West, therefore, is justified by the excessive aggressiveness and brinkmanship of American and NATO anti-Sovietism and by the fact that only the West is capable of yielding to the pressure of popular opinion. It is premised, in other words, on the ethical superiority of the West, not on moral equivalence or neutralism. West Europeans can deplore the oppressiveness, the secretiveness, the lack of respect for human rights and liberties in the Soviet Union, but they can do nothing to influence the Kremlin directly. The Reaganist option is the most dangerous of all, both because it increases the threat to Europe and because it strengthens the very evils in the USSR which it denounces. Undoubtedly Communism generates its own iniquities independently of any Western pressure. But it is equally undeniable, as I have already argued, that the illiberal and oppressive aspects of the Soviet system are worsened and consolidated by the failure of the West to sustain a relationship of détente and peaceful coexistence and to permit the Soviet Union the level of equal security and equal status as a superpower with the United States which it consistently demands. The West has contributed to the problems of Communism, and the current foreign policy of the United States is unwittingly designed to add to the evils it claims to deplore.

To return to the earlier analogy, the position of Europeans, caught between two belligerent giants, may well be analagous to the situation of the cat and the rat and the frightened observer. The confrontation is not in our backyard where we can escape the fallout, however, but in our living-room. And however much we may deplore the character of the rat, it would be less dangerous an animal without the aggressiveness of its enemy. We have no option but to concentrate on controlling the larger and more likeable of the combatants, which is amenable to influence, rather than attempting to control its rival.

The unbalanced criticism of the West by the disarmament movement in Europe implies, too, that the process of de-escalating the arms-race and creating a lasting détente can only be initiated through a strategy of unilateralism. Few concepts in the vocabulary of East-West relations and strategies of peacemaking have been more wilfully distorted than unilateralism. The Kremlin, the White House, the Pope and the defence establishments of almost every European state have joined in roundly denouncing unilateralism as a naive and dangerous policy more likely to cause war than peace, and they have contrasted it with— as they see it— the only realistic and safe programme of multilateralism which must be supported by all right-thinking Communists and Westerners. So diffused is this misunderstanding of unilateralism as pacifism, that there are probably few among the uncommitted who do not immediately associate one with the other.

Who is advocating what so many prestigious political and community leaders are at pains to denounce? Certainly not the major groups in Europe— not even the IKV in Holland, though its slogans go further than most in inviting that interpretation. Least of all is the largest peace campaign in the West— the Freeze Movement in the United States— open to the charge of utopianism and naivety levelled at all whose programme for peace includes an element of independent initiative.

To those who wish to understand and who take the trouble to investigate even superficially, nothing could be more obvious than that almost all unilateral proposals for peacemaking are a form of *qualified* unilateralism, graduated according to realistic judgments of safety and security. The fact that Holland may wish to rid itself of nuclear weapons does not mean that Holland is to be denuded of an army or that the entire Western Alliance, of which it is a part, should deprive itself of the military capacity to resist an enemy. The same can be said of British CND, of the Italian, West German, Danish, Swedish and Irish peace movements. Graduated unilateralism is not only an attempt to initiate the process of multilateral disarmament in stages that are safe and secure. It is also self-evidently the only means by which serious *multilateralism* can proceed. Without the cautious and safe concession, independently offered, multilateralism lacks the very condition which makes disarmament possible. At best it can only mean multilateral talk; more often it is a public disguise for multilateral rearmament. As the history of arms negotiations demonstrates, rigid multilateralism has been more a factor in escalating the arms-race than in controlling it.[27]

Certainly some unilateral proposals are less realistic, less safe than others and, therefore, less likely to win acceptance from responsible statesmen. But this is clearly not the issue which underlies the deliberate distortion of the term and the widespread popular misunderstanding of unilateralism as synonymous with pacifism. The

27. See, for example, Alva Myrdal: *The Game of Disarmament*, MUP, Manchester, 1977. George Rathjens: 'Are Arms Control Negotiations Worthwhile?' in Paul Abrecht and Ninan Koshy eds: *Before It's Too Late*, WCC, Geneva, 1983; David Holloway: *The Soviet Union and the Arms Race*, Yale UP, 1984.

ideologues of West and East do not discriminate between safer and riskier proposals for independent initiatives on disarmament. They smear any positive unilateral move to initiate independently the process of peace with the label of pacifism, intending thereby to consign any proposals but their own to the wastebin of sentimentalism. Since their own effors are a record of failure, and since that historical record shows an increasing tendency for multilateral negotiations to trigger an arms-race in anticipation, in order to strengthen the bargaining position of the negotiators, it is apparent that rigid multilateralism is something of an ideological device to prevent disarmament except on the other side. It denotes the complete absence of any spirit of compromise, or reconciliation, or readiness to take even minimal risks to bring about a long-term reduction in armaments and tension. That some religious leaders fail to recognize the elementary Christian imperative of graduated unilateralism — of taking the first safe step to resolve the conflict with an enemy — is an indicator of how language has been corrupted by ideology. If a US president can reject the mild and cautious programme of the American Freeze Movement on the grounds of its dangerous unilateralism, it is not surprising that his Administration is seen by many as being itself more in need of containment than Communism.

Those who wish to advance the cause of peace are left with no choice between the superpowers. They must choose whatever programme of action is available to them which encourages genuine détente, promotes the spirit of reconciliation at any of the multiple levels of East-West relations which are possible for them, promotes the fact of multilateral disarmament through unilateral initiatives, and opposes the institutionalized mutual hatred which has been the accomplishment of the Cold War. They will find no encouragement for any of these aims in the Kremlin or the White House. Since, as Westerners, they can only correct the evil in their own societies, they have no choice but to focus their efforts for peace on the governments of the West.

5   *War, Peace and Justice**

Paul Oestreicher

The current public debate on war and disarmament is of such immense importance. But unfortunately it is a public debate that is being conducted at an extremely superficial level. It is a public debate triggered by fear — justified fear — of nuclear war and by the immediate emotional and intellectual response to that fear. For that reason the debate is actually very limited in its scope. I want to try to ask some of the more fundamental questions about the nature of peace and about the underlying problems that we must face in our community, if the majority of people are in any real sense to be involved. I think one of the things that you will realize is that those who are engaged in this exploration are a relatively small minority because the subject is profoundly uncomfortable. The majority of people are not eager to face the implications of what is involved in the threat of nuclear war; and, frankly, I don't blame them.

A final preliminary note before the main part of my talk. I am speaking here at the Irish School of Ecumenics in a country which is not a nuclear power, nor is it linked to any nuclear alliance. The threat of nuclear war which you face in Ireland is not very different from that in the United Kingdom. But your contribution to security and peace in the world, your moral option, are obviously influenced by the fact of your neutrality.

I did not come to Ireland to tell you what you should do or to teach you about your own history, your own problems, your own violence and what you can do about it. In general terms, of course, what I have to say will bear upon the particular problem of what Ireland can do to contribute to a more secure Europe and a more peaceful world. But my thinking on peace and war has been shaped largely by conditions in Great Britain and Germany, and if I do not illustrate my talk by reference to Irish history, this is to acknowledge the limits of competence, not the limits of my interest and concern. I

*This is a revised text of the 1983 Peace Lecture given at the Irish School of Ecumenics, 17 September 1983.

shall later refer briefly to that concern for Ireland's role in the peace-making process as I see it emerging from the consideration of war and peace and justice, which are my main theme.

PEACE EMBRACES A WHOLE WAY OF LIFE

I want, first of all, to make clear that there are very many different meanings to the word peace. People use it as though we all agreed what it meant, but we don't, and we shouldn't pretend we do; and I want to explain how the word is used and how I am using it. The superficial and obvious use of the word peace is the absence of war and, actually, I think that is the most legitimate use of the word in the current political climate. But is not the meaning that is attached to the word in a variety of contexts, ideological and theological.

There is, above all, the Jewish-Christian tradition, the biblical tradition. In the biblical context peace means a great deal more than the absence of war. Peace in the Old Testament, the word for which is the Hebrew *shalom*, means something that really embraces a whole way of life. It denotes total harmony. It includes the concept of justice. It embraces a new order. Shalom means that the whole universe is in harmony with God and with itself. It draws in more than human beings. It emanates from God and writes into itself the whole creation — an interesting concept which is being reintroduced today by the ecological movement, by the Greens of various nationalities. Why are we people, they ask, so unique, what is so special about us? Why should we alone lay claim to the privilege of holiness stemming from creation? Why not animals and indeed the inanimate universe as well? That's getting back to the biblical vision of the whole of creation being in some important and profound sense to be worshipped, to be held sacred.

But the idea of *shalom* offers more than scriptural authenticity. It can also function as an instrument of ideology, a means of blunting the cutting edge of the peace movement which, currently, sets itself the clear, narrow path of disarmament and the avoidance of war. Let me explain. Peace as the absence of war is not necessarily a situation in conformity with scriptural ideals. Such a peace can be achieved in the most oppressive societies, with a political system so cruel as to make war seem an attractive alternative. The absence of war is, ideally, the expression of harmony, justice, freedom within the community; it is the reward, the fruit of biblical peace, not its definition, not its sum total. Peace is about all the conditions which make violence unnecessary, and those of us who put forward the pacifist view rejecting violence as itself immoral are in fact narrowing the scriptural dimension.

But conflict over values and resources is an inescapable part of our present human condition. To claim that we can only have peace when all the conflicts have been resolved is to speak of a situation which can only obtain at the end of history — what Christians call the Kingdom of God, others Communism. The rejection of violence as a means of solving disputes is a pacifist principle based on the teaching of Jesus which does not exclude — indeed it requires — resistance to evil. The rejection of war as a means of resolving international conflict — what is sometimes called war pacifism — is a more widely subscribed principle based not only on the Christian gospel, but on the lessons of history that war is an evil which destroys far more than it preserves or creates. In modern times that evil has been multiplied by the fact of nuclear weapons. To suggest that peace must always be understood as *shalom*, that the pursuit of peace must always include the preservation of the values for which human beings have always been willing to destroy and kill is to guarantee the likelihood and the 'justification' of war. It is to make war possible.

I want to turn now to the relationship of peace to justice. It is an element of the *shalom* concept that until there is justice in our world, in other words, until there are right relationships we cannot have peace. The psalmist in the biblical vision has the picture of justice and peace kissing each other in expression of that great fulfilment; a beautiful vision where it is recognized that until relationships are right, until conflict — *necessary* conflict — is properly gone through, there cannot really be peace. That has led in recent years to a great deal of the thinking, both in Christian and non-Christian circles, that justice is an essential pre-requisite for peace, and that in fact to talk of peace without at the same time recognizing that injustice must be righted is to talk moral nonsense. I want to challenge this view, and to suggest that we have to discover a quality of peace that is possible even within injustice, within the political structures of our real world now. In other words, a peace that can exist within a highly imperfect world peopled by very imperfect human beings.

CREATING THE GODS OF WAR

We cannot, I think, embark upon the search for peace without clearly defining at the outset that what we mean by peace is a lack of war, defining war as a process of conflict where human beings, reluctantly or otherwise, accept as a norm that they must destroy those whom they believe to stand in the way of justice. The necessity of war and violence is deeply embedded in human consciousness. I think we have got somehow to break through a kind of sound barrier, an emotional blockage, a thought barrier that takes us right back to the beginning of civilization itself. Because, if you look at the history of warfare — and the history of warfare and man's search for peace are of course coterminus — right from the outset it has been recognized that war is awful and yet, paradoxically, also wonderful, somehow glorious.

This terrible duality of rejoicing in conflict, of almost worshipping conflict, and creating the gods of war, has been a part of human history from the outset. The club that caveman made both to hunt animals and to protect himself and his family against other cavemen somehow became sacred, somehow weapons took on a very special significance, and they came in a strange way to be worshipped, because they represent the preservation of our own kind against the other, against the human being, the group, the tribe, the nation, which challenges our own whatever it is we hold most dear — our identity, our superiority, our own values, but most of all, of course, our bread, our own livelihood, our own economic existence. Marxism is right in claiming that most conflicts have their roots in economics. We may give all sorts of other reasons for conducting those conflicts, but bread — using that as a generic idea of what we need or think we need to live on — is the root of most conflicts. It was probably at the root, symbolically, even of the first murderous conflict between Cain and Abel. That's an awful lot of history and I am really saying that all of human history is, among other things, the history of warfare. And it's not really surprising that to some degree even in today's schools history seems to be a record of battles and war.

The truth that history is a social process in which fighting is only a small part is a relatively modern idea; that social history might matter more than political history and that even political history does not entirely consist of warfare and violence. Nevertheless, wars seem to be the punctuation marks of history, and to learn their dates is actually to learn a lot about the process of human development. I am asking the question today — can the barrier be crossed where we stop that period of history before history itself is stopped? This is the question and the task which faces the peace movement.

Let me say a few words about the tradition I share with you, the Christian tradition, which frames the laws and values of our society. I don't mean by that that most people are Christians, or would claim to live by the standards of the Gospel. But Christianity is the cultural framework in which we still think about the morality or immorality of war. It has its roots again in the Old Testament to which I have already referred. In the history of the people of Israel the dream of ultimate peace becomes stronger and stronger as their story develops, but it remains a dream, an aspiration for some future time. There is still a necessity for armed struggle in order to vindicate God's purpose for the people of Israel. And so we find in the Old Testament a long record of bloody battles being fought on God's behalf. God is, in a sense, the commander-in-chief, and man is simply fulfilling his will to prevail over the heathen, with the heathen, by definition, becoming God's enemies. And so we get war in a highly ideological frame-

work, or religious framework, which more or less amounts to the
same thing.

But there is another strand in the Old Testament. The idea that war is
terrible, war is de-humanizing; we must try to civilize it; we must
learn that even our enemies are human beings like us and they must
be respected. — So we get the tradition developing that creates rules
of warfare — what in the Middle Ages was called chivalry, putting
limits on violence, on what you may or or may not do to your enemy.
The enemy must be treated decently, and if you capture his land you
must not even cut down a tree on it, because a tree is the bringer of
life and fruit, which both your enemy and you will need to eat — a
piece of ecological insight already present in the Old Testament, a
respect for creation, even if it belongs to your enemy.

Already in the Old Testament there are the threads of three traditions about conflict and violence — the tradition of the holy war, a
second tradition of the war that is beastly and ghastly and therefore
must be cilivized, where the evil must be minimized, and where
among other rules we get the one most quoted: an eye for an eye, a
tooth for a tooth. (That was not actually the primitive and barbarous
rule it is commonly judged to be. What was meant was that we may
not do anything to an enemy that is more violent than what the
enemy has done to us; we may retaliate, but we may not do it first.
Now there, if anywhere, is a limitation on violence in war — an ancient
policy of no first use and no disproportionate second use either). So
we have the tradition of the holy war which you must win because if
you don't God is defeated, then the tradition of what we now call the
just war which has to be limited in its evil, and thirdly, just over the
horizon, a vision of a world without war, of a society in which we will
no longer resort to war to settle our conflicts, expressed so movingly
in Isaiah and Micah by the image of the swords beaten into plough-
shares and men learning war no more; the lion will lie down with the
lamb, the whole of creation will cohere within itself.

These are the three traditions we are heirs to and they are not in
harmony with each other. But into this situation comes Jesus of
Nazareth, a crazy young prophet with most unconventional ideas
that were considered to be a threat to the whole Jewish establishment, preaching a very radical gospel and picking up various strands
from the Old Testament, but clearly saying that we have got to start a
new tradition, or rather we have got to build on the old one and transform it. 'You have heard it said "an eye for an eye and a tooth for a
tooth', but I say unto you love your enemies, do good to those who
persecute you.' And St Paul echoing that teaching: 'If your enemy is

hungry, feed him, if he is thirsty give him to drink; do not be over-come by evil but defeat evil with goodness.'

This is a Gospel which, in modern terms, is pacifist, which makes it possible to carry on conflict in a completely new style and because people are sacred — all people, our enemy as well as our friend. This gospel dictated the mood of the first three centuries of Christian life, not least because it included in its teaching a refusal to accept that the secular state, the power of Caesar, was higher than the law of God, and that worship of Caesar was appropriate for a Christian. And of course to worship Caesar was simply a Roman way, in the absence of a God in our sense of the word, of recognizing the highest authority and paying it the highest respect.

Now that view of the state, I contend, has not really changed. We no longer used the word 'worship', but unconditional obedience to the state is still considered by most people a fundamental human duty, and there is no difference between worship and unconditional obedience. It is just a different way of using words. For the first three hundred years of its existence, the Christian Church was in a situa-tion of martyrdom, because it refused this unconditional obedience to the Roman state. An important part of that refusal was the refusal to fight for the Roman Empire. And then the wonderful, and at the same time terrible, happened: the emperor was converted to Christianity and things have never been the same since. From which we might learn that it is better to have heathen rulers! When power and Christianity were united in one and the same structure, when the Empire was now Christian, or called itself Christian, what actually happened was that the Church went back into an Old Testament per-spective, and we are still basically in that situation. This is not to be despised. It would be anti-Semitic to suggest that an Old Testament view is devoid of humanity and goodness. I am not suggesting that, but rather that the peculiar ethic of Jesus of Nazareth was no longer held to be applicable and relevant to public life in the world as it developed since the fourth century, and that is still our situation today.

JUSTIFIABLE WAR

So the Church faced the task of restoring Old Testament doctrine to some kind of real dignity in the new Christian context, and St Augustine was the first great theologian who tackled that problem, and, in the context of war and peace, began to evolve the doctrine which has since been called the just war. It would be better lin-guistically to call it the justifiable war; the war that is indeed sinful because man is sinful, but is a necessary evil in a fallen world. And this war must be limited, it must be subject to strict rules; it must respect constantly the fact that in some way all human beings have a particular dignity and that to destroy them in war is sinful, however unfortunately necessary. And so we got the development of the doctrine of the just war — and I'm not going to take you through it in detail tonight because that would take too long, and there are other accounts of just war teaching easily available. It consists of an elaborate set of conditions which, in theory, drew the moral boundaries for the declaration and conduct of war. Under these conditions, human beings may go to war against each other without regarding their behaviour as conflicting with the Will of God.

Just three of these conditions: the evil that is caused by the war must not exceed the evil that is being combatted — a fairly obvious point meaning that if the war does more harm than the thing you are trying to destroy then the war obviously is counter-productive. Secondly, war must be waged only against those who are actually the enemy, in other words, those who are actively engaged themselves in some evil against us. The non-combatant, the ordinary civilian, the human being who is not directly involved in this evil struggle, must on all accounts be respected, not injured or destroyed. And thirdly, there must be a reasonable chance of achieving the objective for which the war is being fought; sheer idealism is not enough. We must be able to calculate that what we are fighting for is an achievable object. These carefully considered and rational limitations make it clear that total war, with no holds barred, is ruled out, is not permitted for Christians.

THE 'HOLY WAR' TRADITION PREVAILS

Now that view has officially prevailed since the fourth century, more or less, throughout Christendom. But it has been studiously ignored by that contradiction which allows mankind to set up rules and then fail to live by them. Because the other tradition in the Old Testament, the holy war tradition, or, as Christians have known it, the Crusade, is in fact the one that has prevailed. Nearly every war has been turned into an ideological war, into a war for the survival of our deepest values and ideals. We have defined God on our own side and anti-Christ as our enemy and if we go into the cathedrals of our country — I speak as a British Anglican — and into its parish churches and look at the memorials to war, we see the evidence around us. We have assumed that to die in war for our country is in some way more holy, more pleasing to God, than to die in our beds. It is a strange concept, an idea that is in conflict with the doctrine of the just war which certainly does not suggest for a moment that in fighting for our country we are doing something holy, but simply recognizes that we may be doing something that is the lesser of the evils in prospect. But the mood of that doctrine has prevailed into our own time and is still behind the thinking of many decent people, practising Christians, who still seem to think that a readiness to go to war against and to kill the opponents of their own community has some kind of holy quality about it.

In the First World War the element of crusade was clearly present as part of the psychology of waging it on both sides. It was a bloody internecine struggle between European tribes, which spread far beyond Europe and which had, in retrospect, very little of substance to justify it, but in which both sides had to convince themselves that they were fighting God's war. The Germans, who probably had some doubts about this, had to convince themselves by engraving their justification on the belt buckles of their soldiers. If you possess such a thing as a German belt buckle from the First World War, you will see inscribed on it the words 'Gott mit uns' — God is on our side. Of course the British Army had no need for such reminders. If you are profoundly convinced of something you don't inscribe it on your belt buckle. The British have a custom of understating the obvious. And that kind of dual delusion indicates the moral dilemma in our current situation.

The Church of England in its formularies, like all Western Christendom, has no doctrine whatever justifying war as a good and holy enterprise. In fact, the only statement on war of a traditional kind in the Church of England's doctrines is one of the thirty-nine articles of belief formulated at the Reformation. It is interesting that in its original Latin form it says that a Christian man, at the behest of a magistrate, that is the civil power, may take part in just wars. The Book of Common Prayer conveniently omits the word 'just', but there is no doubt at all that that is what was intended. In practice, of course, it actually meant all wars that the nation regards as necessary, that those in power decree shall be fought. During the bitter period of Civil War, with Catholics against Protestants, Cromwell against the King, the war was much more passionately fought, because Christian doctrine was at the heart of it, and the Crusade was its meaning. Civil wars tend to be of that nature, even more ghastly than wars between nations because they are even more irrational by their nature and even more in need of a supernatural excuse, since to butcher your own brother on home ground is psychologically more difficult than to kill some foreigner in another nation. So we need a much more stirring cause which God, in various guises, can provide.

PACIFISM A CONTINUING STRAND IN CHRISTIAN TRADITION

We are heirs to all that and yet, through the whole period of history that I am talking about, there is this continuing strand of pacifism, this tradition of Christians rejecting violence as an appropriate or acceptable means of resolving conflict. We will not kill. We will not recognize that kind of enmity any more. We will try to prevail by other means, whatever those means may be. We think it is possible to live without taking up arms and in a profounder sense to survive. So the pacifist tradition as a minority witness was always there. And in our own century, because war has become so dreadful, and possibly because our moral sensibility has in some ways become more refined, that tradition has grown and gained respect. Conscientious objection to military service, at least in those countries which are inheritors of the Western liberal tradition, has become a part of life. In other words, pacifists, because they are an obviously sincere minority who do not challenge the right of the majority to defend themselves in traditional ways, are tolerated, accepted, even welcomed. They are regarded as a part of the creative community and, within the Church, respected as people who witness to an ultimate ideal that today cannot be achieved, because we live in a fallen world.

And often those who are not pacifists will accept that pacifism is possible for individuals, honourable for individuals, perhaps even the only right way for individuals, but will add that we cannot apply the rules that are good for an individual to a nation because the collectivity behaves and must behave differently to the individual. Reinhold Niebuhr is the great theologian who developed this idea of the restricted applicability of pacifism in the thirties when pacifism was fashionable. He described it in his famous book *Moral Man and Immoral Society*, where he claims that a morally rersponsible leadership cannot effectively function in the world as it is. Moral society is really a contradiction in terms according to Niebuhr, and there is an immense amount of circumstantial evidence about collectivities and individuals in history to suggest that he is right. The Jesus ethic can be applied to individuals, Niebuhr maintains, but it is virtually inapplicable in terms of political power. And that is one of the things I would like to explore.

PEACE THE ABSENCE OF WAR

But I want first to look at how others outside the Christian tradition now behave in relation to the peace problem. One of the inheritors of our Western liberal and Judeo-Christian culture is modern Communism, and it is very interesting that modern Communism conforms to type, to our type. Communism ideologizes the whole of the peace struggle in a way that is very close to our Christian practice. I was in East Germany for a May Day Communist festival last year, a high point of Communist emotionalism, and one of the great slogans all over East Berlin was 'Peace equals Socialism', and, of course, we are invited to turn it round 'Socialism equals Peace'. Socialism is short-hand in Eastern Europe for Marxist Leninism, for the kind of society that is in power. That is to say, when our ideology is properly implemented, then we have peace, and everything that works towards the implementation of our ideology is by definition peaceful. So there is no contradiction in the Soviet SS20 missile being described as a missile for peace, because it is there to protect or promote Marxist Leninism. It is a peace weapon, we must understand.

Peace in the Communist context does not mean the absence of war. It has taken on a new meaning, a richer significance for them just as it has for many of Christians — remember my sharing with you the Shalom idea? Shalom, too, does not mean the absence of war. It is deeper, richer, equally difficult to specify concretely, equally inaccessible in our imperfect world. In theory, they are each, in their own way, noble ideals. In the concrete world of international hatred and brinkmanship they are each ideologies. The Communist Andropov and the Christian Reagan work with similar assumptions. They both ardently desire peace, but not at any price. Not at the price of sacrificing Communism, the Russian way of life, on the one hand, or sacrificing freedom which, in practice, is the ideological code for the American way, on the other.

So peace is fine, but only in terms of achieving the national objec-tive. Peace is fine when it protects my kind of world. We have to ask ourselves whether we can still live with that ideological framework for peace. And I want to say — No, we must end this game of peace definitions and give peace its proper linguistic meaning, and that is the absence of war.

We live in a world where imperfect human beings are often in conflict with each other and yet, somehow or other, will have to resolve their conflict by means other than war. Ethically, this was always the option but mankind has always chosen violence. In realistic terms non-violence has always been regarded as utopian, never achievable. Need I say that in the age of nuclear weapons, in the age when technology dominates, when technology threatens us all, whatever our ideology, we have perhaps a generation in which to work out patterns of conflict resolution which do not depend on the conduct of war. If we fail, then the probability is that there won't be any more problems to solve or conflicts to resolve because we won't be here to do it. We can now extinguish life as we know it on this planet. That is no longer a technological problem, the problem has become how to avoid doing it.

LOVING OUR ENEMIES AN INJUNCTION OF PRACTICAL POLITICS

We have arrived, in Christian terms, at a point where, perhaps for the first time in human history, the injunction of Jesus to love our enemies has become a counsel of practical politics. Until now it has been assumed to be a counsel of perfection that sinful human beings cannot live by. Now perhaps it is becoming the only way sinful human beings can survive in community. If we confront each other in corporate and national terms, if the historic burden of racial or religious division shapes our consciousness and defines other human beings as our enemies, then we have got to learn to resolve the conflicts which arise without going to war against each other, and we must learn to do this as an act of enlightened self-interest, simply as an exercise in conduct. This is a very difficult thing to get across, and you will find if you try it with friends and acquaintances that they will not easily catch on.

Loving an enemy does not, of course, mean pretending your enemy does not exist, that there is no enmity. Such pretence is sentimental nonsense. There are people of whom we have cause to be afraid. To minimize evil in our world of Auschwitz and the Gulag is to be a fool, and a knave. There are enemies. There is real injustice. There are good grounds in traditional terms why we should go to war against each other. And yet that is no longer in our own interest; it is no longer rational. We must find other means of resisting our opponents and combatting our enemies. The study of alternative ways of resolving conflict has made a modest beginning and has become a very important part of tomorrow's history, if there is to be a history tomorrow.

Loving enemies is not a sentimental business of liking the people we dislike and fear and it is our business, not our government's, to determine who to fear, who are our friends and who are our enemies. We are inescapably the targets of clever propaganda from West and East encouraging us to mistrust and to hate those whom politicians need as their enemies, encouraging us to see violence and war as the only realistic defence of our own interest in an age when violence and war have been made the instruments of human destruction.

We must find alternative ways. I learned a lot from a teaching of Mahatma Gandhi, which helped me understand the implications of conflict and violence which I have been trying to share with you. Gandhi once said: 'Not to do battle with evil when you are confronted by evil is to surrender your humanity. To confront evil with the weapons of the evil-doer is to enter into your humanity. To confront evil with the weapons of God is to enter into your divinity.' He was teaching that there are many situations in life in which to go to war against evil is better than not to fight at all. That is a surprising thing to many who see Gandhi as the great pacifist, but who understand pacifism as passivism. Gandhi actually said war is better than non-resistance to evil, but he also said that there is a better way still — to resist evil by other means; to use the power God gives us. Now, this needs to be expressed in the secular language of human development and interest because to many people God is not accessible, metaphysics is not meaningful. We need to find a rational language to show that it is an act of enlightened self-interest to love, that is, to respect the opponent, to see that the security of the opponent is part of our own security, that our security cannot be bought at the price of our enemies' fear.

This is actually the doctrine behind the recent Palme report on the nuclear-free zone in Central Europe. Olaf Palme, the Prime Minister of Sweden, is concerned with mutual security in East and West, each side co-operating to improve the sense of security of the other. This rational consideration for the security of one's political enemies is one of the techniques of alternative methods of conflict resolution.

ARTICULATING A COLLECTIVE ETHIC

It is essentially a political process but it is also a human process and a spiritual one.And it underlines the point that Reinhold Niebuhr was wrong in assuming that collectivities cannot embody a spiritual imperative within their policy framework. The crusade was a spiritual imperative, but it can also be a higher form of struggle that does away with the arms and still continues the struggle. In fact Jesus was part of a tradition in which morality was not seen primarily in personal terms, but rather in collective terms, in which the people of Israel, the nation, was accused again and again by God of departing from God's ways. Israel was God's people, and in the New Testament the Church is seen as the body of Christ, a collective personality having real moral character, emphasizing the fact that collectivities have ethical significance, even if, all too often, their ethical behaviour is negative rather than positive. The great challenge to us in this age is to articulate a collective ethic that can bind politicians in their own interest. We cannot make peace against the politicians, but we can persuade them, in their own interest, to act in our own interest.

Jesus said to his disciples: 'There are many things you cannot now understand, but the Holy Spirit will lead you into all truth.' It took until the nineteenth century for Christians to realize that slavery was dehumanizing and not in accord with the gospel. Within a century and a bit more, perhaps, it is just conceivable that Western civilization, and maybe Eastern as well, will come to see that not only slavery is dehumanizing but war also. That requires a giant leap of consciousness, given that many wars in our world today are being fought against forms of slavery and they are still morally justifiable in terms of the injustice they are trying to right. So we are in between the times when all war has not become inconceivable and totally immoral, when we can respect many people involved in war today, even though I, as a Christian pacifist, could never join them. We can respect, too, the professional military men, who are often more peaceful in their personal relations and disposition than a lot of pacifists I know. They are heirs of their tradition and many of them are capable of re-thinking their position. They know how dangerous war has become and they are often the last to want to engage in it.

So we have a difficult task ahead of us, a tremendous challenge which humanity has not been faced with before in human history. I am not optimistic about the outcome, but because I have a faith I also have a hope. That hope is based, in part, on the courage and strength of the peace movement and on the potential it demonstrates in the smaller non-nuclear states of Europe. And here I want to return to the question of Ireland and the possibilities for this country afforded by your tradition of neutrality. Ireland shares with four other countries of Europe not only the wisdom and benefit of having no nuclear weapons on its territory, but also the privilege of being involved in no military alliance with the nuclear powers.

NEUTRALITY NOT A POLICY OF INDIFFERENCE TO INJUSTICE

I am aware of the vigorous debate now going on about the future of Irish neutrality, of the ambivalent and irresolute attitude taken by past governments of the Republic, of the threat to neutrality posed by your membership of the E.E.C. and of the tempting option facing your politicians to negotiate a final solution to the Northern Ireland problem with Westminster in exchange for a united Ireland committed to Britain's defence policy in NATO or in a supportive bilateral alliance. I am no expert on these matters, as I have said, and it ill becomes a British visitor to lecture Ireland on how it should conduct its international affairs. But some general points deriving from my talk are appropriate.

At first glance the concept of neutrality scarcely commends itself to a Christian. It smacks of indifference and of that cowardice and self-involvement so often attributed to pacifists. No doubt there were some who called themselves pacifists in the 1930s whose only concern was to protect profitable trade with Germany and to save their own skins. And no doubt there are advocates of neutrality in Ireland today who are similarly indifferent to the plight of Europe, and who think neutrality can save them from the holocaust, whatever the merits of the case for East or West or the millions trapped within their conflict.

Neutrality in that passive sense is better abandoned, buried with the paraphernalia of militarism which disfigure our cathedrals and churches and which belong to an age of just war delusions. We live now under the threat of a nuclear catastrophe in which no war can be just and no country can be saved. Not only is passive neutrality ethically indifferent; it is also practically useless as a means of avoiding the effects of war.

But Ireland's tradition and its *de facto* neutrality present a unique opportunity to transform that neutrality into a positive commitment to world peace. Ireland enjoys an influence in international affairs out of all proportion to her size, population and wealth. You have already established a world-wide reputation for the Irish army as an efficient peace-keeping force within the United Nations. Now, with the increasing danger of a world engulfed in nuclear war, you have the opportunity, which few countries enjoy, of extending that role into a service for Europe, a witness to the gospel of peace. Unlike Austria and Finland, Ireland's neutrality is not constrained by treaties or threats by the superpowers. Unlike Switzerland, Ireland's neutrality is not dictated by trade and commerce. Like Sweden, the Irish government can be a force for reconciliation between the superpowers, a resource for imaginative measures in security and confidence-building in Europe. Whether you take this opportunity, or lose it for a quick fix in Northern Ireland, will depend on the pressure exerted by the people of Ireland on your politicians.

Politicians here, as everywhere, take the shortest route to re-election and party survival. If they are offered the glittering prize of a united Ireland, who could blame them for signing away a tradition of neutrality which has been at best a non-violent political expedient, at worst a source of embarrassment in international affairs? If the violence in Northern Ireland could really be halted by Ireland joining the war preparations in alliance with the Western powers, if Ireland's contribution to NATO for a Third World War were a necessary condition for ending the war in Northern Ireland, then such a move would be understandable, if ethically reprehensible.

But that is not the case. The ending of violence in the North does not depend on appeasing the forces of militarism in Westminster or anywhere else. It depends on a positive and wholehearted conversion to peace-making, at home and abroad, wherever violence threatens, whatever the price to our traditional conceptions of sovereignty, nationalism, church allegiance, ideological preferences. It can be facilitated — and certainly not inhibited — if Ireland seizes the opportunity to transform passive into positive neutrality and commits herself and her institutions to involvement with the world as a peace-maker.

6 Why the Christian Church Must Be Pacifist*

Alan Kreider

The case that I have been asked to argue — that the Christian Church *must* be pacifist — is a bold one. Forty years ago it would have been preposterous to make such claim in a place like this. Many Christian traditions would have dismissed a person making such a claim as an irrelevant crank. Some Christian traditions would have been more severe; by arguing a pacifist case in public one would have been running the risk of excommunication and anathema. But today, there is a resurgence of pacifism throughout the world. And I think it is fair to state that in the 1980s pacifism is being taken more seriously by every major Christian tradition than at any point for the past sixteen hundred years.

There are many indications of this; I will give you just two. The first comes from London. In a 1979 Remembrance Day sermon in All Souls Church, Langham Place, the Reverend John Stott, the most widely-respected representative of conservative Evangelical Protentantism, stated that pacifism is one of the two positions which are held by people whom he styled as 'equally biblical Christians'. Pacifism and the Just War, according to John Scott, are the two positions to which Christians must listen today.[1] The second indication comes from the US. In *The Challenge of Peace*, the recent second draft of the proposed pastoral letter of the American Catholic bishops, the bishops state that there are 'two legitimate modes of Christian witness on issues of war and peace', the Just War theory and non-violence. And they conclude that 'today in the Catholic community, when any issue of peace or war is addressed, the non-violent

---

*This is a revised version of a paper given at a conference on 'Peace and the Future of Irish Neutrality' at the Irish School of Ecuminics, Dublin, 12 February 1983.

1. John R. W. Stott: Sermon at All Souls, Langham Place, London, 11 November 1979; printed in *Christianity Today*, 8 February and 7 March 1980, and in *Crusade*, November 1980.

tradition must be part of the discussion.'[2]

Once again I return to the astonishing nature of this development. When one thinks of the dogmatically confident scorn that an eminent Irish theologian such as Jeremiah Newman — as recently as 1961 — could pour on pacifism in the *Irish Theological Quarterly*, one realizes that we have come a long way in the past two decades.[3] Indeed, in the 1980s we are entering a new world in which pacifism may be a uniquely appropriate expression of the Christian faith; for — as I shall argue later — the world of the late twentieth century is in significant respects similar to an older world, the world of the early Christians.

I speak as one who greatly respects the Just War tradition in Christian moral philosophy. At its best it can address the world with great authority, as it did through the writings of the American theologian Fr John C. Ford S.J., who during the Second World War denounced the Western Allies' policy of the obliteration bombing of German population centres;[4] or as it did in the book *The Church and the Bomb*, prepared by a Working Party for the Church of England's Board for Social Responsibility;[5] or as it did in the US Catholic bishops' recent pastoral epistle on nuclear weapons.[6]

But in pacifist Christianity I discern something which comes even closer to Jesus, even closer to the perfect expression of the character and will of the Father, even closer to the fount of our common tradition, than I do in the Just War theory. A striking illustration of this is the bishops' draft pastoral letter itself, in which pacifism follows naturally as an expression and application of the inspiring statement of the Christian gospel with which the bishops begin their statement; the Just War theory, in contrast, enters the discussion as jarring theological *non sequitur*, the product of other sources of ethical reasoning.[7] If pacifism therefore comes closest to Jesus Christ, ultimately it is the most likely — indeed, the *only* — source of healing for our desperately hurting world. To me, therefore, pacifism is not a

2. *The Challenge of Peace: God's Promise and Our Response*, published in *Origins*, 12, xx, 311. This second draft has since been superceded by a fourth and final version, which on 3 May 1983 was adopted by the US National Conference of Catholic Bishops by a vote of 238 to 9. Although at the time of writing this had not yet been published, I was informed by one of the five-bishop drafting committee, Bishop Thomas Gumbleton (Auxiliary Bishop of Detroit), that the final version is substantially the same as the second draft.
3. Jeremiah Newman: 'Modern War and Pacifism', *Irish Theological Quarterly*, n.s. 28 (1961), 181-206.
4. John C. Ford, S.J.: 'The Morality of Obliteration Bombing', *Theological Studies*, 5 (1944), 261-309.
5. Working Party for the Board for Social Responsibility of the Church of England, *The Church and the Bomb* (London, Hodder and Stoughton, 1982).
6. *The Challenge of Peace*, 315 ff.
7. *Ibid.*, 311.

department of moralism; it is good news. It is good news to us all as Christian believers. It is good news even to you, as Irish men and women, as you gather today to consider your nation's security and well-being.

With this as background, I would like to proceed to the substance of my address. In it, I wish not so much to argue why the Christian Church *is becoming* pacifist, and why pacifism has emerged as a serious moral force in the world which politicians must take seriously. There are, it seems to me, four reasons for this surprising pacifist resurgence. In presenting these reasons I will speak descriptively, at times even analytically. Yet you will note that behind each of these four reasons there is a normative element, an element of urgency, of vocation, in biblical terms of *kairos* (the significant moment).

THE FUTILITY OF VIOLENCE

The first of the reasons for pacifism's current growth is the mounting realization, on the part of millions of people, that military violence is futile. This is true both of violence on the 'strategic' level and on the level of more localized — though often excruciatingly tragic and potentially globally dangerous — conflicts.

Let us begin by looking at the military situation on the global level. Never before, it is 'safe' to say, has so much money been spent on military hardware and personnel as is being spent today. Last year the world spent over six hundred billion dollars on armaments.[8] This represents six per cent of the total world output, and is twice as high a percentage of world productivity as was being spent on armaments during the latter stages of the arms race which preceded World War I.[9] Tragically, among the big spenders are numerous small powers, many of them in the Third World, who are emptying their exchequers to buy the most sophisticated weapons that their suppliers will let them have. Often they are buying these on credit, and their large debts are a significant factor contributing to the present precarious state of the international banking system.

It is not only the small powers that are on a military spending spree. Setting bad examples are the two major military powers, who are racing ahead with the militarization of their societies, constantly re-equipping their forces with the latest in 'high tech' weaponry, and cowering in fear of each other.[10] On the part of the two major powers

8. Ruth Leger Sivard: *World Military and Social Expenditures, 1982* (Leesburg, Va., World Priorities, 1982), 5.

9. *World Armaments and Disarmament, SIPRI Yearbook 1980* (London, Taylor & Francis, 1980), xvii; Ruth Leger Sivard: *World Military and Social Expenditures 1981* (Leesburg, Va., World Priorities, 1981), 24.

10. James Fallows: *National Defense* (New York, Random House, 1981).

and their allies there is thus a *vertical proliferation* of weaponry. This is especially true of nuclear weaponry, which will soon be producing, according to Fred Iklé of the US Department of Defence, an unstoppable *horizontal proliferation* of nuclear weapons. By 1985, an estimated forty countries in the world will either have nuclear weapons or be able to produce them.[11] In the world today, there is therefore a military potency of unthinkable magnitude. But, at the same time, as a direct product of that potency, there is a military vulnerability and weakness of equal magnitude. For the first time in history, through nuclear war, there is a real possibility of a humanly engineered snuffing out of human life. Unless current trends are reversed, the planet earth may shortly be a lonely globe on which only insects and grass can flourish.[12]

There is something lunatic about all this. We have been moving in a direction that a recent article in the authoritative US journal *Foreign Affairs* characterizes as being from Mutually Assured Destruction to Nuclear Utilization Target Selection — from MAD to NUTS![13] The consequences of this insanity affect us all. They affect those of us who live in U.K.; they affect the Americans, the Russians, and even you Irish people. Given world-wide fallout patterns, there can be no place, not even in County Kerry, that is not ultimately a nuclear target.

In this situation, people are suddenly coming to realize — and often this happens as a veritable conversion experience — the sheer futility of it all. They are coming to realize that the might of weaponry is illusory, that power (Chairman Mao to the contrary) does not grow out of the barrel of a gun, and that there must be another way of dealing with conflict.

Although I have been speaking so far about the perceived futility of the global arms race, what I have been saying is just as true of many localized conflicts (some of which have geopolitical rami-fications) in various parts of the world. The basic ingredients in these conflicts are the same as those in the super-power rivalry: two hostile groupings, both of whom have a sure sense of their own rectitude, and both of whom construct arguments based on history and morality to justify their armed intransigence. One of these, of course, is on your island. The struggle, I am informed, is between the

---

11. Albert Wohlstetter, et al: *Swords from Plowshares: The Military Potential of Civilian Nuclear Energy* (Chicago, University of Chicago Press, 1979), 126. See also Walter Schütze: 'A World of Many Nuclear Powers', in Franklyn Griffiths and John C. Polanyi, eds., *The Dangers of Nuclear War* (Toronto, University of Toronto Press, 1979), 88.
12. Jonathan Schell: *The Fate of the Earth* (London, Pan Books, 1982), ch. 1.
13. Spurgeon M. Keeny, Jr., and Wolfgang K. H. Panofsky: 'MAD vs. NUTS: The Mutual Hostage Relationship of the Superpowers', *Foreign Affairs*, 60 (Winter 1981/1982), 287-304.

'loyalist' community, whose chief exponent is the M.P. for Antrim
(North) and the nationalist community, whose self-appointed representatives justify their military activities by appealing to Irish history
and the Just War doctrine. An equally insoluble conflict is that in the
Middle East. There we observe the ironic predicament of an Israeli
state which, despite its massive military superiority over its combined enemies (it has the third largest air force in the world), cannot
achieve a secure basis for its national existence, for it cannot reach a
tolerable relationship with its Palestinian neighbours.

In the Middle East, as in Northern Ireland and many other parts of
the world, more and more people are questioning the political efficacy
of military strength. Indeed, military strength is coming increasingly
to seem not potent but futile — because it cannot bring reconciliation.
One cannot bomb hostile neighbours into peaceable neighbourliness.
Nor can the threat of military strength bring reconciliation. It is
impossible to live in peace with someone whose brains you are
threatening to blow out, or with someone whom you fear may at any
moment blow your brains out. In the increasing awareness of this
futility, on both the global and local levels, Christians are beginning
to turn to a different way, a way of creative suffering, a way of non-
violence. They are beginning to turn to pacifism which, in the words
of Jürgen Moltmann, is 'the only *realism* of life left to us in this
apocalyptic situation of threatening world annihilation'.[14]

BIBLICAL AND THEOLOGICAL INSIGHTS

A second reason for the resurgence of pacifist Christianity is the
advent of new insights from the biblical and theological disciplines.
Although these insights come from the study of both testaments,
some of the freshest insights are coming from recent studies in the
Old Testament. The Old Testament, of course, is the classic locus of
Christian justification of warfare. It has always seemed so obvious,
hasn't it? God, it is argued (indeed, it is assumed) in the Old Testament authorized his people to fight; and, by easy extrapolation, we
assume that he similarly authorizes us to fight today using the latest
available military technology.[15] Whenever the Bible seems to provide
us with such self-evident justification of what we had already decided
to do anyway, we are right in querying whether we are reading it correctly. Yahweh is not a household deity! Therefore, when we
approach the Old Testament expectantly and reverently, we must
expect to hear a word of confrontation of our comfortable pre-

14. Jürgen Moltmann: *Following Jesus Christ in the World Today* (*Occasional
Papers*, No. 4) (Elkhart, Indiana, Institute of Mennonite Studies, 1983), 108.
15. For a recent example of this approach, see Jerram Barrs, *Peace and Justice in
the Nuclear Age* (Greatham, Hants, Garamond Press, 1983).

judices. And indeed, according to recent studies, we are hearing just that.

The principal study to which I am referring is *Yahweh is a Warrior* by an American Old Testament scholar, Professor Millard C. Lind.[16] In this careful study of the theology of warfare in the Primary History (Pentateuch and earlier prophets), Lind points out that the conventional use of the Old Testament war narratives neglects to ask what sort of war it was that Yahweh was authorizing his people to fight. In one of the earliest writings that was incorporated into the Old Testament, 'The Songs of the Sea' of Exodus 15, Lind finds the clear outlines of a different kind of warfare. In her song, Miriam proclaims that the Exodus was a battle, a battle which was won not by human prowess but by divine miracle at the Reed Sea. And thus the Exodus, by which Israel was formed as a nation and given its sense of identity and destiny, was a deed of God's grace and not of human works. As Exodus 14:14 puts it: 'Yahweh will fight for you, and you have only to be still'.

During the subsequent wars of conquest and the period of the judges, Israel's victories were gained repeatedly, as in the Exodus, by the miracles of their divine King: by crumbling walls, rumours, swollen streams, a hornet, pestilence, by broken pitchers, torches and trumpets. In these narratives there is record, to be sure, of human violence, often of a genocidal nature. But this human violence was incidental — in fact, it was generally subsequent to Yahweh's miraculous acts which had given Israel victory.

To ensure that Israel would trust in Yahweh even in military matters and thus would be different from the surrounding societies, the Law (Deut. 20:1-9) established procedures that institutionalized Israel's *numerical inferiority* to her opponents. When confronted by an army stronger than her own in both technology and numbers, Israel was instructed to send men home! Those who had just built houses, planted vineyards, or married wives where all to be sent home; so were those who were 'fearful and fainthearted'. Only when Israel had such a small force that she could not conceivably trust in her own prowess must she do battle, for only then would she have to trust Yahweh, who will 'fight for you and give you the victory'. In the book of Joshua (11:6, 9) there is a parallel insistence which institutionalized Israel's *technological inferiority* to her enemies: Yahweh instructed Israel, whose army unlike her foes did not possess chariots, to 'burn with fire' any chariots that she might capture. The issue once again was acculturation; Israel was not to become like her pagan

---

16. Millard C. Lind: *Yahweh is a Warrior: The Theology of Warfare in Ancient Israel* (Scottdale, Pa., Herald Press, 1980). See also Vernard Eller, *War and Peace from Genesis to Revelation* (Scottdale, Pa., Herald Press, 1981), ch. 1-4.

neighbours in their reliance on military strength.

Thus there is admittedly warfare commanded by Yahweh in the Old Testament, but it is not the sort of warfare that people want to justify today. It is a distinctive, cultically-based form of warfare designed to emphasize the reality of God's grace in Israel's historical experience.

A watershed occurred, according to Lind, when Israel rejected Yahweh's kingship and chose to have a human king instead (1 Samuel 8). Samuel, speaking the words of Yahweh, told Israel that the consequences of their choice of human monarchy would be two-fold: the militarization of Israel's society; and the advent of materialism in Israelite society, with flagrant social inequality rooted in the royal court. Israel would thus come to be 'like all the nations'. She would be acculturated, compromised, living by conventional wisdom; indeed, she once again would be in slavery (1 Sam. 8:11-20). This, according to the biblical narratives, is precisely what happened. And in response, prophets arose to speak Yahweh's word of judgement on Israel for her materialism and militarism — for her pride in her own martial prowess and technology, for her reliance on powerful foreign allies: 'Woe to you who go down to Egypt for help or rely on horses, who trust in chariots because they are many and horsemen because they are very strong and do not look to the Holy One of Israel' (Isa. 31:1). The consequence of militarism was military disaster: 'Because you have trusted in your chariots and in the multitude of your warriors, therefore the tumult of war shall arise among your people, and all your fortresses shall be destroyed' (Hosea 10:12-14). In many passages, the consequence of the Israelites' militaristic infidelity is represented as Yahweh's fighting against his own people. If they will not burn their chariots, he will do the burning for them! The result of Israel's militarism is Israel's defeat, exile and subjugation.

A careful reading of the Old Testament thus provides not a justification of military strength, but a critique of militarism. This view is becoming increasingly persuasive to Old Testament scholars.[17]

The perspectives offered by recent New Testament research are not perhaps as novel as those of Millard Lind; but they are equally important in giving theological substance to the revival of pacifism in the Churches. We have known for a long time, for example, that Jesus' life and teaching must be assessed in light of the socio-political circumstances of first century Palestine. But it is only recently that scholars — led by Martin Hengel of Tübingen — have exhaustively

17. For representative reviews, see *Catholic Biblical Quarterly*, 44 (1982); *Interpretation*, July 1982; *Biblical Archaeologist*, Summer 1981.

indicated what those circumstances really were.[18] Jesus' ministry, they have reminded us, took place in a setting of foreign occupation. And, from the Jewish point of view, that occupation was not benign. The Romans offended the Jews' religious sensibilities, fleeced them economically, and ruled them with brutal severity (the two thousand simultaneous crucifixions on the hills just outside Nazareth in 6 A.D., when Jesus was ten years old, is a particularly flagrant example).[19]

In response to this foreign misrule, the Jews responded in various ways, occupying all points on a typical spectrum of religio-political behaviour, ranging from collaboration with the Romans (Herodians and Sadducees) through politically-neutral withdrawal (Pharisees and Essenes) to an increasingly organized and armed revolutionary rejection of Roman rule (Zealots).[20] It is in light of this setting, which was a 'politico-religious tinderbox', that we must read Jesus' challenge to his disciples to 'Love your enemies'.[21] With these words, Jesus was calling on his followers to love the one enemy whom his expectant and observant Jewish compatriots were tempted to resist by collective violence; he was urging them to love the *Romans* and to treat them non-violently.

By doing this, however, Jesus was not endorsing Roman rule of Palestine. In a setting in which Roman sovereignty was being controverted, Jesus' proclamation of the 'Kingdom of Yahweh' must have been politically provocative.[22] Furthermore, Jesus was clear in his rejection of the patterns of rule of the Roman rulers, who 'lord it over their subjects' and style themselves as 'benefactors'. But, Jesus warned them, 'Let it not be so among you!' (Luke 22:24-27).[23] In God's Kingdom, the great would be servants and enemy-lovers, not Roman-style rulers or their supposed Zealot antithesis. The lifestyle of Jesus' disciples would be more radical than either, and would reveal the nature and rule of God.

This could not, of course, happen to them as isolated individuals. In the heart of Jesus' teaching there was thus a communitarian dimension. It would come into being, according to the Mennonite

18. Hengel's foundational statements in English translations are *Was Jesus a Revolutionist?*, trans. William Klassen (Philadelphia, Fortress Press, 1971); *Victory our Violence*, trans. David E. Green (London, SPCK Press, 1975).
19. Josephus: *Antiquities of the Jews*, XCII, x, 5 10, in *Complete Works*, trans. William Whiston (London, Pickering & Inglis, 1960), 371-372.
20. John Howard Yoder: *The Original Revolution: Essays on Christian Pacifism* (Scottdale, Pa., Herald Press, 1971), ch. 1; Hans Küng, *On Being a Christian*, trans. Edward Quinn (New York, Doubleday, 1976), section C.I.
21. Hengel: *Victory*, 56.
22. John Howard Yoder: *The Politics of Jesus: Vicit Agnus Noster* (Grand Rapids, Eerdmans, 1972), 34.
23. Richard J. Cassidy: *Jesus, Politics, and Society: A Study of Luke's Gospel* (Maryknoll, N.Y., Orbis Books, 1978), 39-40, 60-61.

professor of theology at Notre Dame University, John H. Yoder, only through 'the creation of a distinct community with its own deviant set of values and its coherent way of incarnating them'.[24] The Jesuit biblical scholar Richard J. Cassidy agrees: 'by espousing radically new social patterns and by refusing to defer to the existing political authorities, Jesus pointed the way to a social order in which neither the Romans nor any other oppressing group would be able to hold sway'.[25] As Cassidy was intimating, there is an eschatological dimension to this new community/social order. Again and again the Reformed theologian Jürgen Moltmann has returned to this theme. The Church is no more and no less than the 'vanguard [of] the new mankind'.[26] Attempting as it does to 'correspond to Christ as messianic Lord in political and social activity', the Church 'anticipates in history the kingdom of God'.[27] And inherent in this biblical and theological vision for God's people — Yoder, Cassidy and Moltmann ecumenically agree — is pacifism/non-violence.[28]

RETHINKING THE NATURE AND ROLE OF THE CHURCH

The third reason for pacifism's current resurgence is the reconceptualization that many Christians are doing of the Church's nature and role in the world. In this reconceptualization, the Church's role is emerging as simultaneously more modest *and* more ambitious than it has been for the past sixteen hundred years.

In the first place, Christians today are often more modest than they used to be about their own capacity to control events, indeed about the susceptibility of world events to anybody's control. Increasingly Christians are doubting their capacity to know or determine the consequences of their actions. To be sure, over the centuries churchpersons have only fitfully attempted to control these things directly; often they have acted indirectly, providing justification and solace for statespersons whose actions (even actions which have violated the moral principles of the Church) they have sought to direct towards consequences which they considered beneficial.

But in recent years, a series of tragic conflicts has been reinforced by the exponentially growing magnitude of the risk of miscalculation, to force churchpersons to face evidence that has been accumulating for centuries — that it is impossible to know in advance what the con-

24. Yoder: *Original Revolution*, 28.
25. Cassidy: *Jesus*, 79.
26. Jürgen Moltmann: *The Church in the Power of the Spirit*, trans. Margaret Kohl (London, SCM Press, 1977), 196.
27. Moltmann: *Following Jesus Christ*, 77.
28. Yoder: *Original Revolution*, 24; Cassidy: *Jesus*, 80-82; Moltmann: *Following Jesus Christ*, 108.

sequences of an action will be. And as a result, they are returning to an ethic of principle.

Reflection on three recent wars has done much to clarify this for us. The first of these, World War Two, was a war of self-evident justness against an enemy whose evil appeared monstrous and manifest. Indeed, so evil did that enemy appear, and so horrendous were the anticipated consequences of a victory by Hitler, that almost no one protested when Prime Minister Churchill in 1943 told the House of Commons, 'There are no sacrifices that we will not make and no *lengths in violence* to which we will not go'.[29] The enemy, Churchill and his hearers alike were tacitly stating, was so monstrously evil that the Just War principle of discrimination could be held in abeyance. And so, against both the Germans and the Japanese, the Allies engaged in military violence that was limited solely by the available military hardware and technology. In November 1940, after the Germans bombed Coventry, killing four hundred people, some British MPs still had the capacity to protest against the 'indiscriminate and murderous character' of the German attacks.[30] But by 1945 our sense of outrage had become dulled. We had become accustomed to the bombing of civilians; indeed it had come to be a calculated part of Allied policy which aimed to break our enemy's immoral morale. The incinerating in March 1945 of 135,000 Germans in Dresden was simply the most lethal episode in the Allied air forces' sustained application of this policy.[31] Throughout the war the Germans, with wanton lack of discrimination, killed 62,464 British civilians through bombing.[32] In the course of their 'Crusade in Europe', the Allies, with a lack of discrimination almost ten times as wanton, bombed to death an estimated 593,000 German civilians.[33] Despite the carnage, we learned subsequently, Allied calculations had been wrong all along — obliteration bombing had steeled rather than shattered German morale.

But of course, we said defensively, World War Two, savage though it was, was a lesser evil. It was necessary to prevent Hitler, who was killing six million Jews, from imposing his moral order on the world. So, to combat the Hitlerian moral order which was killing six million Jews, we calculated it best to ally ourselves with the Soviet

29. Winston Churchill: Speech to House of Commons, 21 September 1943, in *Parliamentary Debates (Hansard)*, House of Commons, 5th ser., 392 (1942-1943), col. 89 (italics mine).
30. *Parliamentary Debates (Hansard)*, 5th ser., 367 (1940-1941), 540.
31. David Irving: *The Destruction of Dresden* (London, William Kimber, 1963), 237.
32. E. E. Reynolds and N. H. Brasher: *Britain in the Twentieth Century* (Cambridge, Cambridge University Press, 1966), 214.
33. A. J. P. Taylor: *English History, 1914-1945* (Oxford, Clarendon Press, 1965), 591n.

Union whose moral order, we later learned, was killing ten to fifteen million people in the 'Gulag Archipelago'.[34] And the unforeseen consequences of a no-holds-barred contest against Hitlerian immorality is another contest, against our erstwhile Ally, which is morally so important that we are threatening to blow up the world! How, many Christians are asking, in light of our past miscalculations can we be so sure?

The same fallibility of calculation became evident during the Vietnam War of a decade ago. When the United States decided to become embroiled in the war, she was led by people who were jocularly known as 'The Best and the Brightest'.[35] These men — liberal-minded academics trained at universities such as Harvard and Yale — were men of unimpeachable character. Equally impressive was their confidence in their capacity to calculate the consequences of their actions and to use force to control events. The were brilliantly misguided. As the United States sank deeper and deeper into the morass, they found themselves not controlling events but being controlled by them. Their experience was harrowing and chastening, and has led these representatives of the traditional American establishment to a belated modesty. In the United Kingdom today, there is a comparable undercurrent modesty about calculations. To be sure, the UK 'won' the Falklands/Malvinas war. But she got into it by diplomatic miscalculation. She fought it against an enemy armed in significant measure with British weapons, which Britain had calculated would never be used against herself. And the result of her victory is a 'Fortress' which, according to current assessments, she is not sure that she has the resources to defend. And as a result of the war, the goals of British policy in the region are farther from realization than they were before the fighting began.

Despite this history of miscalculation and the ever-present peril of cataclysmic nuclear miscalculation, some politicians persevere with brave calculation-talk. Professor Richard Pipes of the US National Security Council, for example, has said that a nuclear war would not necessarily be that bad; it would be like an amputation, traumatic but not fatal.[36] Another American, a general, observed that the foreseeable result of World War Three for the United States would be no

34. Robert Conquest: *The Great Terror*, rev. ed. (Harmondsworth, Middx., Penguin, 1968), 713.
35. David Halberstam: *The Best and the Brightest* (London, Barrie & Jenkins, 1972), 32: 'There was a sense that these were brilliant men, men of force, not cruel, not harsh, but men who acted rather than waited ... We seemed about to enter an Olympian age in this country, brains and intellect harnessed to great force, the better to define a common good.'
36. *Time Magazine*, 29 March 1982.

worse than a return to the economic standards of the Great Depression![37]

For some time, however, many Christians who have pondered the same historical experience and wrestled with the same nuclear-age predicament, have come to sense the arrogance of this confident calculation. One of the earliest of these was the American theologian Reinhold Niebuhr, who in the early 1950s was reflecting on the omnipresence of 'irony' in history.[38] Three years earlier, in a brilliant series of broadcast talks, the English historian Herbert Butterfield — with World War Two and nuclear weaponry equally in mind — had been thinking along similar lines. 'The hardest strokes of heaven,' he argued, 'fall in history upon those who imagine that they can control things in a sovereign manner, as though they were the kings of the earth, playing Providence not only for themselves but for the far future — reaching out into the future with the wrong kind of farsightedness, and gambling on a lot of risky calculations in which there must never be a single mistake.'[39] In 1959, the American sovietologist and diplomat George Kennan confessed to similar misgivings in an address at Princeton Seminary. 'I can testify from personal experience that not only can one never know, when one takes a far-reaching decision in foreign policy, precisely what the consequences are going to be, but almost never do these consequences fully coincide with what one intended or expected'.[40]

A similar predictive modesty underlies both the draft letter of the American bishops and the English Anglican statement, *The Church and the Bomb*. Both of these statements base their recommended policies at least in part on the anticipated consequences of those policies. But in the case of both statements, it appears in the final analysis to be principles, rather than consequences, that determine the outcome of the argument. In this, they are representative of the current Christian retreat from consequential ethics. Since events have proven to be so unknowable, and consequences have been seen to be so unpredictable, Christians of many traditions have come to be more consciously guided by the principles which shape their ethical reasoning. Christians, knowing the outcome of events is incalculable, can only bear testimony to what they believe, modestly but very deeply, to be right.

37. Interview in film, *War without Winners* (Washington, Center for Defense Information, 1979; available from Concord Films, 201 Felixstowe Road, Ipswich, Suffolk IP3 9BJ.
38. Reinhold Niebuhr: *The Irony of American History* (London, Nisbet, 1952), x.
39. Herbert Butterfield *Christianity and History* (New York, Charles Scribner's Sons, 1950), 104.
40. George Kennan: 'Foreign Policy and Christian Conscience', cited by James W. Douglass, *The Non-Violent Cross* (New York, Macmillan, 1969), 264.

Although Christians are in this sense becoming more modest than they used to be, in another sense they are becoming more ambitious. Their liberation from the tyranny of consequences has freed them for prophetic statement and action. Less and less are Christians willing to provide reasoned justifications for war and preparations for war; instead, they are opposing these things, not as a means of withdrawing from the real world, but rather as the only means of significant Christian involvement in it. Indeed, among both clerics and laypersons today a rediscovery is taking place of the Christian vocation to prophecy.

This prophetic calling, it is arguable, is the unifying characteristic of the 'new church' which is emerging in our time. The 'new church' is prophetic because it is in costly fashion re-asserting its divine mandate to Jesus-centred social nonconformity. It is a movement that, though present within existing denominations, is also trans-confessional, drawing together men, women and communities from various Christian traditions. It it is a movement which is fuelled by spiritual renewal, both charismatic and contemplative. It is a movement comprising both small and great, workers and archbishops — for both are speaking and living in a way that confronts as well as comforts the world. The American Catholic bishops have well discerned the shape of this emerging church (and their words have a resonance in many other countries, even, it seems to me, in Ireland): 'It is clear today, perhaps more than in previous generations, that convinced Christians are in a minority in nearly every country in the world — including Christian and Catholic nations. In our own country believers can identify rather easily with the early church as a company of witnesses engaged in a difficult mission'.[41] No mission can be more difficult — or ambitious — than that of a 'company of witnesses' re-asserting their prophetic self-identity!

Around the world, for an increasing number of Christians, communities functioning as 'companies of witness' are a tangible reality. In them, men and women are hearing God's prophetic message for our time, providing mutual support for each other, and encouraging each other to be faithful to the God who is calling them to persevere in 'difficult mission'. They are assisting each other to live the kind of life ('justice, peace and joy in the Holy Spirit' [Rom. 14:17]) that will triumph when God's Kingdom comes in fullness. They are, in Moltmann's potent phrase, 'the presence of the future in the conditions of history'.[42] As signs of God's future, these cells of newness are alert to other signs — in the secular as well as religious sphere — of the kind of Kingdom that will come when all things are reconciled to God in

41. *The Challenge of Peace*, 322.
42. Moltmann: *The Church in the Power of the Spirit*, 193.

Christ (Col. 1:20). And as they become engaged in the world, they can recognize these secular signs, give thanks to God for them, and actively work for them in the political arena. An illustration of these secular signs is the reconciliation that has taken place within the past generation between Germany and France.[43] We are so accustomed to this by now that we forget that for a millenium these two nations were irreconcilable enemies; but today they are friends, with unguarded frontiers, whose major battles are verbal ones about wine prices. In the past Christians have been at the forefront of secular ventures for reconciliation. The same is true today, as Christians strive for the breaking down of dividing walls between the irreconcilables (Americans and Russians, etc.) of our time.

But whatever happens in the political realm, the primary calling to God's people today is to live the biblical vision now, in renewed community life and in a prophetic summons to modesty and faithfulness. Is it too late? That is not the question. What is vital is that cells of believers make it their all-encompassing ambition to appropriate God's promise that he 'has chosen things low and contemptible, mere nothings, to overthrow the existing order' (1 Cor. 1:28).

RECONCEPTUALIZING PACIFISM

The fourth reason for pacifim's current resurgence is that pacifists are reconceptualizing their position. There was a time when pacifists were viewed — and often viewed themselves — as saints and sectaries, who at the price of irrelevance were willing to withdraw from the world to preserve their personal purity. But today pacifists are reconceiving their role in the world to be one not of withdrawal but of purposive involvement. They are seeing their position as one which, in our apocalyptic age, may well have more relevance than any other approach to world problems. And they are sensing that their position is arguably the only one which enables a contribution to the world that is distinctively Christian.

In the past, pacifist withdrawal has often been the product of a faulty anthropology. Pacifists have optimistically posited a goodness in humankind which they expect will lead to a reciprocity of benevolence: if we are civil to our enemy, he will be civil to us. We have learned better. This alas is not the way that individuals or nations behave, even it appears when their interests are not being threatened. According to scripture and orthodox Christian teaching, humankind — though not beyond conversion of heart, life and life-style — is profoundly sinful. Among God's people there must thus be

43. Professor James O'Connell: 'Progress towards Disarmament', speech to the Shaftesbury Project Study Group on War and Peace, London, 4 July 1981.

sober realism as well as a hope for renewal.

But the pacifism that is emerging in the churches today is the product of a growing realization among Christians, not that they and their enemies are fundamentally good, but that they and their enemies are not good enough.[44] As they examine before God their own motives, they are discovering that there is much in themselves that is impure. They are sensing that a good case can be made for their enemies as well as for themselves. Indeed, orthodox Christian anthropology should lead us to the insight that there is a fundamental sameness between us and our enemies. There is sinfulness in us and sinfulness in them; there is goodness in us and goodness in them. This is true even of Adolph Hitler. As Dale Aukerman has argued in a profound book, 'It is crucial for us to recognize not only the continuity between the darkness deep in each of us and the darkness in Hitler, but also a continuity between positive impulses and longings within us and those, even if to a large extent atrophied, within Hitler'. [45] Pacifists are therefore increasingly conscious that they do not have sufficient moral authority to take the life of someone who might repent or be the instrument of their own repentance. The enemy might (in God's time, *will*) become our brother/sister, for reconciliation is God's historical goal (Eph. 1:10).

Today it is not the pacifists who have faulty anthropology. It is the advocates of 'defence' policies that — unless current trends are reversed — may well kill billions of people and deface the cosmos. A prime example is Mr. Paul Johnson, Mrs. Thatcher's favourite church historian, who asserted recently that 'Soviet totalitarianism is a moral threat humanity has never contemplated before'.[46] Statements such as Johnson's are common these days, and are necessary to bolster us in our willingness to commit the ultimate mortal sin with a sense of rectitude. But Johnson's anthropology is as unchristian as his history is dubious. How shallow it is to claim that original sin ends at the Elbe River? In the words of a Jewish scholar, statements such as Johnson's are 'early warnings of holocaust'.[47] Those who are unlike us we can with a good conscience incinerate. The growing pacifist movement today is a response to the lethal arrogance of this position.

The second element of the pacifists' reconceptualization of their position has to do with the development of the theory and practice of

44. This insight recurs in the writings of Thomas Merton, e.g. in *New Seeds of Contemplation* (New York, New Directions, 1962), 122.
45. Dale Aukerman: *Darkening Valley: A Biblical Perspective on Nuclear War* (New York, Seabury Press, 1981), 19.
46. Paul Johnson: 'Christians, Awake', *Times*, 29 January 1983, 8.
47. Rabbi Marc H. Tanenbaum, in preparatory documents for International Conference on the Holocaust and Genocide, Tel Aviv, 20-24 June 1982.

nonvioient resistance.[48] To understand the significance of this for
pacifists, it is helpful to visualize a spectrum of responses to evil.

PACIFISM			JUST WAR	TOTAL WAR
persuade	boycott	blockade	combatants	noncombatants

do		kill		destroy
nothing				creation

At the one extreme is utter inactivity (ignoring the evil); at the other
extreme is blowing up the world (combating the evil by committing
not only suicide but cosmocide). Adherents of the Just War and
pacifists both find themselves between these extremes, for both have
limits which they will not transgress. Just War theorists will not
knowingly kill noncombatants; pacifists will not kill. But as pacifists
have been discovering in recent years, this limitation nevertheless
affords the resourceful pacifist with a wide variety of actions, all of
which can be consistent with loving and caring for the enemy.
Pacifists can thus persuade, rebuke, demonstrate, boycott, block
entrances to military bases or enter them illegally for prayer, engage
in selective acts of civil disobedience. All of these methods of sub-
lethal resistance can cause the enemy to question the legitimacy of his
position; all of them can make it difficult for him to attain his ends.
But none of these methods is likely to inflict lasting physical harm on
the enemy; none of them will dehumanize him or deny him the chance
to explain or change his position. As a result of this reconceptualization of the pacifists' position, pacifists are now emerging from their
virtual withdrawal from public life to play a variety of roles which are
politically challenging and which may be politically effective.

The pioneer theoretician and exponent of this position is of course
Mohandas K. Gandhi, who steered India towards its independence
and who through Richard Attenborough's film is inspiring this
generation.[46] Gandhi's approach was most effectively imported into
the West by Martin Luther King, who inspired the civil rights movement of the 1960s and who thereby permanently altered the shape of
American society.[50] But even before King, others in the West had
been developing techniques of nonviolent resistance. According to Sir

48. For recent theoretical treatments, see Anders Boserup and Andrew Mack: *War
Without Weapons* (London, Francis Pinter, 1974); Joan V. Bondurant: *Conquest of
Violence*, rev. ed. (Berkeley, Cal., University of California Press, 1965); P.
Regamey: *Non-Violence and the Christian Conscience* (London, Darton, Longman
& Todd, 1966).
49. M. K. Gandhi: *Non-Violent Resistance* (New York, Schocken Books, 1961).
50. Martin Luther King: *Strength to Love* (London, Fontana, 1969).

Basil Liddell Hart, who is arguably the most significant British strategic thinker of our century, it was these techniques which during World War Two had been the most effective means of resisting Nazi rule in occupied territories (and which might, he mused, be the only form of genuinely viable defence in a nuclear age). In a paper which he wrote shortly before his death, Liddell Hart reflected:

> When interrogating the German generals after the Second World War, I took the opportunity of getting their evidence about the effects of the different kinds of resistance which they had met in the occupied countries. Their evidence tended to show that the violent forms of resistance had not been very effective and troublesome to them ... Their evidence also showed the effectiveness of nonviolent resistance as practised in Denmark, Holland and Norway — and to some extent in France and Belgium. Even clearer, was their inability to cope with it. They were experts in violence, and had been trained to deal with opponents who used that method. But other forms of resistance baffled them — and all the more in proportion as the methods were subtle and concealed. It was a relief to them when resistance became violent ... Violent forms of resistance tend to work on the assumption that all members of the occupying forces are enemies. But if one regards them as fellow human beings, and gets this human feeling spreading, it is enormously valuable ... It is necessary to demonstrate as clearly that [nonviolent civilian defence] is a workable policy, and that it is more workable than military defence.[51]

Within the past fifteen years, this line of thinking has been developed and given an elaborate theoretical and historical framework by an American political scientist, Gene Sharp of Harvard University. Sharp has argued passionately that pacifists will never really be taken seriously until they become as serious about the effectiveness of non-violent resistance as politicians and soldiers have always had to be about the effectiveness of violence. From Sharp's perspective, non-violence must not be viewed as an idealistic mode of conflict; it must be seen as the most realistic method of opposing an enemy. In his massive study, *The Politics of Nonviolent Action*, Sharp buttresses his case with a thousand pages of evidence drawn from virtually every era of global history.[52] And on the basis of this evidence, Sharp vigorously contests two theses that are so basic to our patterns of

51. B. H. Liddell Hart: 'Lessons from Resistance Movements — Guerrilla and Non-Violent', in Adam Roberts, ed., *The Strategy of Civilian Defence* (London, Faber & Faber, 1967), 205, 209, 211.
52. Gene Sharp: *The Politics of Nonviolent Action* (Boston, Porter Sargent, 1973).

nurture (in our homes, the media, school history lessons, etc.) that they are rarely stated explicitly or examined: the thesis (briefly put) that violence 'works'; and the thesis that nonviolence 'doesn't work'. And behind even the incidents of nonviolent action that 'failed' there lurks the challenging question: what if those who were engaging in nonviolent action had persisted a bit longer, on the basis of deeper understanding of and firmer commitment to nonviolent principles?

In a speech in London, Sharp reminisced about his encounter in Accra in the mid-1950s with Frantz Fanon, the psychiatrist from Martinique and author of *The Wretched of the Earth,* who was then providing an intellectual framework for the revolution in Algeria.[53] When Sharp asked Fanon how the Algerian revolution was progressing, the latter responded that 'we had a demonstration, and the French troops killed two hundred people. We've tried nonviolence and it doesn't work'. So the Algerians turned to violence, and in the course of the revolutionary war which eventuated in independence from the French, approximately one million people were killed.[54] The Algerians and most outside observers have concluded, typically, that violence works and nonviolence is futile. Two hundred killed — nonviolence doesn't work; one million killed, one out of ten Algerians — violence works. What might have happened, Sharp mused, if not two hundred but two thousand — or even twenty thousand — had been willing to be killed through purposive nonviolent action that accepted 'the necessity of suffering'? Such a re-examination of history has powerful implications. I would be surprised if it did not offer similarly fresh perspectives on the Irish past and present, but that is something for you to do.[55]

What is clear is that the case for nonviolent action is becoming increasingly influential. George Kennan, for example, has recently argued that the United States in the nuclear age should seriously consider adopting a policy of 'national defence through passive resistance".[56] Seminars on this mode of defence have been held in such unlikely places as the U.S. Military Academy at West Point; articles are being written about it in periodicals such as the *Journal of Strategic Studies*;[57] and the forthcoming report of the Alternative Defence Commission will be illuminating in its application of non-

---

53. Gene Sharp: 'Nonviolence as a Means of National Defence', speech at Westminster Cathedral Conference Centre, London, 19 March 1983.
54. Sharp: *Politics*, 552.
55. For a starting attempt at this kind of thinking, see 'Nonviolence in Irish History', *Dawn*, Nos. 38-39.
56. George Urban: 'From Containment to Self-Containment: A Conversation with George Kennan', *Encounter*, 47 (September 1976), 37.
57. Gene Keyes: 'Strategic Non-Violent Defense: The Construct of an Option', *Journal of Strategic Studies*, 4 (June 1981).

violent methods of the U.K.[58]

Thinking is thus beginning to change in the world of defence studies, and in significant ways it is converging with conceptual change that has simultaneously been taking place in the anti-militarist world. But you will be aware that, as I have been discussing these changes, the focus of my attention has been shifting. Earlier in this talk I had been talking about theology; now I am discussing strategy. Earlier I had been querying the capacity of humans to anticipate the consequences of their actions; now I am thinking in consequentialist terms of effectiveness and results. As I do so, I, as a pacifist Christian, am uncomfortable. For I know that nonviolent activists are no more immune than anyone else from the prideful allurement of attempting to control history through calculated action. In this case, to be sure, the calculations of the practitioners will not lead them to violent means; their range of options will not include killing or maiming the people whom they are attempting to deny the capacity to rule, construct missile silos, etc. But what if they miscalculate? What if they fail? What if they, despite their use of the most refined nonviolent techniques after thorough preparation, do not gain their objectives? Might not some of them begin to meditate critically on their failure? Might they not be tempted to escalate the struggle by crossing the ill-defined firebreak between nonviolent action and 'just a little' violence? Might this temptation not be especially irresistible for those activists whose drive towards a political end is more deeply rooted than their commitment to nonviolence?

To pacifist Christians, who are intensely conscious of the mysterious nature of change which ultimately takes place through suffering and grace, these are obvious concerns. They are the counterpart of the nonviolent activists' concern — that the pacifist will forever remain immobile in the purity of isolated irrelevance. Between these concerns and convictions there is room for conversation, and indeed for an overlapping of emphases. In fact, such a merging is taking place, even in our understanding of Jesus of Nazareth. For Christians whose rejection of violence is rooted in an espousal of biblical revelation have been coming to realize that Jesus, though not a calculator of consequences, was nevertheless a practitioner of nonviolent resistance.[59] At the close of my discussion of the reconceptualization of pacifism, and at the end of my address to you today, I would like to re-fix our attention on him.

Jesus' non-violent resistance is best demonstrated in his cleansing of the Temple (Mark 11:15-17, parr.; Jn. 2:13-16). This incident, since it shows Jesus prepared to resort to 'violence', has often been

58. *Defence without the Bomb* (London, Taylor & Francis, 1983).
59. Cassidy: *Jesus*, 80-82.

used as an antipacifist proof text, and many pacifists have been embarrassed by it. A closer reading of the text, however, and an understanding of the spectrum of responses to evil, lead to the conclusion that this embarrassment is unnecessary.[60] In this incident, Jesus in boldly prophetic fashion showed his authority over Israel's most holy place. Clearly he was filled with righteous anger by what he found there — the cheating of the pious poor (through iniquitous exchange rates and exorbitant charges for sacrificial animals) and the exclusion of the Gentiles from their court: God's house, which was to be 'a house of prayer *for all the nations*' had been made into 'a den of robbers' (Mk. 11:17). If pacifism denotes inactivity in the face of evil, clearly this incident shows that Jesus was no pacifist. Going into action, Jesus wielded a whip of cords and overturned the money-laden tables of the proprietors of the Temple *bureau de change*. One can imagine the resulting noise and confusion, with sheep bleating, pigeons flapping their wings, and money-changers groping in the dust for errant coins.

And yet the story makes it clear that Jesus was more morally nuanced than to imagine that there is no essential difference between a prophetic demonstrative action and killing. Even armed with a whip, Jesus could not possibly have overcome by physical force the numerically superior corps of temple businessmen; his power in this situation was obviously an expression of his moral authority. Furthermore, careful exegesis of the Greek text (reflected in recent translations — NEB, NIV, TEV) makes it clear that Jesus was directing the whip at 'all the animals', not at the people; at the end of the incident Jesus is speaking to the pigeon salesman (Jn. 2:16). This then was an action that fits easily into our understanding of nonviolent demonstrations. But, significantly, Jesus apparently undertook it without carefully calculating the consequences. According to the synoptic gospels, within a week he was being crucified.

This demonstratively prophetic, nonviolent dimension of Jesus' life must be taken seriously by all Christians, not least by pacifist Christians. But more deeply, the Christian Church as a whole must rediscover the full impact of the fundamental New Testament insight which should be the context of our entire discussion. This is the insight that ultimately the meaning of history is revealed to us, not in Caesar or the revolutionary Barabbas, but in the suffering servant Jesus — not in the sword, but in the cross.

The cross, on which Jesus 'disarmed the pricipalities and powers' (Col. 2:15) and brought salvation to humankind, was not a calculated device to manipulate history. Or was it? Let us re-read a familiar passage in St. John's gospel (11:47-50): 'The chief priests and the

60. *Ibid.*, 44-45; Jean Lasserre: 'A Tenacious Misinterpretation: John 2:15', *Occasional Papers*, No. 1 (Elkhart, Ind., Institute of Mennonite Studies, 1981).

Pharisees gathered the council, and said, "What are we to do? For this man performs many signs. If we let him go on thus, every one will believe in him, and the Romans will come and *destroy both our holy place and our nation*". But one of them, Caiaphas, who was high priest that year, said to them, "You know nothing at all. You do not understand that it is expedient for you that one man should die for the people, and that the whole nation should not perish".' As this passage makes clear, there *was* calculation in the cross. It was the calculation of security-minded authorities who were concerned about their nation's freedom of worship and political integrity, and who thought that they would be able to control the situation by getting rid, by a small blood-letting, of one inconvenient person. They were wrong, as people who calculate the consequences of 'lesser-evil' actions will be wrong. But unbeknownst to themselves and at a deeper level than they could comprehend, they were also right, for divine 'irony' was at work. That 'one man' Jesus did indeed die for the people, overcoming sin and death, and becoming the pioneer whose pattern of faithfulness has been the model for his followers ever since (Heb. 2:10-15).

Pacifist Christians are those who in every area of their lives — personal and political — seek to 'walk in the same way in which he walked' (1 Jn. 2:6). Looking at Jesus, we sense ourselves confronted with the deepest mysteries of life and history — through God's grace there is liberation through suffering, healing through elective pain, power made perfect in weakness. Aware of the hurts in the world, we affirm that those hurts cannot be healed through the infliction of yet more hurt. They can be healed solely through the 'aggressive vulnerability'[61] of those who, in the power of God, head into that hurt and in faith take it upon themselves, not knowing what is going to happen, not being able to calculate the outcome, but confident that Jesus went there ahead of us and we are called to follow him.

61. Faith Lees: *Break Open My World* (London, Marshall, Morgan & Scott, 1982), 38.

7 Christian Discipleship in a Nuclear World

Jürgen Moltman

Responsible support of the world orders of economics, society, culture and politics or consistent, undivided discipleship of Christ in economic, social, cultural and political conditions? This is the question today in view of the growing number of nuclear plants, further economic growth at the cost of poor peoples and the preparation for nuclear warfare. Should we boycott nuclear energy? Must we come up with alternative economic systems? Should we live without armaments? Can we afford to buy no products of apartheid? Or is it the case that we may not and cannot drop out and must therefore exist responsibly with nuclear energy, live with the bomb and use our economic relationships with South Africa to improve the conditions of the blacks there? Where are the limits of Christian responsible political engagement?

REFORMATION REFLECTIONS

Responsible participation in the world or undivided discipleship? That was the question which stood behind the consequential and controversial Article 16 of the Augsburg Confession. Unfortunately it is not clearly recognizable and therefore overlooked by many that the Lutheran Church on this question took an unambiguous but also one-sided position. The reason for this was that with this confession at the Augsburg Reichstag the Protestants wanted to enter into discussion with the Emperor and Rome, but not with the 'Left Wing of the Reformation', which was at that time still a widespread Anabaptist movement prepared for peace. Together with the Catholic Church the Protestants united themselves in a common condemnation and persecution of the Anabaptists. Who were the Anabaptists and what did they teach?

Article 16 of the *Augsburg Confession* is an answer to Article 6 of the *Schleitheim Articles of 1527* (the 'Brotherly Union'), which Michael Sattler drafted for the first Anabaptist synod. Within a year (four months actually) Sattler was burned at the stake in nearby

Rottenburg-am-Neckar. We begin with a systematic comparison of these two articles.

1. "THE SWORD IS A DIVINE ORDER OUTSIDE OF THE PERFECTION OF THE CHRIST" (Schleitheim Article 6).

This sentence summarizes the lived witness of the Anabaptists. The perfection of Christ can only be lived in the consistent and undivided discipleship of Jesus. This means that a Christian cannot serve two lords. If a person confesses 'Christ alone' as his or her Lord, then he or she must live solely according to the wisdom of Christ as it is expressed for the life of discipleship in the Sermon on the Mount. A Christian is not a person with a divided conscience. Therefore a Christian cannot commit an act of violence, not even to impede or punish others doing violent acts. It follows that a Christian cannot accept and practice a calling in economics and politics; this would compromise his or her faith by forcing him or her to use violence. For the Anabaptists of that time this meant no participation in public affairs which necessitated the use of the sword; hence this meant refusal to participate in the army, serve in the police functions or hold positions in the court and the state.

The perfection of Christ can only be lived in the voluntary community of brothers and sisters. In this visible community of believers there is only admonishment — no force, only forgiveness; no judgment, only love; no calculation, only obedience. This voluntary community which is constituted by faith, discipleship and baptism is the true, visible body of Christ. This voluntary community of Christ is the visible alternative to the society of laws and compulsions: 'It shall not be so among you . . .' (Mt. 20:26 ff.). Many Anabaptists demonstrated this alternative in their own life communities: the Hutterite Brothers from Mähren created the *Brüderhöfe*, which still exist in the United States and Canada. The Mennonites founded their own village communities in Russia, Paraguay and the United States. The current movement of basic communities and alternative rural communities on the land has Anabaptist origins.

The perfection of Christ is proven through the refusal of participation in state acts of violence. The Christian's ministry of peace demands the consistent defencelessness of life. The Anabaptists did not believe with Luther that executioners and soldiers could be in a 'holy station'. They refused participation in such public offices which 'necessarily force one to sin'. They refused to take oaths and repudiated that private ownership of land and tools which made other human beings into slaves.

Finally, the perfection of Christ can be witnessed in this violent world only through fundamental readiness and willingness for suffering and defenceless martyrdom. Patience, tolerance and 'forbearance' were considered signs of the true church. Indeed the Anabaptists are the martyrs of the Reformation times — persecuted, condemned and executed by Protestants and Catholics alike. The *Book of Martyrs* and the moving Anabaptist song of 1527, 'How precious is the consecrated death . . .' speak a most impressive language. When Michael Sattler was interrogated at Rottenburg about how to defend against the danger of the Turks stirring out of the East, he replied, 'Live defenceless!".

Love of neighbour, defencelessness, readiness for suffering were for the Anabaptist the signs of discipleship of Christ based on personal faith and one's own decision. Is this responsible Christian existence? There remain open questions. The community of Christ and this world stand in exclusive opposition. Only in apocalyptic times has the Christian community experienced such alternatives. From this perspective the community of Christ must separate itself from this world. Is this world thus lost? Is this world, despite its violence and inhumanity, not God's good creation? If the community of Christ separates itself from society, does it not then show only its own great refusal, but not the criticism of this violent world in light of the judgment and kingdom of God?

2. '... ALL ESTABLISHED RULE AND LAWS WERE INSTITUTED AND ORDAINED BY GOD ...' (*Augsburg Confession*, Article 16).

This sentence appropriately summarizes the witness of the Lutheran responsibility for the world. If all established rule is from God, then the participation of Christians in ruling offices and their conduct according to public laws cannot as such be considered sinful. To civil offices and to actions according to public laws also belongs the Christian's right to 'render decisions and pass sentence according to imperial and other existing laws, punish evil doers with the sword, engage in just wars, serve as soldiers, buy and sell, take required oaths, possess property, be married, etc.' None of this contradicts the gospel because the gospel teaches an 'eternal righteousness in the heart'. The perfection of Christ is not external, but rather internal. It is the 'proper fear of God and real faith in God'. Because 'the gospel does not teach an outward and temporal but an inward and eternal mode of existence and the righteousness of the heart', it does not overturn the worldly regiment but requires that the political and economic orders be kept as 'true orders of God' (*Conservare tamquam ordinationes Dei*) and that love be practised *in* these orders. Thus Christians are obliged to be subject to civil authority and obey its commands and laws. Fortunately, the Augsburg Confession also added a phrase at the end of this wholesale declaration of civil authorities, namely, 'except when they command to sin' (*nisi cum jubent peccare*). 'When commands of the civil authority cannot be obeyed without sin, we must obey God rather than men', says Article 16.

We have here in classic form the basic ideas of Christian responsibility for the world: Every political power contains an element of order without which there can be no common human life. Civil authority is created by God and equipped with a monopoly of force so that social peace might be preserved and political justice established. It belongs to Christians as such to respect and responsbily maintain civil authority. The political obligation of Christians is not the great refusal but responsible cooperation.

But according to which criteria should Christians cooperate? The gospel offers no new perspectives for the transformation of structures but rather only obligates Christians to love *in* structures. Love penetrates all political and economic orders but does not transform them. It presupposes that in the normal situation God speaks through the gospel internally in the heart with the same language with which the authorities created and set in place by God speak externally. In cases of doubt, one must obey God more than human beings, that is, the gospel more than the authorities.

But if Christian world responsibility means leading a responsible life *in* the world orders, then this means that God, not the human being, is responsible for it. Christian responsibility for the world thereby gains a fundamentally preserving tendency: against the temptation to disintegrate (*dissipare*) political and economic orders, it conserves them by explaining them as 'God's orders'. This conservative orientation is grounded in the faith that the preservation of the world by the divinely ordained authorities is willed by God until the end of time (*conservatio mundi*). The criteria for Christian responsibility for the world are thus love and reason. There is no such thing as a peculiarly Christian view of justice or a wisdom which is specifically Christian. This formulation of Christian responsibility for the world makes the Christian unrecognizable in worldly callings and positions, for in ordinary situations he or she chooses to do exactly the same thing that non-Christians do.

The critical questions which arise here are numerous: If the gospel really teaches only the righteousness of the heart, then the thought of the actually lived, incarnated — that is, also political and economic — discipleship is sacrificed. A faith which is made so internal delivers over the external world to other powers which it must then explain as divine orders; these then must be obeyed, but 'without sin'. But can just any group — militaristic and even terrorist perhaps — who come to power by the use of arms be regarded as a divine order? Should the text be understood to say 'all authorities', or only legitimate governments, *legitimas ordinationes*, as the Latin text says.

So just as the Anabaptists stand in danger of pulling themselves back out of the world quietistically and without criticism, so the Lutherans stand in danger of going along with the world as it is and cooperating without criticism. The 'silent ones in the land' and the 'pious state underlings' thus in the end have little to contribute to peace and justice in economics and politics in the world.

Further, this conflict of the Lutherans and the Anabaptists over responsible participation or undivided discipleship provides no direct way to address the problems of Christian witness in the nuclear age. However, for Christians today the patterns of both of these decisions are always close at hand. These great alternatives constantly obtrude in many individual decisions; the basic thinking for these decisions remains similar to that of the sixteenth century.

NUCLEAR WEAPONS AND DISCIPLESHIP

We begin with the major pronouncements of the Reformed Church of the Netherlands (1962, 1978), of the Protestant Church in Germany (1969, 1981) and of the Reformed Alliance in Germany (1982). According to these pronouncements we must assume that peace is the order and promise of God: God wants to live with human beings in a kingdom of peace. Because of this the people of God are given their task of peace. Peace means not only the absence of war but also the overcoming of suffering, anxiety, threat, injustice and oppression. Peace is the blessed, affirmed, good, splendid life with God, with human beings and with nature: Shalom. It is the commission of Christians to serve this peace in all dimensions of life, to promote it and protect it, but in particular to resist war, the most dangerous form of the lack of peace. Christian churches have always viewed their position against war as only one part of their comprehensive service of peace.

In view of the fact and possibility of war there have been among Christians two different approaches:

(1) *Principled pacifism* (from the traditional peace churches). This approach refuses every act of violence, including those acts of violence by which violence is to be prevented. Here the discipleship of Christ is given priority over political responsibility for one's own people. The responsibility for the consequences of this discipleship is given over to God: 'Do not have anxiety . . .'

(2) *The doctrine of just war.* Whoever is not a pacifist always explains himself or herself with a kind of doctrine of just war. This doctrine does not intend to provide a justification for war — we must be clear about this — but seeks to apply the moral criteria of justice and injustice to the conduct of war. With this doctrine the moral norms of good and evil are , applied to the execution of war. According

to this theory, war must be conceived as a means of politics or a continuation of politics by other means. Yet we should be aware of the fact that the doctrine of the just war was not developed for the justification of war but for the limitation of war, because no one is allowed to participate inan unjust war. (Both the Vietnam War and the Falkland's War, for example, were, according to this tradition, unjust wars because war was never declared.)

The decisive elements of the doctrine of the just war are:

1. War must be declared by a legitimate authority; it must serve the common good of the state.

2. It must be conducted with a good intention.

3. It must be conducted with the expectation of a good outcome; the general situation after the war must be better than the situation before it.

4. All peaceful means for a resolution of the conflict must have been exhausted.

5. The means of the war my not be worse than the evil which is supposed to be overcome by it, that is, the means must stand in the right proportion to the end.

6. There must be a distinction between soldiers and citizens. The civil population must be protected.

Points 1-4 relate to *jus ad bellum* (the right to war), point 6 to *jus in bello* (justice in war) and point 5 relates to both. Those who find these considerations somewhat macabre in the world today may apply these points to a doctrine of the just liberation struggle and think, for example, about the struggle of the Sandinistas against Samosa in Nicaragua. But we in the Federal Republic of Germany and the United States have to come to grips with the possession of nuclear weapons, and now quite specifically the refusal of armament or disarmament; we must in this situation live out our service of peace as Christians and churches of Christ. Our efforts to find the right way have taken place within the context of five related considerations, in the church and in the world generally: 1. The doctrine of the just nuclear war. 2. The doctrine of just moral armament. 3. The apocalypitc threshold. 4. To live without armaments.

1. *The Doctrine of the Just Nuclear War*

According to this doctrine nuclear war is not to be directly justified but rather confined to prescribed limits. The possession of weapons is not refused: Having weapons is part of the present deterrent system which 'secures peace'. The use of the weapons is subjected to the norm of the appropriateness of the means and the norm of the differentiation between military and civilian population. This means that the massive destruction of large cities is not allowed; only the selective use on military objectives is allowed. The strategy of 'massive retaliation', therefore, is not to be justified.

As a result of the strategic attacks on military installations, however, civil population will be destroyed, and this is inevitable. This inevitability is thus a part of the deterrence strategy because it provides an additional threat to the opponent. But mass destruction cannot be espoused. Hence it is prohibited to be the first one to use nuclear weapons. If this is prohibited, then it is also prohibited to prepare for a first-strike capacity. These considerations, arising from the application of the just war theory, do not exclude, however — to this point in the discussion — nuclear armament as such.

By its further development of nuclear weapons the government of the United States (and the USSR as well) is obviously following the position of just nuclear war: the neutron bomb, the Pershing II and the Cruise missiles can be employed with precision against military objectives without causing massive destruction of civil population. Out of the old strategy of massive destruction has developed the more finely tuned strategy of "limited nuclear war". Nuclear weapons are thus made useable. Accordingly, the process of increasing armaments is organized more and more. With this, however, the threshhold of the beginning of a nuclear war has come considerably nearer. And because no one knows whether a 'limited nuclear war' can be kept within limits, the situation in Europe has become not more secure but less secure. As far as I am aware, no one in our European churches is a proponent of a 'just nuclear war', because the limiting of such a war cannot be assured.

2. The Doctrine of Just Nuclear Armament

While the doctrine of the just nuclear war has been refused, the doctrine of just nuclear armament is nevertheless maintained in both pronouncements of the Protestant church of Germany (EKD) of which we have spoken (1969, 1981): By means of the parity of armaments the present peace is preserved; only a situation of parity will alow negotiations for disarmament; and, further, the mutually incredible horror of attack prevents a nuclear war. Because disarmament steps can be taken only on the basis of military parity, armaments must be increased. But this can be justified only if the breathing space or grace period is used to move from armed peace to a security system without nuclear weapons and to build an international order of peace.

According to this doctrine, therefore, only the possession and threat, but not the use of nuclear weapons, may be allowed. If, however, one is not ready to use what one possesses, no deterrence results. To this extent there is an illusion here. On the other hand, it was already recognized in the 1969 pronouncement: 'The expectations which in the early 1960s were connected with international politics on the basis of "armament control" can no longer be maintained'. The breathing space or grace period was not used for peace — not because of bad will, but because the possibility did not actually exist: In the midst of the armaments race one can hardly speak of disarmament. The speed of increased armaments is always many times greater than the speed fo disarmament talks (compare, for example, the relationship between the Geneva talks to limit intermediate-range missiles while at the same time development plans proceed for space war missiles!).

3. The Apocalyptic Threshold

Among many people today the impression is growing that increased armaments of nuclear weapons do not secure peace but rather lead more and more into a collective insanity. The deterrent systems have their own laws. Within their logic it is not asked whether something serves peace and life but whether it increases the enemy's fear of one's own strike capacity. Kurt Biedenkopf is right when he calls peace based on nuclear deterrence an ultimate threshold, because nuclear deterrence presents the threat of the enemy as world destruction. A securing of peace by means of threatening world destruction can never be stabilized as a permanent condition. This situation is therefore unsuitable as the foundation of a permanent order of peace. That an apocalyptic peace of deterrence is not even 'capable of gaining democratic consensus' shows that among the peoples of the world there is still a healthy human understanding.

There is ethically no conceivable justification of a possible destruction of humanity and of life on earth in order to protect the rights and freedom in one of the social systems in which human beings live today. A peace which is bought with the threat of world destruction is no peace. The peace of deterrence through mutual fear may technically be non-employment of weapons, but it is not peace. Mutual deterence through fear is a condition of extreme lack of peace, because it increases potential realities of violence. Even without nuclear war the stock-piling of armaments already destroys the life of human beings and the natural environment. The military-industrial complex spreads itself like a concerous growth and infects all dimensions of life. Unnoticed, a total mobilization has come into being.

We call, therefore, for 'withdrawal from the apocalyptic threshold', a gradual nuclear disengagement as a first step and then the gradual dismantling of conventional armaments. But is such a withdrawal still at all possible? Does not the turning back away from an apocalyptic death zone unto life mean a comprehensive transformation of the whole system in which we live? If for a moment we imagine that the nuclear threat did not exist, we would then have to disband the military budget, free our souls from anxiety and aggression, and . . . But because this idea sounds so utopian, it is clear that we have never thought through it seriously; this shows that we quite pessimistically believes that the point of no return has already been reached and we have become prisoners of the deterrence system. In terms of political rhetoric, the 'force of the issue' and the momentum have already taken the place of free, responsible decisions.

4.   *To Live Without Armaments*

A person who recognizes that mutual deterrence through fear is based not on a parity of armaments but on an armaments race which is already now bleeding the nations to death and can lead to no good end stands before the decision either to go along with it or to protest against it. It is therefore understandable that the old movement which worked under the slogan 'Ban the Bomb' is being resurrected in Europe today under the self-obligating formulation 'live without armaments' (*Ohne Rüstung Leben*). The logic is clear: The use of nuclear weapons is irresponsible and sin.

But if the use is irresponsible and sin then the possession also cannot be considered responsible, for the possession binds the possessor to rearmament, counter armament, modernization, proliferation, etc., and also, in the long run, to their use. If, however, the possession is not be considered responsible, then one must withdraw from the universal arms race and devote all of one's efforts to an alternative service of peace just at the Anabaptists and Mennonites who were prepared for peace have done for a long time.

To live without armaments can have two dimensions, a personal and a political dimension.

First, Christians who place the discipleship of Christ over responsibility for the world can deny themselves without making their own denial a model and a law for all human beings, Christians and non-Christians. That was the way of the Anabaptists. Defencelessness, bound up with the readiness for suffering and martyrdom, is the way of faith, and this faith is not everyone's thing (we can expect it from those who believe, but not from those who do not have the strength of faith; it is a personal commitment, but not a political proposal).

Second, Christians and non-Christians who want to end the arms race can deny themselves and seek to make their readiness to live without armament a political injunction for all human beings of their nation.

In the first case the risk is personal; is the second case it is also political. In the first case one takes the consequences upon oneself; in the second case one must think of the consequences for others.

Wherein does the risk lie in the second case? Whoever disarms unilaterally and brings to the enemy preliminary achievements for peace can of course by this very action provoke the foe to aggression (for instance, it is sometimes said that England's and France's peace initiatives in 1939 provoked Hitler's aggression). Even if no aggression results, one can thereby become subject to blackmailing and extortion through the threats of the adversary. In this way one delivers oneself and one's own to the more powerful foe.

Therefore whoever believes that nuclear war can be prevented only through unilateral disarmament must be ready to sacrifice not only himself or herself but also his or her own people. Such a person must risk the freedom, the rights and the security of his or her own country in order to save the whole of life on this earth from nuclear death. To be sure, this risk is not yet provable because as of yet no one has made the experiments, but it is a fear which cannot easily be laid to rest as long as the adversary is believed to be capable only of the worst, but not of the rational. And this leads to the controversy over what we, the West, can expect of the Russians — the worst or the rational?

REMEMBERING THE SERMON ON THE MOUNT

Up to now both sides of this issue have made their calculations as if neither Christ nor the Sermon on the Mount existed. With Christ, however, there comes into the calculation a factor which suspends the whole process and changes everything: It is the reality of God which actually supports us all.

'You are children of your Father in heaven', says Jesus. This remembrance calls us out of the conflict. Whoever engages in a struggle and arbitrates a conflict stands under the law of retaliation. Otherwise the parity in conflict cannot be maintained: eye for an eye, tooth for a tooth, armament — counterarmament, proliferation — counter proliferation. When we engage an enemy on the basis of the law of retaliation, however, we enter into a vicious circle from which we can no longer escape. We become enemy to our enemy and horrified by our own fear. We threaten what threatens us and we hate what hates us. We are more and more determined by the enemy. When evil is retaliated with evil, then there arises one evil after another, and that is deadly. We can be freed from such vicious circles only when our orientation to the foe ceases and another one becomes more important to us.

The love which Jesus puts in place of retaliation is the love of the enemy. The love of friends, mutual love, is nothing special; it is only retaliation of good with good. The love of the enemy, however, is not recompensing, but is rather an anticipating, intelligent and creative love. Whoever repays evil with good must be really free and strong.

Love for the enemy does not mean surrendering to the enemy, submission to his will. Rather, such a person is no longer in the stance of reacting to the enemy, but seeks to create something new, a new situation for the enemy and for himself or herself. Such a person follows his or her own intention and no longer allows the law of actions to be prescribed by the foe. Jesus did not die with a curse upon his enemies but rather with a prayer for them. In his life, his passion and his dying Jesus revealed the perfection of God: 'Be perfect, even as your heavenly Father is perfect'.

Of what does God's perfection consist? In no way is a moral perfectionism meant. It consists of that love which is long-suffering, friendly and patient, which does not add to evil or carry a grudge, which bears all things, believes all things, and hopes all things (1 Cor. 13). God's perfection lies in the fact that he loves his enemies, blesses them, does good to them and does not return evil for their evil. It is precisely from this that we all live. The whole world lives from this divine reality, even if it does not know it. As Jesus said, God is like the sun rising on the evil and the good, or like the rain pouring down upon the just and the unjust. Hence God bears all and maintains all because he hopes for each one. God's perfection is his limitless ability for suffering, his almightiness is his patient suffering for and with all things. God's uniqueness is his inexhaustible creative power of love. This is the new orientation: We do not only live in two divided and hostile worlds: Free world here — communist bloc there; First world here — Third world there. We actually live on this one earth. We breathe the same air, the same sun is rising in life. Let us become children of this one earth and overcome our divided, hostile worlds.

In former times, we have asked only: What serves our security, what serves our survival? But now in listening to the Sermon on the Mount and seeking to experience God's love for the enemy, we must rephrase the basic question: What is the most helpful thing for 'the enemy'? In what way can we best bless those who curse us? How do we do good for those who hate us? To remain concrete for my situation in Germany: Since we Germans fear the Russians (and otherwise almost nothing on the face of the earth), we must ask: What helps the Russian people to gain peace more, our further armament or our disarmament? In what way can we bless the Communist who curses us? In what way can we do good for the peoples of the Third World who consider us their exploiter and enemy?

The politics of national security is, to a large degree, a politics of anxiety and fear: Because we have anxiety we demand security. Because we demand security, we increase our armaments. As we increase our arms we give terror to our adversary. Therefore our adversary also increases his arms. Quite to the contrary of this system, creative intelligent love arises out of freedom, out of the freedom to be a child of the eternal God, and that means out of the freedom from the fear of temporal death. Out of this freedom can come love for the enemy and the work for peace.

Can one, however, really become free from this anxiety? One can become at least a bit freer from it when one recognizes the danger and consciously enters into the risk. To the degree that the risk of the vulnerable, defenceless but creative life becomes conscious to us, the more free and patient we become. Only the unknown and the repressed make us really anxious. In this sense I am personally willing and ready to live without armaments.

TO PROCLAIM PEACE

I come now to the 1981 Declaration on Peace by the Society of Protestant Theology and the statement of the Reformed Alliance in Germany from August, 1982. These two groups have made clear statements against nuclear war and armament and for disarmament. What follows represents, first, the Declaration of 1981.

> Jesus Christ, as he is witnessed to us in the Holy Scriptures and lives among us in the Holy Spirit, is our peace (Eph. 2:14). In him the eternal God has reconciled the world with himself (2 Cor. 5:14). Through him the world will be redeemed. Through the gospel he makes his peace to be proclaimed among us (Eph. 6:15).
>
> There are no dimensions of our life in which we cannot be certain of the peace of God. There are no conflicts of our life, neither personal nor political, which are not embraced by God's will for peace with human beings and his whole creation. There are no enemies, neither personal nor political, for whom God's will for peace does not apply.
>
> We deny God's peace when we secure ourselves before our enemies by becoming enemies to them, when we encounter their threat with counter-threat and their terror with horror. God's peace rather makes it possible for us to love our enemies creatively by understanding their suffering, by thinking through our own position critically, and by making every conceivable effort to dismantle their and our enmity. Love of the enemy is an expression of the sovereign freedom of the children of God and has nothing to do with weakness and submission.
>
> From the modern, military means of mass destruction comes not only a deadly danger for humanity and all life on earth; it threatens us also with immeasurable guilt (and this reflects our experience as German Christians from World War II, after which we must ask how we can come to the judgment of God).

The Reformed Declaration says:

> In the face of the threat to peace posed by the means of mass destruction by both conventional weapons of mass destruction and nuclear weapons, we as a church have often kept silent for too long or not witnessed to the will of the Lord with sufficient decision. Now as the possibility of atomic war is becoming a probability, we come to this recognition: The issue of peace is a confessional issue. In our opinion the *status confessionis* is given to it because the attitude taken toward mass destruction has to do with the affirmation or denial of the gospel itself.

What is the significance of these official Chruch statements? What are their convictions? If the use of the means of mass destruction is sin, then the possession of the means of mass destruction for the purpose of threatening and deterring the enemy cannot be justified as Christian. Because this threat is effective only if one is also ready to use the weapons, the threat itself is immoral and must also be viewed as sin.

The modern military means of mass destruction have changed war so much that the real nature of war is revealed now before everyone's eyes. We have reached the point, therefore, where we must go back and say that all war is irresponsible, is sin, and there can be no justification of it. Every martial threat and positioning which includes the possibility of escalation to universal nuclear war is irresponsible. The current peace through mutual deterrence is also irresponsible.

The planned spiralling of nuclear armaments threatens us all as never before. We therefore demand immediate and binding arms talks among the great powers. We advocate a European disarmament conference with the declared goal of establishing a zone free from the means of mass destruction. We support a gradual disarmament in the area of conventional arms and the agreed upon building up of cooperation in Europe and Asia, in particular in areas of economic justice.

The service of peace then must become the content of life in the community of Jesus Christ. Church institutions and organizations can do no other than encourage and help in the formation of this sevice of peace among Christians. Service of peace which is alive in the congregation and which is being supported by the church leadership should have these three emphases in mind:

1. *Learning the love of the enemy.* Wars are spread through friend-foe thinking. Through artificially concocted images of the ene.ny, fears are used and aggressions called forth. Through psychological warfare human beings are led to the disregard for life and mobilized for killings. The command of the love of the enemy enables

the dissolution of these images of the enemy and the fears and aggressions which are engendered through them.

If anxiety before the enemy is made the counsel of politics, not only external but also internal peace is imperiled. The loyalty of the citizens to the government which has been elected by them is then no longer won through fulfilling the mandate to govern but forced through the spreading of fear, be it fear of enemies of the state, or be it the fear to be considered as an enemy of the state. The spreading of psychological unrest and public mistrust are the results. Whoever wants, on the contrary, to spread peace will resist the use and engendering of fear in our people. Sober historical and political analyses can also free us in Germany from the fear of Russia and the horror of the communists, and make us capable of the necessary concrete political encounter.

2. *Recognizing the real danger and cooperating on overcoming it.* While taking up again and intensifying this East-West conflict, the great powers have repressed from the public awareness the much more dangerous North-South conflict and the danger of the ecological catastrophe. The politics of the new armament functions at the expense of help for the Third World and leads to its further exploitation. The poor are already today paying for the arming of the rich. Already today time, intelligence and capital are being wasted for instruments of mass destruction and not spent for overcoming hunger in the world. The Christian's service of peace in such a situation must also become the voice and advocate of the silent and dying peoples in the midst of the conflict over spiralling armaments.

3. *Becoming a peace church.* The more the church moves from being a church bound to the state to a free church, the clearer can become its witness to peace and the less ambiguous its initiative for peace. We believe that the church of Jesus Christ can become a church of peace without sectarian isolation from the world. It will become a peace church to the degree that it confesses Christ and Christ alone as its and the whole world's peace and shows the necessary consequences of this confession.

One final remark. I believe that so-called pacifism is no longer an illusion or utopia. Pacifism is the only realism of life left to us in this apocalyptic situation of threatening world annihilation. Pacifists are the realists of life, and not merely voices of utopia.

8 Changing Perceptions of Irish Neutrality

Bill McSweeney

'Ireland's future membership of NATO would not be inconsistent with Irish neutrality during the Second World War and thereafter'. This statement, which occasionally appears for discussion in the assessment of students of the Irish School of Ecumenics, represents a view which most Irish people would find peculiar, even objectionable. We were neutral, after all, and we cannot remain neutral if we join NATO. Yet it is an opinion which is becoming commonplace among academics, and is accepted with little difficulty by politicians in office — though they tend to question it in opposition.

As a statement of historical fact, it is nearer the truth than most Irish people would like. But neutrality, though it is fashioned and conditioned by history, is not merely a historical question; it is also a possibility, an instrument of policy in an international arena constantly changing and presenting new problems and new opportunities. The world and our awareness of it today are radically different from the circumstances in which Ireland declared and maintained her neutrality in the past. Moreover, that policy was not itself consistent throughout the post-war period, and one could say that the truth of the statement above depends on which part of that period since the Second World War is being considered. A final point of ambiguity: Irish neutrality since the Second World War was not simply a policy conducted by government; it was also a value, fostered by government, which acquired some moral and cultural significance among the people. It matters if an element of a people's identity — however inconsistent it may be with the reality of foreign policy — is discarded by government when it has outlived its political usefulness.

There is no doubt that neutrality was an immensely popular measure among the Irish people and that in some degree it was appropriated as a positive symbol, not merely a negative fact. If academics have now discovered a significant truth about our post-war past, and wonder at the popular resistance to it, they should remember that theirs is a truth about government, not about Ireland. In the social world, if not in the physical, things often are what they seem — as the sociologist W. I. Thomas put it: if people perceive things as real then they are real in their consequences. As we shall see, the capacity to change perception into reality would later influence government tactics on neutrality and related matters.

NEUTRALITY AS A POLITICAL INSTRUMENT

Nonetheless, it is true that what people believed the government was doing, what they understood as a principle of foreign policy from the foundation of the state until the present day, was expressed in the idea of neutrality. It was not simply a descriptive term for a policy executed by De Valera and his wartime government; in popular understanding, it was felt to be a general attitude to war and military alliance which was a feature of the identity of the state in international affairs and a continuing commitment of Irish governments. It had little significance in peacetime and was not seen as contradicting, or being compromised by, other traditional values such as cultural links with the United States, trade preference with Great Britain, religious ties with Rome and the rest of the Catholic world and a profound anti-Communism. Neutrality was a principle, it was felt, not a tactic. But it was a negative principle, relevant only to what Ireland would not do in time of war, but not functional for the conduct of foreign policy in peacetime. In this sense it was a popular value and it was popularly believed that governments valued neutrality in like manner.

Irish politicians have encouraged this opinion in the past forty years by referring to neutrality in such terms as 'a basic principle', 'a tradition to be maintained', even extending its function in peacetime by describing it as the foundation of our impartial role in peacemaking. The available historical evidence, however, leaves no room for this interpretation of policy. Neutrality in Irish history was a political instrument, first employed as a means of attaining sovereignty, later reaffirmed and never entirely abandoned in the interests of Irish unity. Successive governments and Ministers of Foreign Affairs have sought to exchange it for political or economic benefits; and only in periods when no adequate returns or penalties were likely have they been consistently supportive on the neutrality issue.

Irish sovereignty was established with the 1938 treaty handing back the control of Irish ports to the Dublin government and thus achieving the first of the political goals of which neutrality was a means. The first notable hint that neutrality might be more than a mere expedient came with De Valera's response to Churchill at the end of the Second World War. During the war, Ireland's refusal to enter formally into military alliance with the Allies was stubbornly and cleverly defended by De Valera, despite growing international criticism and threatening pressure from Britain to force Ireland into a common cause against Nazism. It was defended by repeated declarations of the injustice of partition and the impossibility of alliance with a government responsible for that state of affairs. This defence was backed up by some ostentatious displays of military impartiality and other, less public, concessions to the Allied cause which were deemed necessary to pacify an outraged Westminster government. Had an Allied victory been predictable during the early years of the war, the pressure on De Valera to yield to Churchill's pleas and threats would have been even greater.[1]

By the end of the war, neutrality, though it had continuing tactical possibilites for the Irish government, had served its basic purpose for the Irish people. De Valera faced an international world dominated by the victorious Allies in which the rewards of victory were seen as the rewards of virtue and the exclusion of the conquered from the spoils of war as an indictment of their cause. Every moral issue which hindsight offered as a noble reason for opposing Hitler was now appropriated to define the motives why Britain had declared war on Germany and to point the finger of cowardice and contempt at Ireland and at the idea of neutrality. De Valera faced an Irish people relieved at the ending of war, grateful for his statesmanship in protecting them from its worst effects, now anxious to recover from their isolation and to rebuild their self-image in a world in which neutrality had become a term of abuse. It was time for neutrals, too, to re-write history.

De Valera's argument that neutrality was not only a principle of foreign policy but that it constituted a basis of Ireland's moral concerns and international involvement, rather than indifference and isolation, was understandably seen as a triumphant rebuke to Churchill and a welcome emphasis on the ethical status of a major element of national policy which no longer had immediate practical benefits to offer. The moral propriety of a neutral policy had not been an issue in Ireland during the war but it was good for the Irish to hear it so clearly stated at the end and by such an authority.[2]

Three years later, with the formation of NATO and the emergence of a more acceptable enemy in the forces of Communism, and a more acceptable ally in the United States, neutrality re-emerged as an expedient. The only impediment to Ireland joining NATO in a military alliance against the Soviet Union was the fact that member-

1. See Robert Fisk: *In Time of War*, Deutsch, 1983, p. 463 ff. The best and most balanced account of Irish neutrality to date is Patrick Keatinge's *A Singular Stance: Irish Neutrality in the 1980s*, IPA, Dublin, 1984.
2. Fisk, p. 463 ff. Also Ronan Fanning: 'Irish Neutrality — an historical review' in *Irish Studies in International Affairs*, RIA, 1982.

ship was incompatible with the fact of the continued partition of Ireland by another member-state. If Britain could be prevailed upon by the US to concede the Northern six counties, then a unified Ireland would be happy to join. The tactic failed.[3] It was an appeal over the heads of the Westminster government to a country with the closest cultural links with Ireland, which had also viewed the outbreak of war in Europe as a neutral. But America's sporadic neutralism vis-a-vis Europe had disappeared with its emergence as the world super-power. Neutrality was no longer a refusal to aid imperialism and colonialism. It was now a refusal to take sides when the moral issue was clear; as Foster Dulles would describe it seven years later, it was the fallacy that 'a nation can buy safety for itself by being indifferent to the fate of others'.[4] If Ireland still loomed large in American sentiments, it was of little strategic significance for NATO and weighed nothing when set in the balance of foreign interests against Great Britain. We were then, in US policy terms, what we continued to be through the sixties and seventies — a friendly neutral — or, as a more candid American diplomat later put it 'small potatoes'.

Not for another thirty years would neutrality again suggest itself to Irish politicians as an instrument of policy which could be used for internal political ends. Neutrality was now a firmly established feature of Irish policy, not because of any commitment to it in itself, but because the only alternative now available was NATO. And NATO without an end to partition was now eliminated from the range of policy options for any Irish government — however threatening the Soviet Union might appear to some, however godless Communism might seem to many in the leading Fine Gael party in the 1948 coalition.

For the first decade of that period, a decade of severe economic and social depression, the fact that Ireland was not involved in a military alliance seemed an irrelevance to most politicans and, probably, to most of the Irish people. Repeated attempts to join the United Nations were vetoed by the Soviet Union for the understand-able, though unstated, reason that our neutrality was internationally regarded as American, not impartial or non-aligned. At a time when nuclear weapons were seen as dramatically altering the nature of war and the strategic significance of territory, no one seemed to care enough for our military potential to make an offer we wouldn't refuse. At a time when Europe was receiving massive Marshall Aid to boost its recovery and Ireland was sinking under a stagnant economy with little to offer half its labour force but the prospect of reconstructing

3. Dáil Debates, 324, 23 February 1949. This was the so-called 'sore thumb' strategy of trying to arouse international sympathy for the fact of partition.
4. Laurence W. Martin, ed: *Neutralism and Nonalignment*, Greenwood, Westport, p. 18.

Britain, neutrality would have seemed a small potato indeed if anyone was prepared to pay for its abandonment. But with the US and the Soviet Union in agreement about our allegiance, with Britain in no hurry to divest itself of a still-useful remnant of its first colony, and with Irish anti-Communism of the early fifties second only to American McCarthyism for the piety and indiscriminateness of its expression, it is not surprising that there were no offers for our military services.

THE LUXURY OF NEUTRALITY

It was in such a context that Ireland's entry into the United Nations took place in 1955, and it was the start of a brief and creative period in international affairs when neutrality − unnecessary now for our own security, apparently useless for anything else − was transformed into an argument for peace and a symbol of status in the international forum. For four years under the leadership and inspiration of Frank Aiken, the Irish delegation to the UN pressed the issue of peace and disarmament in the world, and neutrality as a positive token of Ireland's commitment to it, with a vigour and imagination that stirred the hearts of some compatriots at home. The period coincided with, and perhaps contributed to, a general reawakening of the Irish people, a psychological rebirth which lifted the cloud of depression and humiliation of the post-war years and spread to every sector of Irish society, giving it a new sense of identity and purpose for the sixties.

With the birth of new ideals, however, came a new economic possibility which promised unprecedented prosperity, but which, at the same time, placed a question mark on neutrality. Unlike the war, the EEC offered few tangible rewards to those who opted out, particularly if, like Ireland, their economy was underdeveloped and their pattern of trade was strongly linked to an existing or potential member. If Britain joined, it was argued, then Ireland must follow. But if Ireland joined a community which clearly aspired to political unity and collective security, how could the policy of neutrality be maintained? Neutrality might be termed 'positive' at the United Nations but at home it now seemed to be acquiring a negative value. If the other four European neutrals saw the logic of European membership and could afford the price of staying out, Ireland had no option, it was said, but to choose between economic survival and outdated traditions.

In the event, no such clear choice was made: Ireland joined the EEC with Britain and fudged the question of neutrality. The preparations for membership were begun formally with the first application to the Community in 1961 and were continued for the next twelve years in the gradual accommodation of significant Irish institutions to future participation in the Common Market. The most notable transformation was in the enlargement and reorientation of the Department of External Affairs, as it was then called, towards its new focus on Brussels and Europe. Other departments of government similarly adjusted in anticipation of the new problems and opportunities. A new interest in Europe began to emerge in academic and cultural circles and the debate on the pros and cons of EEC membership was carried enthusiastically by the media — now expanded by the new television station. Long before Ireland's emissaries negotiated in Brussels or declaimed in Strasbourg, the ground was cleared at home and the institutional support for their activities was constructed. Under Prime Minister Seán Lemass, Ireland was serious about the EEC.

No comparable seriousness accompanied our other foreign policy interest at the United Nations. The Aiken policy declined when Brussels beckoned, not for lack of commitment to it on the part of the UN delegation but because it was never a very serious commitment on the government's part in the first place. Neutrality drifted into a cloud of free-floating symbolism after the end of the Second World War and after the failure of the coalition government in 1949 to trade it for unification. No one cared much about it one way or the other and if Frank Aiken and some far-sighted intellectuals could put it to worthy purpose at a time when the country was demoralized and the outlook bleak, then he might as well do so. What he said at the United Nations was hardly likely to improve matters for Ireland and there was no thought in the government's collective mind that their delegation's utterances in New York needed any institutional support at home other than the airfare.

The historical basis of this gap between reality and expression — between the ideological and institutional conditions at home, on the one side, and the ringing phrases of Ireland's diplomats in New York on the other — is important for our understanding of Irish neutrality. Ireland was simply not neutral in the sense implied by Aiken's policy, whatever De Valera may have said in the particular circumstances of Churchill's attack at the end of the war. (He corrected that virtuous interpretation later when there seemed to be a possibility of exchanging neutrality for reunification.)[5] While Aiken was denouncing the superpowers for their conduct of the arms-race, initiating the Non-Proliferation Treaty and supporting Communist China's entry to the UN, his government was avoiding an occasion of sin at Dalymount Park when Ireland played Communist Yugoslavia, his compatriots were denouncing Russia's crushing of Hungary and his Cardinal was

5. Fanning, *op. cit.*

denouncing him for voting for Red China in the name of Catholic Ireland. Things might have been different. Had De Valera pressed home the idea of positive neutrality after his broadcast reply to Churchill it might have stirred the imagination of his colleagues in government and stimulated the conditions for its successful implementation in foreign policy. But Aiken's leap of the imagination in the mid fifties was too big and too late for the government to accomplish it at home and he was left to play with symbols in New York while his colleagues in Dublin got on with the real business of reacting to balance-of-payments crises, appeasing the hierarchy and counting the emigrants.

This history — and Aiken's role in it — was encapsulated in the famous three principles announced in 1956 to govern the conduct of affairs on Ireland's behalf at the United Nations. The first is a simple acceptance of the obligations of the Charter. The second reflects the known preferences of Frank Aiken and expresses the innovatory character of his UN policy:

> We should try to maintain a position of independence, judging the various questions on which we have to adopt an attitude or cast a vote strictly on their merits, in a just and disinterested way . . . to avoid becoming associated with particular blocs or groups so far as possible.

The third principle upholds the more traditional values of Catholic Ireland in support of Christian and anti-Communist ideals and Western liberties, and the readiness to defend them against the unnamed aggressor. As a principle of foreign policy, of course, it makes nonsense of the second:

> To do whatever we can as a member of the United Nations to preserve the Christian civilization of which we are a part and with that end in view to support wherever possible those powers principally responsible for the defence of the free world in their resistance to the spread of Communist power and influence . . .
> We belong to the great community of states, made up of the United States of America, Canada and Western Europe.[6]

Commenting on the explanation of these principles given in the Dáil by the then Minister for External Affairs, Liam Cosgrave, Conor Cruise O'Brien notes that, taken together, they were intended to signal Ireland's intention to fall in behind the United States in the

6. Conor Cruise O'Brien: 'Ireland in International Affairs' in Owen Dudley Edwards ed: *Conor Cruise O'Brien Introduces Ireland*, Deutsch, London, 1969, p. 128.

voting on all important issues. But Aiken's opportunity came with the victory of Fianna Fáil in 1957 and, until 1961, his UN delegation effectively ignored the traditionalist third principle.

Without serious support at home, however, his policy had little hope of surviving the changed circumstances. Modern diplomacy works on a tight rope; it has little room for wandering into areas not controlled and approved by the government. Where such excursions are sustained, either the diplomats or the government must eventually fall into line, otherwise diplomacy risks becoming empty rhetoric and government loses the opportunity of defending its real interest. In Aiken's case, it was he who toed the line marked out by the government of Sean Lemass, and the UN delegation after 1961 resolved the contradiction of second and third principles in favour of the third. Aiken's policy between 1957 and 1961 was possible because Ireland was still in the vacuum of international identity and purpose left by the war and its aftermath, and because the international market for the only property of value we had for sale — neutrality — had collapsed. We were ready to join NATO to end partition; but while partition lasted, NATO had no need of the rest of Ireland.[7] Aiken's policy could only last, furthermore, if it served the real interest of the government and of the society it represented. For Lemass, those real interests were reflected in neither the second nor the third principles nor even the United Nations itself. What mattered was economic development, and the place to turn to for that was Brussels, not New York.

O'Brien seems puzzled, nonetheless, by the speed of change and the fact of the decline of the UN in Irish foreign policy. 'Ironically, this came about at a time when Ireland had greater freedom than ever before to pursue a genuinely independent policy', he writes. Referring to the EEC factor in forcing the decline of independence and the adoption of a subservient role to American interests in the UN, 'it would be difficult to imagine a more absurd argument . . . The United States cannot get Ireland into the Market and France, which can, is not likely to be favourably impressed by displays of subservience to America's supposed interests'.[8] This is true as a statement of major-power relations but it takes no account of the historical fact that the UN policy in question was not Ireland's but Aiken's — and O'Brien's, too, for he was a senior member of that famous delegation.

Diplomacy must be grounded in the institutions for which it speaks, if it is to be effective and lasting. Aiken's diplomacy, at worst, was seriously at odds with public opinion at home and irrelevant to, or incompatible with, the majority view in government and the values embodied in the major institutions; at best, it was a tolerable excur-

7. Fanning, *op. cit.*
8. O'Brien, *op cit.*, p. 133.

sion into territory unknown and unappreciated by his government, which could bring some minor benefits of a symbolic kind, but which must cease when a new policy option seemed to demand all the resources of government for its realization. Lemass would permit nothing which might put at risk a successful application to join the Common Market. O'Brien is right, of course, when he claims that entry to the EEC did not of itself entail disengagement from the existing policy at the UN. But given the dominant perspectives and values of the government and people of that time, it is not surprising that disengagement occurred and that all the talents of External Affairs and government went into the preparations for a role in international affairs which they could understand, which the people would appreciate and from which all could profit materially.

NEW PRESSURES ON NEUTRALITY

The independence of Aiken's UN policy was predicated, moreover, on the fact of Ireland's neutrality. We could make a real contribution to world peace, it was argued, because we were neutral. But from the outset, Ireland's application for membership of the EEC cast doubts on the appropriateness, if not the viability, of our neutrality. All other members and potential members were already in NATO and the vague aspiration for political unity, which was part of the Community vision in its origins, was gradually being defined — both in Europe and in Ireland — in terms of common defence and security. While the immediate threat of a military alliance was still some years away, the clouds were forming in 1962 when Lemass made the first of several attempts to break that link between partition and neutrality promoted by De Valera and exploited without success in 1949. His stress on the inevitability of abandoning neutrality on joining the Common Market underlines the point made above. Though EEC rules clearly permit membership to a neutral country and in no legal sense whatever bind such a country to a military alliance or defence agreement, even in the long term, nonetheless Lemass and his government, and successive governments thereafter, were happy to see the EEC in that light. He stated in 1962, in an interview with the *New York Times*:

> We recognize that a military commitment will be an inevitable consequence of our joining the Common Market and ultimately we would be prepared to yield even the technical label of neutrality. We are prepared to go into this integrated Europe without any reservation as to how far this will take us in the field of foreign policy and defence.[9]

9. Quoted in Trevor Salmon: 'Ireland — a Neutral in the Community' in *Journal of Common Market Studies*, 20 March 1982, p. 210.

There is no suspicion here or elsewhere that Lemass mourned the passing of Aiken's active neutrality diplomacy or that he mobilized the Department of External Affairs for the EEC campaign with any reluctance, with any regret for opportunities lost. It is not even the case that Lemass's preoccupation with the European Community alone led him to exaggerate the obligations and cost of Ireland's membership. For, in February of the same year, he had already given a quite different reason for his distaste of neutrality and for his eagerness to be rid of it. He said in the Dáil:

> I think it would be highly undesirable that remarks made here should give the impression in Europe that there is a public opinion in this country which regards membership of NATO as something discreditable. The view of the government in that regard has been made clear. We think that the existence of NATO is necessary for the preservation of peace and for the defence of the countries of Western Europe, including this country. Although we are not members of NATO, we are in full agreement with its aims.[10]

It would be politically damaging today for any party leader to be so frank, though it is quite clear that Lemass's views are shared by many in the leadership of Fine Gael and would not be difficult to accommodate, less explicitly, in Fianna Fáil. They are essentially an echo of the third UN principle, which is itself as deeply rooted in Irish culture as anti-Communism in America or anti-imperialism in the Soviet Union. Most people were for Christian civilization, Western values and the defence of the free world, and therefore − if they thought about it at all − they were against the expansion of Communist power and against the Soviet Union which seemed to threaten it. Only in the early eighties did world events take a turn which seriously questioned the facts and the moral implications of this simple equation.

As Ireland prepared its people and institutions energetically, over the following decade, for a successful application to the EEC, every effort was made to display abroad the characteristics of a worthy candidate for acceptance in Europe and to allay at home the fears that more might be given away by treaty obligations or compromise than the government was admitting. The government made it clear that the Treaties of Rome and Paris, which govern membership of the EEC, did not entail any military or defence commitments and no such undertaking was involved in Ireland's acceptance of membership.[11]

Clearly, however, different pressures were being exerted informally in the European corridors which were ineffective on Ireland's

10. Dáil Debates, 193, 14 February 1962.
11. Dáil Debates, 258, 421 ff., 255, 1856.

politicians when in opposition, but irresistible when they formed the government of the day. With few exceptions, the leading politicians of the two main parties are on record as supporting the equivocation on neutrality when in office and using it to embarrass the government when in opposition. Lemass had no ethical qualms about linking the defence of the European Community to the defence of Western Europe by NATO, as we have seen. His successors in government tried to separate NATO — by now a politically sensitive concept to deal with — from Europe, by arguing that the defence of the EEC territories was already implied in the willingness to defend Ireland and its interests. Such defence had nothing to do with the Cold War or with NATO, it was claimed. Thus Jack Lynch, as Taoiseach, saw neutrality as being no more compromised by the intention to defend Europe than to defend our own territory; and his Minister for Finance, Charles Haughey, rejected the idea of joining NATO but recommended participation in the common defence of the EEC.[12] The attempt was being made, therefore, to define neutrality in terms of its 1949 history — to define it, in other words, as a policy related to NATO, not as a policy related to war and military alliance. Since Europe had nothing to do with NATO, in government reasoning, then it was perfectly consistent to join the EEC, defend Europe and be neutral, all at the same time.

The strained logic of a defence pact with the EEC, which is not effectively a defence pact with NATO, is explicable only in terms of the desperate resolve of a government and its Civil Service aides to avoid exclusion when Britain joined the Community. Juggling with labels and playing with language were a favoured tactic of both major parties in Irish politics, before and after 1973. Neutrality was defined in opposition to NATO, not to any other military alliance which might well be itself a pillar of NATO or in alliance with it.

By 1973, NATO was well established as a politically unacceptable aspiration in Ireland, a dirty word in the media and in the Dáil which could be used judiciously to allay or sow suspicions about the real intentions of government. And neutrality was virtuous, for some, a cherished tradition with overtones of high moral principle — at odds with the facts of history — a tradition which could only be abandoned now by a combination of official stealth and ingenuity. Why did so many Irish politicians in office since 1962 advance the cause of a NATO or European military alliance — openly at first, then furtively behind a screen of qualifications which their opponents could remove with delight, only to find themselves taking office in turn and echoing the same phrases, the same equivocations? When there was little popular demand for abandoning Irish neutrality — and none of a legal

12. Dáil Debates, 241, 1155 and 230, 1098 ff.

kind from the EEC or NATO — why were they all so keen to do it?

THE SOURCES OF PRESSURE ON NEUTRALITY

There can be little doubt that the constant factor persuading politicians in government to equivocate on neutrality, but not within whispering range of the politicians in opposition, was the civil service and, predominantly, the Department of Foreign Affairs. This is no answer to the question, of course. It merely shifts it, leaving unresolved the problem of why an unpopular and apparently unnecessary drift into military alliance was allowed to dominate the political process. Who was persuading the civil servants to ensure that Ireland's neutrality would be no barrier to full EEC membership when the time was come?

After the failure of the NATO negotiations in 1949, there was little sign of concern within the Atlantic Alliance that a neutral Ireland posed any strategic problem for the West and little indication within Ireland that the NATO card was of much value. For twenty years — 1961 to 1980 — the objective basis of official Irish misgivings about neutrality lay in the committees and institutions of the EEC, and primarily within the process of political integration formalized with the birth of European Political Co-operation at the 1969 Hague Conference. Since there is no clearly defined obligation arising from Community participation or from EPC directives, one can reasonably conclude that an element in this pressure was also the subjective perception by the policy-making bureaucracy in Ireland of the hidden agenda and long-term goals of EPC, in so far as they consitute a necessary condition of full and fruitful involvement in Europe.

From one point of view it is more important to identify the process in Ireland of full integration in Europe — including the abandonment of neutrality — than to locate its instrument in the civil service. But this would suggest that the Irish civil service merely communicated to government the unavoidable and unquestionable pressure on neutrality emanating from the EEC, and that there was not an *interpretation* of that pressure and a consequent increasing of it on the part of the Dublin bureaucracy. There are some features of Irish orientation to Europe since 1961 which suggest that the nature of the initial commitment to Europe, and the fact that it was promoted and developed with minimal public debate behind a screen of codes and ambiguities, has created a dynamism within the bureaucracy which itself adds to the pressure originating in Europe. In other words, on the issue of a future military alliance, the Irish public is now faced with pressure of unknown quantity from Europe and, in addition, a bureaucracy in Dublin moving towards that particular goal with the inertia of twenty years, making it increasingly reluctant to question its initial perception of the implications of Europe or to examine alternative policy options which do not entail an alliance incompatible with neutrality.

Ireland's European commitment was unreserved from the outset, and it succeeded in mobilizing support at home because it was seen, from the beginning, in terms of Ireland's self-interest, not in terms of some abstract moral ideal. It was a positive Europeanism, promoted with a clear image of the economic benefits and political costs and with a willingness to create the conditions for its success. (This realism stands in sharp contrast to the UN policy of the fifties.) And this vision of the quid-pro-quo nature of membership of the European Community — and of the precise costs which future benefits entail — still operates as a counsel of caution and stealth where the delicate issue of neutrality is involved.

EPC AND NATO

The Irish perception of EPC is in line with that of most other EEC countries. Though officials and government politicians never say so, EPC is moving towards a level of defence or military cooperation which is not compatible with neutrality. Since all the other countries are members of NATO, it is not surprising that they have little difficulty, in principle, with such a trend. From the perspective of Europe, the slow progress on this and the inhibitions in stating this objective more clearly and emphatically arise in part from the Irish factor, partly also from uncertainty in Europe about the implications it will have for the solidarity of NATO. But clearly the military defence of the territories and interests of the EEC member states is the goal of EPC, and if the US reaction urges caution, it is also true that European dissatisfaction with the American leadership of NATO has been an important factor in suggesting the goal in the first place and in stimulating progress towards it in recent years.

The consistent acceptance by Irish governments since 1962 of a defence obligation in the context of Europe, coupled with carefully qualified and sometimes dismissive references to neutrality leave little doubt that Ireland finds its odd-man-out status in the EEC problematic. The legal terms of membership may not oblige Ireland to fall in line but certainly the perceived limitations of being neutral in a Community which aspires to political unity as the complement of economic co-operation, which is already, apart from Ireland, a major territorial part of a military alliance and, in that regard, shares a peculiarly European perspective on defence — in such a Community the Irish tradition of military neutrality is perceived as counterproductive, a serious limitation on Ireland's bargaining capacity. Thus Padraic MacKernan, the Political Director of the Department of Foreign Affairs, in the guarded terms mandatory on this subject, spoke of the relationship between the EEC and EPC:

> ... because of the interaction between the economic and political components of Community membership and EPC, the credibility of the Irish contribution in both frameworks is inter-linked. Thus if our contribution to co-ordination of foreign policy amongst the Ten is a credible one, it can enhance our credibility when we advocate particular solutions to Community problems in the Treaty framework.

As we shall see below, the term 'credible' as a description of Irish foreign policy in EPC can be decoded to mean 'compatible with the defence interests of the other Nine'. MacKernan continues in the same paper to relate Ireland's foreign policy in the European Community to our foreign policy in the United Nations:

> The United Nations continues to be a principal framework for the conduct of Irish foreign policy and remains the forum in which Ireland encounters most of the major international issues of the day, particularly those which arise outside our own region. But since the other members of the Community are also members of the United Nations, and given that the means available to European Political Cooperation are the normal instruments of diplomacy, it is inevitable that the United Nations in this era of continuous multilateral negotiations and global inter-dependence should be a primary focus for the collective diplomacy of the Ten.[13]

While collective diplomacy at the UN does not currently prevent the members of EPC from acting independently — EPC works as an informal consultative process with the aim, but without the obligation, of consensus — nonetheless it represents a trend away from independence which will be considerably more pronounced when moves to strengthen the existing machinery of cooperation result in a more formal process of decision-making in which the wishes of the

13. Padraic MacKernan: 'Ireland and EPC'. Paper read to RIA Conference on European Political Co-operation, 20/11/1981. This paper, given the weight of Ireland's Political Director behind it, has become something of a gospel text for supporters of government policy. It is an exercise in ambiguity and allusiveness within a discursive framework which suggests openness on the sensitive issues, carefully defining neutrality in negative institutional terms (non-membership of NATO/military alliance) to permit the conclusion that EPC poses no threat to it.

smaller countries will inevitably have little influence.[14] Collective diplomacy at the UN may not result in any change of Irish policy before that time — but that is because Ireland's foreign policy since 1961, including UN policy, has been consistently oriented to the EEC. Collective diplomacy is simply a more visible indicator of the decline of the United Nations as a focus of Irish concerns.

Ireland entered on European Political Co-operation as a duty and opportunity deriving from a decisive commitment to maximizing the economic benefits from the Community in general. While there must be serious misgivings about any political process which systematically conceals information on a central part of its purpose in order to create a *fait d'accompli*, it must be recognized that such practices are fairly normal in all democracies today. The process of manipulating public opinion to accept policies defined by bureaucratic and political elites is increasing in the West, particularly through the recruitment of the media, over which governments have a measure of control which is hidden, subtle and effective.

But public opinion can also be influenced, when need be, by a strategy of gradual institutional change or modification which creates the conditions in which the policy goal becomes more desirable, or less objectionable, as the case may be. A rather crude version of this can be seen in the Israeli policy of massive housing construction on the West Bank, in order to strengthen the argument for occupation against public opinion at home and abroad. The other extreme and the more acceptable form of gradual persuasion, advocated by enlightened Irish nationalism, consists in developing economic and cultural conditions in the South, with appropriate British support and cooperation in the North, in order to persuade the Northern majority to vote for some form of united Ireland. The official policy on European integration is, similarly, one of gradual persuasion in which the policy objective is suggested but never clearly affirmed, while a climate of public opinion is formed by the piecemeal construction of a new profile or package of elements favourable to the objective and too costly to discard. It is not by any means an oppressive practice, but neither is it democratic. And it is difficult to sustain strong ethical objections to the method if the goal is desirable, apart from making a rather purist point about the role of elites in modern democracy.

Undoubtedly the economic benefits of European integration constitute a desirable goal for the majority of Irish people. The question arises about the desirability of the defence pact and the abandonment

---

14. Several initiatives in this direction have already been tabled following the 1975 Tindemans Report which proposed, explicitly, the development of a common foreign policy, with an *obligation* on EPC members to agree common positions, thus ending the voluntary co-operation. See European File no. 13, 1983.

of neutrality which seems to accompany it. More immediately, there is a serious question about the necessity of the whole EPC process towards military alliance as an *unavoidable* accompaniment of gaining the benefits of economic integration.[15] And these questions raise another point about the undemocratic nature of the process: had there been due consultation and public debate outside a small circle of bureaucrats and politicians, other policies or substantial modifications of the same general objectives might have been formulated with wider appeal and without the ethical difficulties of EPC; but these are now at a considerable disadvantage in gaining public acceptance because they lack the institutional preparation that has supported the existing European commitment.

Certainly EPC has not yet moved to the fulfilment of its goal as the defence community of EEC territories and interests. And the Irish government, therefore, can easily dismiss arguments about the reality of its EEC policy by drawing attention to this fact — to the current flexibility and informality of the EPC arrangements, to the absence of any formal requirement on neutrality from any authoritative organ of the Community and to the evidence of a benign and tolerant attitude of the other member-states towards the odd-man-out off the west coast of Britain. Such evidence is contained in the Report of 1981 concerning the scope of foreign policy questions in EPC, which the British Foreign Secretary, Lord Carrington, interpreted as an affirmation of flexibility which would not embarrass the Irish.[16]

But the defence commitment of EPC is a goal opposed in some practical respects by a European lobby which could be strengthened by too hasty a move towards its realization. EPC has no power over its participants; it functions currently to create a climate which will gradually persuade the other NATO members to drop their fears of US reaction and NATO weakness and to move gradually through stages towards a defence alliance. Similarly, a high profile for responsible collective diplomacy at the United Nations and for EPC involvement in the Helsinki process will demonstrate to an Irish lobby that neutrality is not relevant in the EEC context, as Jack Lynch said, or at least will make more people ask, with Charles Haughey, 'what is wrong with nations getting together and deciding they are going to

15. A two-tier Europe has been mooted by other European nations when their own interests were threatened. It has never been seriously examined by the Irish as a means of preserving and strengthening neutrality while still retaining the economic and cultural benefits of the European Community.
16. EPC London Report, 1981. See the paper by Patrick Keatinge, in this volume, for the text of Carrington's press comment.

have a common bond of defence between them?"[17] A European defence pact, organizationally distinct from NATO, would obviously pose less problems for Ireland than any direct link with NATO. While the difficulties of such a development for other EEC countries have been mentioned, it is worth noting that increasing consideration of such a proposal has been aired from a variety of sources recently, linking its desirability to the question of a common arms procurement policy, outlined in the Fergusson Report, and to the need for greater European commitment to — and NATO reliance on — conventional armaments. Hans-Dietrich Genscher, the West German foreign minister, who was principal architect of the famous Genscher-Colombo plan proposing a major advance on the level of foreign-policy integration, recalled in a recent article the view of President John F. Kennedy that the NATO alliance would be strengthened if it could be transformed from a single, global organization into an alliance of two equal pillars, a European and a North American.[18]

While such a development is highly unlikely in the near future — not least because of difficulties with NATO solidarity created by the deployment of Euro-missiles — and the airing of such views can only be regarded as kite-flying, the frequency and convergence of similar proposals touching on future stages of EPC are significant as an element in the creation of a suitable climate of opinion. They may lack the authority of law but, like EPC in relation to Irish neutrality, they have the power of persuasion. The Fergusson Report too, like the Genscher-Colombo proposals, called for an advance on political cooperation in its first draft which far exceeded the level of integration of foreign policy and the distinction between the Community and NATO currently obtaining. Finally, the first of the more recent Haagerup reports (January 1983) includes a resolution on EPC which was adopted by the European Parliament and which contains the following statements relating to EPC and NATO:

> As all present and probable Community Member States *but one* are members of the Atlantic Alliance, it is urged that a more effective co-ordination take place between the consultation in EPC and the Atlantic Council when political and economic subjects touching on matters related to European peace and security are under discussion.
>
> Consultations in EPC must not negate political consultations within the Atlantic Alliance but should on the contrary strengthen such consultations . . .[19]

17. Dáil Debates, 241, 1155 and 230, 1098 ff.
18. Cited in *Peace and Security and Europe*, Ecumenical Commission for Church and Society in the European Community, Brussels, 1983, p. 14.
19. Niels Haagerup: European Polical Co-operation and European Security, 1-946-82, January 1983.

These are only some of many kites hovering over European capitals — harmless things in themselves, but attracting attention where it matters. They serve to create a consensus of influential opinion in defining the role of the Community and harmonizing into a familiar whole elements which, as long as they are separate, can be considered irrelevant or inapplicable by those who so wish for reasons of their own or their constituency's sensitivity. Gradually the elements build their own links, the kites form their own pattern and, in the absence of alternative patterns and competing possibilities which are not financed by Community resources, they will come to be seen as the way things are, a *fait d'accompli* which is too troublesome or costly to demolish.

(Here it may be useful to insert a note about conspiracy-theory. We are familiar with two kinds of conspiracy views of politics: the fundamentalist kind, for which no evidence is offered or possible, such as the global designs of Jewish/Communist/Banking interests. The popular use of the term 'conspiracy-theory' suggests that all views of conspiracy necessarily belong to this irrational category. The other kind is familiar in social theory as a means of uncovering a strategy of power exercised covertly by groups with common interests and a common purpose. A case in point is the well-documented argument that the British Foreign Office is linked by common background and interests to other key sections of the political establishment and government policy is often influenced by this factor. An important point here is that such a conspiracy may occur without conscious or cynical planning on the part of the principal agents. Conspiracy of this kind is difficult to prove incontrovertibly, since it works by exploiting a calculated ambiguity that allows for the innocent explanation. But where there is evidence of a convergence of interests and actions, the possibility of conspiracy cannot be denied merely because it is unprovable or sounds sinister. The most effective denial of conspiracy is openness, clarity, access to relevant information. The most damning indicator of it is systematic resistance to such access and consistent equivocation.)

As already noted, the major link being forged by this process is that between NATO and the European Community. The proposed enlargement of the Community by the inclusion of Spain and Portugal is referred to in the Haagerup Report above in the phrase 'probable Community Member States'. The official motive for the enlargement stresses the laudable aim of the EEC to protect the young democracies of the South, stabilize their new liberties and advance the common ideal of peace and unity.[20] This is a prettier

20. 'The Enlargement of the European Community', *European File*, November 1983. See also Bulletin of the European Community, Supplement, 1/78, 86.

picture than that which emerges from the discussions and negotiations on enlargement. The central concern is to draw into the orbit of West European economic and defence interests a critical area of Southern Europe which 'might be lost to Western Europe and become hotbeds of continuous political unrest, providing points of departure or even landing stages for aggressive Soviet influence'.[21] The last enlargement with Greece was part of the same EEC concern to secure its Mediterranean flank. Alleviating the poverty and protecting the democracy of these three poorer countries is the reward offered for their participation in a common political union, in EPC, ultimately in NATO. This was clearly perceived in the candidate countries themselves and it explains why Greece restored its military force to NATO shortly before its accession, and why Spain, whose membership was resisted for economic reasons by France, quite openly made its membership of NATO conditional on entry into the EEC.[22] (That Ireland's accession was permitted without too great insistence on joining NATO can be explained by the enormous strategic importance to NATO of Greece and the Iberian territories and by the fact that NATO already controls part of Ireland and the rest is of no great significance as long as partition lasts.)

Another indication of the centrality of the EEC/NATO link lies in the growing desire within the Community to co-operate on arms design and production, already mentioned. Already an Independent European Programme Group (IEPG), controlled by NATO, is engaged in arms design and production with the co-operation of all EEC members except Ireland. Now the Fergusson Report has proposed the linking of IEPG to EPC and the idea is being floated – and made respectable under the heading of rationalization and cost-efficiency – that the needs of NATO and of a future European defence community would provide a market for the combined technology and productive capacity of the EEC, which is not available to the individual European arms exporters at present.

In theory, of course, there can be no objection to efficient production of weapons and the benefits in employment and profit for all which will ensue. Arms are an important element even of a viable neutrality and, while pacifists reject them on ethical grounds, most of them would tolerate defensive weapons on grounds of political realism. In theory, too, the anarchy of the arms-trade could be controlled by the rational harmonizing of weapons production on the part of a responsible community of nations. It all depends on how much weight one gives to the

21. L. Ruhl, *Das Parlament*, No. 33/4, 16 August 1980.
22. Spain's relationship to the EEC is similar to Ireland's in a second way also. Spanish claims on Gibraltar would be advanced by joining NATO. 'The military negotiations . . . will be important for a decisive advance on the matter', according to Foreign Minister Perez-llorca. *The Irish Times*, September 1983.

pretty self-portraits which are the acceptable face of the European Community. There is little reason to believe that the EEC, which cannot avoid butter-mountains and wine-lakes in the production of food, will avoid arms-dumps which will then be used to stock the arsenals of Third World dictatorships and, in the process, multiply enormously the evils of the arms-trade. There is even less reason to believe that EEC cooperation in arms production will respect the separation of NATO and the Community and will not, in fact, escalate the arms-race — either by establishing a third superpower jointly threatening the East with North America, or by direct input into the existing NATO force, with the real likelihood of moving from conventional to nuclear production as the benefits of cost-efficiency and profit dictate.

Enough has been said, in think, to indicate the force and nature of the pressure on Ireland to abandon its neutrality as a consequence of its integration into the European Community. It should be clear, however, that this is not an unavoidable consequence — the pressure exerted in Europe and interpreted to government by civil service circles in Ireland is of a socio-political kind, a convergence of complex forces arising from committee-bargaining, status considerations, personal friendships and the unrelenting flow of information and documents which focus on a message that gradually sinks in: Ireland is the odd-man-out. The pressure is nonetheless real for being socio-political, but it is certainly not the case — at least, not yet — that neutrality and the EEC are incompatible. There are other possibilities which would allow Ireland to retain EEC membership and to retain, even strengthen, neutrality if the will and the commitment is there. I shall make some suggestions in this regard in the final paper in this volume, which takes up this argument again, in summary form.

It remains to return briefly to the historical sketch of neutrality in Ireland and to bring the debate up to date. What has been discussed so far can be simply summarized: until 1949, internal political considerations made neutrality a bargaining tool for the achievement of particular political goals. After the failure to realize its potential to end partition, it became an unsaleable but still attractive feature of Irish life. It was there, like the soft rain in the West. We liked it, some tourists liked it, others thought it peculiar; but there was nothing much we could do with it. For a brief period, 1957-61, it was used to advance, and account for, an active peacemaking role in the United Nations, but without the institutional support at home. From 1961, it became something of a liability, apparently endangering our entry into the EEC with Britain, threatening, after 1973, to limit our bargaining potential in Europe, particularly with the development of EPC as a major concern of all the other member-states. For our politicians and bureaucrats in Europe, neutrality offered no leverage, partition aroused no support. They were both a nuisance, more like bad breath than a sore thumb, evoking irritation rather than sympathy.

A NEW PREMIUM ON NEUTRALITY

The scene changed somewhat with the beginning of the eighties. A number of factors contributed to altering the context of neutrality as a foreign-policy issue, to sharpening the public debate and to resurrecting the idea of neutrality as a positive instrument of policy — either as a tradeable commodity or as the condition of a new involvement in international affairs.

A growing despair over Northern Ireland, with no end in sight of the violence which defeated every effort to elicit or impose a solution; the awareness in the South that the European party was over and that the rewards of EEC membership, which had ended emigration and encouraged migration from the North, were running out and would not come without a struggle in the future; the emergence of Margaret Thatcher's presidential style of leadership, with her uncomplicated view of a world of staunch allies and sworn enemies which matched the fundamentalist style of Ronald Reagan; the decision of NATO in December 1979 to deploy Cruise and Pershing missiles in Europe which created a new mass-awareness of the threat of nuclear war and launched the modern peace movement in Europe and the United States; and, finally, the election of Charles Haughey as leader of Fianna Fáil and Taoiseach.

Haughey was elected with a reputation as a skilled manipulator and a survivor of political scandals which would have destroyed the career of a less astute politician. Despite the odds, despite the unprecedented attack on his character and background in the Dáil debate on ratification of his leadership, he achieved power and, with it, the opportunity to consolidate his hold over the party and rectify his reputation in the country. He was in a hurry.

With the UK government in a quandary over Northern Ireland and no solution in sight to the mounting costs of direct rule, a bold initiative, cut to Thatcher's measure, seemed worth the gamble. For a party which guarded the symbols of Irish republicanism and nationalism and for a leader who was charged with conspiracy in illegal importation of guns only ten years previously, it was quite a leap to sense the new possibilites of being Britain's ally in a common cause. The first hint of Haughey's ambitious plan came in a report by the political correspondent of the *Sunday Times* in May 1980, announcing the proposals for a bipartisan agreement, which surprised journalists in Dublin as much by the fact of the leak as by the nature of the proposals. No hint was conveyed to the media in

Ireland, only a sense of optimism later expressed in Foreign Affairs Minister Brian Lenihan's famous phrase 'everything is on the table'. But the media could only speculate and the government ensured that, for the Irish people, everything was firmly under the table and would remain there, for reasons that are not difficult to infer. Haughey's proposals envisaged a general degree of cooperation with the UK which would have been intolerable to the nationalist element of Fianna Fáil voters; more specifically, they included Anglo-Irish cooperation on defence and foreign policy which would have solved the EPC and the Northern Ireland problems at a stroke and still avoided the unacceptable label of NATO.

It is small wonder that the 'inextricable link' between Ireland and Britain, which the official communiqué after the summit in December 1980 conceded to the news-hungry media, required extreme secrecy if Haughey and his party were to continue in power to develop it. The conditions which encouraged the UK delegation to share the Irish hope — if not the euphoria — for a successful outcome, included the commitment of Haughey to defeating the IRA and his demonstration of goodwill on that score in providing for unprecedented cooperation on border security with British troops and Northern police. The first phase of the H-Block hunger strikes did nothing to dampen enthusiasm for Haughey's plans or Mrs. Thatcher's enthusiasm for the Fianna Fáil leader who had extended Anglo-Irish cooperation to levels never conceived by his predecessors. It is no surprise that Charles Haughey, in her view, was 'a remarkable man'.[23]

The relationship soured as events combined to remove Haughey from power and his party from government. By November 1982, a coalition of Fine Gael and Labour under Garret FitzGerald had taken power and begun the task of repairing the damage to Anglo-Irish relations caused by the failure of Thatcher to back Haughey on the H-Blocks issue and Haughey's impulsive retaliation in withdrawing support for her military action in the Falklands. The hunger-strikes had taken their toll on Fianna Fáil in the 1981 election when Haughey failed by a narrow majority, represented by the two seats won by H-Block candidates in a wave of sympathy for the needless deaths which Thatcher could have prevented. In refusing to make concessions to the prisoners, Thatcher cost Haughey the leadership of the government and stimulated a new interest in neutrality in the Fianna Fáil party which was at odds with the role of Britain's ally cultivated only a short time previously. Now, in opposition, neutrality was becoming 'a long and honoured tradition' yet again.

Returned to power in February 1982 after the fall of FitzGerald's coalition, Haughey faced the Falklands crisis in no mood to help a

23. *The Sunday Times*, 13 December 1980.

Tory Prime Minister who had betrayed his trust. Ireland's solidarity with the EEC countries in imposing sanctions on Argentina before the outbreak of military hostilities was, arguably, consistent with a minimal definition of neutrality in the context of EPC, though it caused serious misgivings within the Fianna Fáil party. After military action had begun, it seemed clear to the Fianna Fáil leadership that too much could be lost, and nothing gained from an unhelpful Tory government, by supporting a foreign army – particularly a British one – in armed conflict. With some truth, Haughey told the Dáil that the 'people of this country are deeply attached to our neutrality, and they are not prepared to see it eroded'.[24]

Almost single-handedly, Charles Haughey did more than anyone in recent years to bring to public attention the issue of Irish neutrality and its implications for the two major foreign-policy questions of the post-war years: partition and conflict in Northern Ireland, and participation in the European Community. And he did it first by gambling on the support of a Tory Prime Minister and, second, by retaliating in kind when she failed him. It is still, in January 1984, impossible to predict the consequences of his decisions, because it is impossible to gauge the degree of popular support for neutrality which would resist further involvement in EPC and, in doing so, create a movement for a positive neutrality going far beyond any comparable trend in Irish history.

What is certain is that a responsible and mature electorate should make a decision on this question. But the Irish people will not have the opportunity to be adequately informed if they rely on their political leaders, who have a record of secrecy and equivocation on this vital matter in sharp contrast to their occasional avowals of the need for an informed public debate if foreign policy is to reflect Irish interests and be responsive to democratic control.

24. Quoted in *The Irish Times*, 20 May 1982.

9 *Irish Involvement in European Political Cooperation* *

Desmond Dinan

That Ireland is still formally neutral, outside any military alliance, is as much a factor of historical accident and geographical location as of political design. Ireland's commitment to military neutrality during the Second World War was indeed intense. Subsequently, however, enthusiasm waned. A move away from economic protectionism in the late 1950s brought Ireland into the mainstream of contemporary European developments. Ireland applied for membership of the European Economic Community (EEC) as early as 1961, and finally became a member in January 1973.

The issue of Irish neutrality was ´occasionally raised in the domestic debate on Community membership in the 1960s and early 1970s. The compatability of neutrality policy and Community membership was seriously cast in doubt. At the time, the Irish Government made no secret of its willingness to jettison neutrality by joining NATO if EEC entry could only be achieved in that way.[1] As it happened, no real external pressure was exerted on Ireland to do so. We therefore joined the EEC with our neutrality policy intact, despite widespread public indifference about it.

Ten years later, public and political attitudes towards neutrality are changing. So too is awareness of some of the initially unseen obligations of Community membership growing. In particular, European Political Cooperation (EPC), the foreign policy coordinating process of the EEC, and Ireland's participation in it, have focussed attention once more on the neutrality issue. This article examines Irish neutrality in the context of EPC. The extent to which neutrality policy retains any meaning or value in view of Ireland's willingness to coordinate foreign policy with nine other states, all members of NATO, is questioned. The full implications for Irish

*This is a revised version of a paper given at a conference on 'Ireland and the Significance of Europe' at the Irish School of Ecumenics, Dublin, 12 May 1984.

1. See, for instance, Trevor C. Salmon: 'Ireland: A Neutral in the Community?', in *Journal of Common Market Studies*, Vol. 20, No. 3, March 1982, pp. 205-228.

foreign policy of EEC membership, and EPC participation, are therefore assessed.

'OUR NEUTRALITY IS SACRED'

Irish neutrality defies precise definition. It is, apparently, neither political nor ideological, but theological. That seems a reasonable paraphrase of some of the best known official statements on the subject, particularly Foreign Minister Gerry Collins' assertion in April 1982 that 'our neutrality is sacred'.[2] Professor Patrick Keatinge, in his most recent contribution to the debate, *A Singular Stance: Irish Neutrality in the 1980s*, maintains, to an extent, the theological theme. He identifies two increasingly irreconcilable appraisals of Irish neutrality. The official definition is narrow and specific, the popular, party political perception is broad and nebulous. Officially, Irish neutrality is negative, amounting to little more than non-membership of a military alliance. Popularly, it is a positive, 'more far reaching concept . . . a basic principle of all Irish foreign policy . . .' Keatinge labels the latter 'fundamental neutrality'.[3]

The maximalist or fundamentalist view of neutrality — that neutrality should be the guiding principle of our foreign policy — is gaining ground.[4] The onset of the 'New Cold War' in the late 1970s increased public awareness of Irish neutrality, and of its potential for ameliorating international conflict. Domestic political developments, in the context of Anglo-Irish relations, reinforced this trend. The apparent willingness of our then Taoiseach, Mr Charles Haughey, to barter Irish neutrality for unification of the country in December 1980, during his summit with Mrs Thatcher, clearly lacked public support. Less than three months later, Mr Haughey acknowledged in Dáil Éireann 'the deep attachment of the majority of the people' to the policy of neutrality.[5] His own zealous conversion to the faith of neutrality during the undeclared Falklands War threatened to denigrate the concept once more to a sophisticated level of Brit-bashing. Instead, unintentionally, it fuelled a debate on the merits of neutrality, quite apart from the specific issue of sanctions.

The brand of neutrality currently gaining support in Ireland is not 'traditional', as many of its proponents would have it. An obsession with justifying policy options on the basis of established tradition is a peculiar feature of Irish political culture. Each side of the great

2. Collins interview on 'Today Tonight', 20 April 1982. Quoted in Patrick Keatinge: *A Singular Stance: Irish Neutrality in the 1980s* (Dublin, 1984), p. 1.
3. Keatinge: *op. cit.*, p. 32.
4. See, for instance, Dennis Kennedy: 'Irish Neutrality and European Union', paper delivered at a conference of the ICEM, 29 April 1983, p. 7, and the IMS survey of April 1984, published in *The Irish Times*, 8 May 1984.
5. Dáil Debates, 11 March 1981.

neutrality divide is thus busily hijacking history in order to disprove and discredit the other. In fact, the case to be made for the 'new neutrality', like the contrary arguments in favour of full European Union, relates primarily to the present and future, not to the past. A striking point about the European Movement in Ireland, for instance, as emphasized by Dr Miriam Hederman-O'Brien in her book, *The Road to Europe,* is the almost total lack of any tradition of European integration in this country.[6]

Unfortunately, greater awareness of Irish neutrality has not facilitated a proper understanding of its meaning or scope. Advocates of active neutrality are occasionally accused of utopianism, of gross ignorance of the unplatable facts of international life. A complementary charge is that of unilateralism and isolationism. Dr Garret Fitzgerald, in a stinging rebuke of the Labour Party Leader, Mr Cluskey, in the Dáil in May 1980, attacked those in the House who would have Ireland pursue a foreign policy of isolation. 'We can't put ourselves in political purdah', the then leader of the Opposition thundered, 'by adopting an isolationist position that ignores the realities of the East/West crisis and the need to work constructively to moderate tension',[7]

Dr Fitzgerald was being disingenuous. The Labour Party can hardly be accused of wanting to go the way of Albania. In the controversial Dáil debate on defence policy in March 1981, Mr Cluskey at least made the point that Labour policy was not one of Irish withdrawal into 'a neutralist cocoon'.[8] Yet Dr. Fitzgerald's criticism reflects a common mistrust of neutralists' motives, as well as a misunderstanding of neutrality itself. There is no contradiction in being neutralist and internationalist. One can be a good Irish neutralist without being a bad Irish-European. By the same token, neutrality is no less pragmatic for being principled, no less prudent for being positive.

AMBIGUITY CONCERNING EPC

An assessment of Irish neutrality and European Political Cooperation is complicated by the confusion surrounding both concepts. EPC, like Irish neutrality, means all things to all men. The problem, again, is one of conduct, scope and content. Because EPC 'occurs in an aura reminiscent of nineteenth century diplomacy', ambiguity is bound to arise.[9] Informality, confidentiality and, presumably,

6. Miriam Hederman-O'Brien: *The Road to Europe: Irish Attitudes towards European Integration, 1945-61* (Dublin, 1983). See especially pp. 21-42.
7. Dáil Debates, 1 May 1980.
8. Dáil Debates, 11 March 1981.
9. Patrick Keatinge: 'New Directions in Irish Foreign Policy', in *Irish Studies in International Affairs,* Vol. 1, No. 1, 1979, p. 76.

conviviality, are the hallmarks of EPC. Obfuscation, deliberate or otherwise, is the result.

The procedure of EPC is, at least, well known. It is based on the Luxembourg Report of 1970, the Copenhagen Report of 1973, and the London Report of 1981.[10] Business is conducted at four levels. The highest, but not necessarily the most productive, meetings take place in the European Council. Established by the Heads of Government in Paris in 1974, and consisting of themselves, their Foreign Ministers and the Commission President, the European Council convenes thrice yearly. Important issues in international relations are discussed, in the context of either economic or political cooperation.

Foreign Ministers meet separately in EPC at least six times a year, and have further opportunities to discuss foreign policy questions at the monthly meetings of the Council of Ministers. In the opinion of former Foreign Minister Brian Lenihan, 'these informal (EPC Ministerial) meetings are the most important of all. They are the key meetings'.[11] Below the level of Foreign Ministers, but perhaps equally influential, are the Political Directors of the Ten Foreign Ministries. They comprise the Political, or Davignon, Committee, and meet once a month, on two consecutive days, for 'informal gastronomic get-togethers'.[12] According to one participant, the privacy and exclusiveness of such occasions provide an ample opportunity 'to discuss sensitive subjects'.[13]

At the lowest level, fourteen working groups and the group of European correspondents prepare meetings of the Political Committee. Working groups cover such topics as the UN, UN-Disarmament, CSCE, and Eastern Europe. Their task is made easier by the COREU telex network, linking the Foreign Ministries of the Ten Member States. Needless to say, much work is also conducted by tele phone, most of it undocumented.

EPC meetings, at all levels, are chaired by the country holding the Presidency of the Council of Ministers. Chairmen play a pivotal role in reconciling the divergent views of participating states. By virtue of her small size and few vested international interests, Ireland aspires to such a mediatory function. Brian Lenihan, when Foreign Minister, described Ireland's position with EPC as 'middle of the road'. The Irish try, he said, 'to reconcile various attitudes and to ensure that a

10. See European Parliament, Committee of Institutional Affairs, *Selection of Texts Concerning Institutional Matters of the Community from 1950 to 1982* (Luxembourg, 1983), pp. 145-157, 538-542.
11. Quoted in the *Sunday Tribune*, 30 October 1983.
12. This description of Political Committee Meetings was given by Mr Van Miert (NL) in the EP on 24 October 1979.
13. Franz Pfeffer, 'The European Ten's Foreign Policy', article forwarded by the West German Embassy, November 1983. Dr Pfeffer is Head of Directorate General 2 at the Federal Foreign Office.

moderate stance is taken, . . . that . . . is how a small country . . . within the Community can exercise its talents best. We play that sort of role: bringing people together, trying to achieve a consensus'.[14] With the growth of two related cleavages within the Community, between the 'progressive' and 'conservative', 'small' and 'large' Member States, however, Ireland's mediatory position is by now illusory. We are firmly on the side of the small, progressive states on most North-South and East-West issues. With mounting pressure in the Community to consider military and defence questions, Ireland's Presidency of the Council of Ministers, and of EPC, was unwelcome in several EEC capitals.

Regrettably, much less is known about the conduct and content of these copious EPC meetings. As a rule, communiqués are useless. Agreed statements are sometimes issued, but details of their formulation are rarely revealed. The end result of the EPC process, a Community demarche or a Presidential speech, for instance, often provides one of the few official indications of the extent of agreement reached.

The purpose of EPC is to harmonize the foreign policies of the ten Member States. The metaphor usually employed is for Europe to speak with one voice. This is achieved by compromise and consensus. The voice might sound as one, if it is heard at all, but each Member State contributes a decibel. As a result, issues likely to prove contentious, notably relations between the Member States themselves, are not tackled. EPC is therefore most successful when dealing with an event or development of equal concern, or unconcern, to the ten participants. Condemnations of Soviet actions in Afghanistan and Poland are examples.

There is no majority voting in EPC. Instead, lengthy negotiations in a search for consensus create 'informal pressures to agree'.[15] Consensus is therefore 'one of EPC's fundamental rules . . . no one can be outvoted, but no one likes to be isolated. There is a strong tendency to follow the balanced opinion of the majority'.[16] This is compounded in Ireland's case by the vast material benefits of EEC membership. In order to get more out of the CAP, there is surely a temptation to put more into EPC. As Mr Paddy McKernan, Assistant Secretary and Political Director of the Department of Foreign Affairs, put it, 'because of the interaction between the economic and political components of Community membership and EPC — the credibility of the Irish contribution in both frameworks is interlinked. Thus if our contribution to [EPC] . . . is a credible one, it

14. Quoted in *The Irish Times*, 29 July 1980.
15. William Wallace: 'EPC — A New Form Of Diplomacy?', RIA Conference Paper, 20 November 1981, p. 12.
16. Pfeffer, *op. cit.*, p. 3.

can enhance our credibility when we advocate particular solutions to Community problems in the Treaty framework'.[17] Professor J. J. Lee made a logical extension of this point, though much less diplomatically, when he noted, in the context of the recent superlevy controversy, that our partners' patience with Irish neutrality might be wearing thin: '. . . whereas neutrality roused little resentment when the Irish appeared to be anxious to make a genuine contribution to Community thinking', Professor Lee argued, 'a feeling can now be detected that the Irish want to have their snout stuck permanently in the trough, but they also want to shoulder none of the burden of keeping other snouts away from the trough'.[18]

The greatest ambiguity about EPC, indeed, is the extent to which 'snout security' is discussed. The 1981 London Report included the statement that EPC embraces 'certain important foreign policy questions bearing on the political aspects of security'. Contrary to accusations levelled in the ensuing Dáil debate, this 'flexible and pragmatic approach' has characterized EPC since its inception. In London, the Foreign Ministers agreed merely to 'maintain' the dubious differentiation between the military and political aspects of security.[19] It was not a new departure.

In claiming an artificial distinction between the military and political aspects of security, we are back once more in the realm of theology. In theory the distinction is valid, and allays the fears of those who uphold the narrow view of Irish neutrality. It was the Irish Foreign Minister, after all, who pressed the formula on his sceptical Community colleagues, 'having regard to the different situation' of his own Member State.[20] In practice, the distinction is dubious, although Irish representatives at EPC meetings on disarmament and East-West relations are managing to maintain it on an operative level. It is difficult, on this point, to disagree with Lt-General Carl O'Sullivan, former Army CoS. In his now famous *Irish Times* interview of February 1982 the General pointed out that 'In Europe at the moment defence is indivisible from security. They interlock — just as defence against internal and external aggression interlock. It would seem to me,' General O'Sullivan concluded, 'that when politicians talk about political security, they must talk about defence. Perhaps they can manage not to talk about defence, but I wonder how it works'.[21]

Widespread concern with the apparent irreconcilability of Irish

17. Padraic MacKernan: 'Ireland and EPC', RIA Conference Paper, 20 November 1981, pp. 4-5.
18. Joseph Lee: *Reflections on Ireland in the E.E.C.* (ICEM, 1984), p. 12.
19. EP, Selected Texts, *op. cit.*, p. 539.
20. *Ibid.*
21. *The Irish Times*, 2 February 1982.

neutrality and EPC is relatively recent. It has much to do with the deployment of Cruise and Pershing missiles in Europe, and with the role of the EEC group at the Stockholm Disarmament Conference. By contrast, in the early days of Community membership, Ireland entered lightly into the obligations of EPC participation. Our primary concern in the early 1970s, as reflected in the Government White Paper and subsequent public debate, was the economic imperative of entry. There was little knowledge of what EPC involved, or indeed how the procedure operated.

INVOLVEMENT IN EPC A COROLLARY OF ENTERING THE EEC

Mr Paddy MacKernan, in a 1981 Royal Irish Academy conference paper that has since become essential reading on the subject, stated that 'Irish involvement in EPC was at once a consequence and corollary of entry into the European Economic Community'.[22] We had no option, in effect, but to participate in EPC, regardless of its extra-Treaty, or extra-constitutional, status. For it was no accident that the development of EPC coincided with the entry into its final phase of the Common Market, and the eventual first englargement of the Community.[23] On the contrary, EPC was intended to become the 'second dimension' of European integration, added to the 'first dimension' of economic cooperation, at precisely the time when the Six became Nine. After the frustration and stagnation of the 'decade of de Gaulle', feeling in the Community, expressed particularly at the Hague and Paris Summits of 1969 and 1972, was that wider should not mean weaker.[24]

A second, parallel road to European Union was thus laid. Yet the course of each varied enormously. While the 'constitutional' road of economic integration quickly encountered large obstacles in the form of the CAP, MCAs, the vice of the veto and Britain's budgetary contribution, the 'extra-constitutional' road of EPC progressed comparatively smoothly. So smoothly, in fact, that the future of the Community seemed to lie in the further development of EPC, irrespective of the difficulties besetting economic integration. Successive Irish Governments have firmly resisted such efforts to widen the distance between both roads. Speaking in his native Cork in April 1984, Mr Barry, the Foreign Minister, reiterated that 'development in the scope and content of our political cooperation must go hand in hand with growing convergence and greater community of interests at the

22. Mackernan, *op. cit.*, pp. 4, 28.
23. The Luxembourg Report stressed 'the correlation between membership of the European Communities and participation in (EPC)'. *Selected Texts*, p. 150.
24. *Ibid*, pp. 136-138, 241-248.

economic level'.[25] If political cooperation will therefore not be allowed to get too far ahead of economic cooperation, neither will it ever fall behind. The symbiotic relationship persists. In the same way that membership of the EEC was conditional upon participation in EPC, so today is continued Community membership conditional upon continued EPC participation, and *vice versa*. 'It is inconceivable that a country withdraws from the EC but continues to participate in EPC', Dr Heinz Dröge, Deputy Political Director of the German Foreign Office, told an Irish audience in 1981, 'just as it is inconceivable that a member of the EC boycotts EPC'.[26]

It was generally accepted, well before we became a Member State, that a policy of neutrality is incompatible with the achievement of European Union. Irish neutrality, for that reason alone, would seem to be negotiable. It is apparently temporary. Although the precise model of European Union, whether federalist, confederalist, or an innovative mixture of both, has never been properly spelled out in this country, its attainment would evidently involve a radical revision of Irish security policy. As the target date for the dawn of European Union recedes, however, and support for the 'new neutrality' grows, sanguine assessments of the expendability of Irish neutrality are increasingly cast in doubt. The response to the recent Spinelli Report of the European Parliament, the latest attempt to 'light the beacon' and point the way to European Union, illustrates this point.[27] Spinelli's Draft Treaty for European Union, after all, merely proposes an institutional outline for a new political entity that the Member States have already agreed should exist. Yet surprise and concern were expressed in Ireland that such an entity would involve cooperation in armaments procurement and defence. As the reality of European Union sinks in, regardless of how distant its realization is, domestic support for Irish neutrality will almost certainly increase, not decrease.

In the meantime, during the first decade of our EEC membership, while European integration firmly remained a means to an end, neutrality appeared a tenable policy. Only gradually did EPC impinge upon it. The first problem was one of perception. As Patrick Keatinge has pointed out, 'diplomatic credibility is derived at least in part from appearances'.[28] The credibility of Irish neutrality inevitably suffered as our foreign policy merged more and more with that of eight, and later nine, other western European countries, all of whom are NATO member states. By participating in the EPC group

25. Quoted in *The Irish Times*, 16 April 1984.
26. Heinz Droge: 'The Future of European Political Cooperation', paper delivered at the RIA Conference, 20 November 1981, p. 13.
27. EP Debates, 14 September 1983.
28. Keatinge: *Singular Stance*, p. 93.

at various international fora, notably the UN and CSCE, we lost much of our unique, neutral identity. According to the London Report of October 1981, one of the achievements of EPC is that 'the Community and its Member States are seen by third countries as a coherent force in international relations'.[29] Professor Dooge, then Foreign Minister, put this point more strongly some weeks later when he described how third countries perceive the EEC as 'a distinct collective political grouping' in the international arena.[30]

Third countries thus see Ireland as belonging to an association of states that is, apparently, a sub-group of the Atlantic Alliance. Neither the US, nor the Community itself, makes much of an effort to dispel that image. For economic and strategic reasons, the US set Europe on the road to unity in the early post-war period and, despite the vicissitudes of later Euro-American relations, never looked back. As recently as March 1984, during Chancellor Kohl's US visit, President Reagan reiterated American support for European integration, which he portrayed as 'a stabilizing element in the free world'.[31] A decade earlier, at the Copenhagen Summit of December 1973, Community Foreign Ministers agreed that 'the growing unity of the Nine would strengthen the West as a whole and will be beneficial for the relationship between Europe and the US'.[32] Shortly thereafter, the NATO Council, meeting in Ottawa, declared that 'further progress towards (European) unity . . . should, in due course, have a beneficial effect on the contribution to the common defence of the Alliance on those of (the Community) who belong to it'.[33] Although not a NATO member state, Ireland was nevertheless seen as participating in a process destined to solidify the Atlantic Alliance.

Apart from recent efforts to involve EPC more directly in NATO affairs, political cooperation, since its inception, has portrayed itself, and been perceived by others, as a pillar of the Atlantic Alliance. By virtue of its contribution to the ultimate goal of European Union, it can hardly be considered otherwise. Moreover, on several occasions throughout its brief history, EPC has benefitted the US diplomatically. In an important speech to the Foreign Policy Association in New York in September 1981, appropriately entitled 'EPC: Why America Should Welcome It', Lord Carrington outlined the advantages, 'to America and to NATO', of Community foreign policy

29. *Selected Texts*, p. 539.
30. From 'Introductory Remarks by the Minister for Foreign Affairs', RIA Conference on EPC, 20 November 1981, p. 2.
31. Quoted in *The Irish Times*, 5 March 1984.
32. *Selected Texts*, p. 270.
33. Quoted in Resolution of the EP on the Effects of a European Foreign Policy on Defence Questions (Gladwyn Report), in *Selected Texts*, pp. 392-393.

coordination.[34] In particular, the British Foreign Secretary cited the benefits for the US of EPC initiatives on the Middle East, Afghanistan, and in CSCE. Presumably the same points are put to the State Department during their consultations with the President-in-Office of the Council before each quarterly meeting of Foreign Ministers in EPC. No mention was made in Lord Carrington's article of Ireland's peculiar position within the Ten. Perhaps this is also the case in the regular State Department-EPC exchanges.

Ireland's apparent pro-NATO position is not lost on the Soviet Union. Although membership of the Community provided a strong impetus for an exchange of Ambassadors, so that Ireland would be represented in Moscow during our Presidency of the Council of Ministers, it did not result in a noticeable improvement in Irish-Soviet relations.[35] This is partly because, unlike other European neutrals, we participate in a political and economic organization to which the USSR is implacably opposed. Just as European integration and its distant goal of European Union are lauded in the US, they are loathed in the Soviet Union. EPC, as the 'second dimension' of European integration, is similarly distrusted. Neither can the Soviets be much pleased with Chinese support for the EEC, nor with Japanese efforts to become closely associated with EPC.[36]

What is the reality behind the appearance? That is the second, more substantive problem of Irish neutrality in the context of EPC. At first, Ireland attached herself happily to the EPC train, unaware of any real dilemma. Due to the tentative, incremental nature of the process, no great difficulties were initially encountered. Many of the questions raised in EPC were new for Ireland, and did not contradict established policy or practice. Yet in the UN, where Ireland traditionally enjoyed independence of action, a conflict of interest seemed inevitable. Instead, compromises were worked on both sides. Making a virtue of necessity, these were trumpeted as instances of Irish scrupulousness, on the one hand, and EPC flexibility, on the other. A number of studies of the voting record of the Community Member States at the UN during the 1970s illustrate the point.[37]

What has lately become Ireland's greatest difficulty with EPC, however, concerns an issue central to the mythology of our active,

34. Lord Carrington: 'EPC: Why America Should Welcome It', in *International Affairs*, 58(1), Winter 1981/2, pp. 1-6.
35. See Micheál O'Corcora and Ronald J. Hill: 'The Soviet Union in Irish Foreign Policy', in *International Affairs*, 58(2), Spring 1982, pp. 254-270.
36. Wallace: *op. cit.*
37. See, for instance, Leon Hurwitz: 'The EEC and Decolonisation: The Voting Behaviour of the Nine in the UN General Assembly', in *Political Studies*, Vol. 24, No. 4, December 1976, pp. 435-477. Also Beate Lindemann: 'Europe and the Third World: The Nine at the UN', in *World Today*, Vol. 32, No. 7, July 1976, pp. 260-270.

independent, UN policy during the 'Aiken years'. That issue is
disarmament. The seeds of the present problem were sown in the
early 1970s, when we joined the EPC group in the CSCE. It was our
first real venture into the world of East-West negotiations.[38] Again,
the specific questions raised were relatively novel. There was thus no
great dilemma for Ireland in dealing with the minutiae of the various
'Baskets', under the aegis of EPC. A possible exception was the
second part of Basket I, devoted to security issues. The CSCE participating states endorsed certain confidence-building measures
designed to remove some of the secrecy surrounding military
activities, and made a number of general pledges with respect to the
importance of arms control and disarmament. Here Ireland's participation in the EEC group, rather than in the group of Neutral and
Non-Aligned nations (NNA), seemed incongruous. But the relative
paucity of the proposals, together with the prevailing climate of
detente in East-West relations, saved the day.

By the time the second CSCE Review conference opened in
Madrid in November 1980, Ireland was not so fortunate. The international situation had seriously deteriorated. The Soviet invasion of
Afghanistan, continued deployment of SS-20 missiles, and the
retaliatory NATO dual-track decision brought East-West relations to
a new nadir. Shortly after the Review conference opened, President
Reagan was inaugurated. At the end of his first year in office, martial
law was declared in Poland. In these strained circumstances, the
Madrid meeting lurched from crisis to crisis.

An important consequence of the 'New Cold War' was a shift of
emphasis to disarmament, arms control and confidence-building
measures as virtually the only issues in East-West relations in general,
and CSCE in particular. Given the distance between the American
and Soviet positions in Madrid, and the overall polarization of
opinion, Ireland, as a participant in EPC, was almost completely sub-
sumed into the Western camp. For the EEC group itself, the
remainder of whose members also belonged to the NATO group, lost
its identity. As discussions centred on a French proposal, presented
by NATO, for the establishment of a separate CSCE confidence-
building and disarmament conference after the Madrid meeting, only
the NNA group retained a credible position between East and West.
Ireland's active support for the French proposal was indistinguish-
able from that of the NATO member states. The impasse on this and
other issues at the Madrid meeting was broken by the NNA group,
which put forth a draft concluding document in December 1981
(RM-39), and a revised version in March 1983 (RM-39 Revised),

38. See Patrick Keatinge: *A Place Among The Nations: Issues of Irish Foreign
Policy* (Dublin, 1978), p. 167.

that finally bridged the gap between both sides.[39] Ireland's position outside the NNA group was more anomalous than ever.[40]

\ At the current Conference on Confidence- and Security-Building Measures and Disarmament (CDE) in Stockholm, Ireland's invidious position is fully apparent. As its imposing title implies, the CDE deals exclusively with military and security issues. Most national delegations therefore include military advisers. Ireland's security specialist is Colonel Noel Bergin of the Defence Forces. The first stage of the Stockholm Conference, from January 17 to March 16 1984, explored new confidence- and security-building measures which, in their scope and content, would further contribute to a reduction of international tension, and lessen the risk of war. With the breakdown, only two months before, of the Strategic Arms Reduction and INF Talks, the CDE assumed great importance as the sole remaining forum of East-West security negotiations.

Rigid polarization between East and West is adversely affecting the Stockholm Conference. Inevitably, the EEC Group has fallen victim. Although it continues to function, nine of its members prefer to coordinate their positions on substantive questions with their fellow NATO States. The EEC Group as a whole has accordingly lost much independence and identity. It meets, briefly, once a week, while the NATO Group, which includes nine of the EEC member states, meets thrice weekly.

As a result, Ireland's position is problematical. Participation in EPC obliges us to operate with the EEC Group in Stockholm. Yet the EEC Group is effectively operating within NATO. At the first session, for instance, three sets of proposals on confidence- and security-building measures were made. The official NATO and unofficial WTO proposals were mutually unacceptable. A separate NNA submission was closer to the Western point of view, but was nonetheless a valid alternative. Because nine of the Ten subscribed to the NATO proposals, no EEC submission was made. Ireland, although more in sympathy with the NNA position, was well and truly left out in the cold.[41]

Were the EEC Group to assert itself in Stockholm, Ireland's dilemma would not be reconciled. For the establishment of a common EEC position would clearly involve tackling the military aspects of security. Yet such coordination, officially at least, is outside the

39. See USIA Policy Notes, 'Conference on Security and Cooperation in Europe' (American Embassy, Dublin), September 1983.
40. For a discussion of Ireland's role at the Madrid Conference, see Salmon, *op. cit.*, pp. 224-226, and Keatinge, *Singular Stance*, pp. 51-52.
41. The NATO proposals were submitted on January 24 (CSCE/SC.1); the unofficial WTO proposals were submitted by Romania on January 25 (CSCE/SC.2); the NNA proposals were submitted on 9 March (CSCE/SC.3).

confines of EPC. At the CDE, Ireland is therefore attempting, on the one hand, to retain a credible EEC identity, independent of NATO, in order to justify participation in the Group, while, on the other hand, to prevent discussion of the substantive, military aspects of security, in order to maintain the appearance of neutrality. At the same time, for the same reason, Ireland supports, as much as possible, the NNA Group.

It is in this light that official Irish statements at the CDE must be seen. Thus Mr Barry, in his inaugural address, endorsed the 'common approach' of the EEC Group, but went on to assert Ireland's 'own distinctive perspective and particular concerns'. The Foreign Minister then attempted to strike a balanced note between both sides. The US and USSR were jointly criticized for a lack of 'realism, consistency and moderation' in their recent relations.[42] Mr Pat McCabe, spokesman for the Irish delegation, went farther in stressing Ireland's intermediate position. In a speech on 5 March, he emphasized that although any agreement reached would have 'to take account of the preceived needs of (the) Alliances', it would also have 'to respect the particular, and sometimes different, needs of neutral and non-aligned participating states'.[43] Four days later, Mr McCabe warmly welcomed 'the highly valuable contribution' of the NNA Group, and expressed his appreciation 'to these countries, to whose thinking my (own) country is close'.[44]

The CSCE process, including the Stockholm Conference, is a valuable case study in a number of respects. For one thing, it shows the use to which a policy of positive neutrality, as practised by the NNA countries, can be put. For another, it shows the limited extent to which the policy of Irish neutrality is interpreted and implemented. Our participation in the NNA Group should be logical, and would be laudable. Instead, alone of the European neutral and non-aligned participating states, Ireland is part of the EEC or, in the prevailing circumstances, NATO Group. Without doubt EEC foreign policy coordination at the current Stockholm Conference is making nonsense of Irish neutrality.

The serious deterioration in US-Soviet relations since 1979 is indirectly responsible, through CSCE and EPC, for showing up the superficiality of Irish neutrality. In addition, the 'New Cold War' threatened to destroy that policy entirely by fundamentally altering

42. Statement by the Minister for Foreign Affairs, Mr Peter Barry, TD, at the . . . (CDE), Stockholm, 18 January 1984, published in the Bulletin of the Department of Foreign Affairs, 1/84.
43. Delegation of Ireland, Statement by Mr P. McCabe, Member of the Delegation of Ireland to the (CDE), Stockholm, 5 March 1984.
44. Delegation of Ireland, Remarks by Mr P. McCabe, Member of the Delegation of Ireland to the (CDE), Stockholm, 9 March 1984.

the scope and depth of political cooperation. Specifically, the present 'Atlantic Crisis', itself the culmination of long-standing unease in Euro-American relations, brought to a head by the sudden freeze in East-West relations, is forcing Europe to reassess its own security. Pressure to undertake such a review is coming neither only, nor largely, from the US, but primarily from within Europe itself.

RESENTMENT BETWEEN U.S. AND NATO PARTNERS

The US has long been dissatisfied with Europe's contribution to the Atlantic Alliance. Latent resentment first came to the surface in the early 1970s. A desire to cut troop levels in Europe, both for the appearance of detenté and the reality of economy, criticism of the EEC's growing commercial power, and an external manifestation of the domestic 'Vietnam Syndrome', resulted in the celebrated 'Nixon Doctrine'. In future, Western Europe would have to pay its proper share of the collective NATO defence. Ironically, speaking in Limerick at the end of his 1970 European tour, President Nixon proclaimed that 'a strengthening of European defence is the prime requisite for maintaining American troops in Europe'.[45] In 1973, the 'Year of Europe', Henry Kissinger made his famous call for a greater European defence effort.

A decade later, Euro-American relations are even more strained. The appearance of NATO unanimity on the deployment of Cruise and Pershing missiles belies the reality of growing distrust, East and West of the Atlantic. The US despairs of Europe's seeming weakness and irresolution. Europe, for its part, feels that the US is not seriously committed to reducing tension and reaching an arms control agreement with the USSR. There is widespread suspicion in Europe that the US is willing to risk nuclear war in the erroneous belief that it could be confined to this continent. Americans hint, and Europeans speculate, that the Administration will shift its primary focus of attention in the opposite direction, towards Japan and the Pacific Basin.[46]

President Reagan's 'Star Wars' speech, as much as any other single statement or event, shook European confidence to the core. West Germany, in particular, sought to temper the apparent excesses of US security policy. With growing domestic disagreement on the Cruise and Pershing issue, the German Government considered an

---

45. Quoted by Helmut Schmidt in 'New Tasks for the Atlantic Alliance', in *The Year Book of World Affairs 1975* (London, 1976).
46. For a similar European and American assessment of the 'Atlantic Crisis', see Christopher Tugendhat: 'Europe's Need for Self-Confidence', in *International Affairs*, Vol. 58(1), Winter 1981/2, pp. 7-12; and Henry Kissinger: 'A Plan to Reshape NATO', in *Time*, 5 March 1984, pp. 14-18.

immediate initiative essential. Moreover, the general deterioration in East-West relations, with its renewed emphasis on confrontation rather than conciliation, threatened to end the valued, hard-won benefits of *Ostpolitik*.

The ensuing German proposal was not new. 'We should recognize that the US desires a strong European pillar within the Atlantic Alliance, not a weak one', Herr Genscher told the Carl Schurz Society in Bremen on 10 April 1984. 'Instead of lamenting that the US is turning its back on Europe', the Foreign Minister continued, 'we should do all in our power to make Europe a united, strong and self-confident partner of the US . . . the more firmly the European pillar is embedded, the firmer and more effective is the Alliance in preserving its defence capability and in continuing the dialogue with the East. Strengthening the European pillar . . . means primarily ensuring greater cooperation on security policy in Europe'.[47]

France and Belgium strongly supported such an initiative. The French are particularly concerned to ensure that German dissatisfaction with the US is channelled into a policy of Europeanization, rather than neutralism or unilateralism. Successive French statements have advocated close Franco-German cooperation as an essential ingredient of Europe's contribution to East-West stability and international security. For the French also, a strong European pillar is essential. '. . . if I had been re-elected', Valery Giscard d'Estaing told the Council on Foreign Relations in New York in April 1983, 'I would have devoted a large part of my time . . . (to establishing) a new approach to (Europe's) problems of defence and political unity', which would be 'a major contribution to a better balance of power and a closer understanding in trans-Atlantic relations'.[48] In the event, President Mitterand has devoted himself wholeheartedly to the cause that his political adversary espoused. The Belgian Prime Minister, Mr Leo Tindemans, added his voice to the chorus of support for a European security initiative when, in a speech on 5 April, he too called for the establishment of a 'a *European Pillar* in the heart of NATO'.[49]

American statesmen and strategists have been equally vociferous in putting forward such proposals. A recent call was made by Henry Kissinger in an article in *Time* magazine, in March 1984. Kissinger's 'Plan to Reshape NATO' involved 'a more significant role for

47. Speech by Foreign Minister Genscher to the Carl Schurz Society, Bremen, 10 April 1984.
48. Valerie Giscard d'Estaing: 'New Opportunities and New Challenges' in *Foreign Affairs*, Vol. 62, No. 1, Fall 1983, pp. 176-199.
49. Speech by Mr Leo Tindemans to the Eighth Annual Conference of European and American Journalists, Knokke, 5 April 1984, p. 7.

Europe' within the Alliance. This would be achieved by 'greater (European) identity and coherence . . . responsibility and unity . . . in the field of defence'.[50] Thus, on both sides of the Atlantic, there is general agreement that 'greater political cooperation and integration in Western Europe (is) needed to assure Europe of a more weighty role in the formulation of Atlantic (Alliance) policies. Only this (seems) likely . . . to retain American respect for the partners overseas, European respect for an alliance with the US, and German reassurance within the collective framework of the West'.[51]

REVIVAL OF WESTERN EUROPEAN UNION

The unresolved question, however, is what institutional form the strengthened European pillar will take. The most convenient and promising platform is EPC.[52] This was apparent as soon as EPC began to operate in the early 1970s. That was the time, coincidentally, of the first major crisis in Euro-American relations. Not surprisingly, with the onset of the second crisis in the last couple of years, EPC was considered an ideal structure on which to build a new European security system within the Atlantic Alliance. Hence the Genscher-Colombo proposals of November 1981.[53]

The fate of these proposals is well known. They were emasculated by the combined opposition of Denmark, Greece and Ireland. Instead, based on a Franco-German initiative, the dormant Western European Union (WEU) is being revived.[54] Already the resuscitation of WEU has been endorsed, in principle, by its five remaining member states. The US Administration has been kept well informed, notably by Chancellor Kohl and President Mitterand, during their recent, separate Washington visits.

The rebirth of WEU is taking the spotlight off EPC, but only temporarily. The EEC and EPC, by virtue of their increasing membership, soon to include nearly all the European members states of NATO, their latent political power and huge industrial potential, are far better suited to building the Euro-American 'two-way street' in armaments procurement, and the 'European Pillar' in the Atlantic Alliance, than is the WEU. Significantly, in his speech of 5 April, Leo Tindemans made no secret of his preference for basing his proposed new European security system on the EEC Ten, rather than the

50. Kissinger, op. cit., p. 17.
51. Christopher Bertram: 'Europe and America in 1983', in Foreign Affairs, America and the World 1983, 616-631, p. 630.
52. See Karl Kaiser: The European Community: Progress or Decline? (RIIA, 1983).
53. See Selected Texts, pp. 490-499.
54. See 'Europe Takes Lessons in Self-Defence', in the Observer, 4 March 1984.

WEU Seven. He further stated that 'an action linked on three levels, WEU, the Ten and NATO, would doubtless be the best answer . . .'.[55]

Far from EPC and, by extension, Irish neutrality being unaffected by these developments in Euro-American relations, it therefore seems only a matter of time before the larger EEC Member States return to the charge. When they do, Ireland might be much less fortunate. The present plan to develop EPC into a European security system failed due to Greek recalcitrance, Danish reluctance, and Irish resistance. On its own, Irish opposition could hardly have been sustained. But social-democratic parties will not always be in the ascendant in the Greek and Danish parliaments. When they fall, support for Ireland's peculiar position within EPC will evaporate. Will Dr FitzGerald, or his successor, then storm out of a European Council if Irish neutrality seems endangered? Has his stand on the superlevy issue made withdrawal from an EPC meeting more or less likely? Is neutrality a 'vital national interest'? In the meantime, it is a sad reflection on our commitment to neutrality that its fate appears to rest in the hands of the Danish and Greek electorates.

ELECTORATE, DÁIL AND EUROPEAN PARLIAMENT ILL-INFORMED ON EPC

What about the Irish electorate? The Irish electorate voted overwhelmingly, in 1972, for Community membership. The issue then was economic, not political. EPC was in its infancy; few realized how important it would subsequently become. Twelve years later, there is no possibility of a social-democratic party, committed to the maintenance and strengthening of Irish neutrality, being elected to form a government. The Labour Party, a junior partner in the present Coalition, espouses such a policy, but is hardly making its presence felt.[56] The essential cleavage in Irish politics, in any event, is not along Right-Left lines. The two main parties, Fianna Fáil and Fine Gael, are conservative. When in opposition, their commitment to neutrality seems intense. When in office, it is dubious. Thus Mr Bertie Ahern, Fianna Fáil Chief Whip, recently reaffirmed support at a meeting of the party faithful in Longford, for a 'positive and active' policy of neutrality, as opposed to a more 'minimalist role'.[57] This statement is in marked contrast to those of his party leader when Fianna Fáil was last in power.

The electorate, and for that matter the Dáil, are ill-informed of

55. Tindemans: op. cit., p. 9.
56. See The Labour Party, 'Ireland — A Neutral Nation', Policy Paper No. 1 (Dublin, undated).
57. Quoted in The Irish Times, 16 April 1984.

developments in EPC. Apart from media coverage, which tends to be sporadic, EPC is given a separate chapter in the semi-annual Government report, 'Development in the European Communities', submitted to the Oireachtas under Section 5 of the European Communities Act (1972). The chapter contains only a general survey of the functioning and scope of EPC. No details are divulged. On the contrary, more information is already available in other Community and Member State publications. The emptiness of such EPC coverage was clearly evident in the 20th Report's treatment of the 1982 sanctions debâcle. In less than a page, under the sub-heading 'Falklands/Malvinas Islands', the sole reference to Ireland's independent action was that 'At (a meeting on 17 May), Ireland and Italy made declarations to the effect that they would no longer apply sanctions against Argentina'. No explanation was given, and no mention of Irish neutrality was made.[58]

Given the limited extent of official information, it is not surprising that the level of Dáil debate on EPC, in particular, and foreign affairs in general, is abysmal. Making EPC a domestic political football hardly helps. On the credit side, the Coalition Government undertook to hold two annual debates, exclusively on EPC issues. While this is a laudable move, unless TDs are encouraged by their constituents to take an active interest, the standard of such debate cannot be expected to rise much above that of the celebrated 1981 exchanges.

Electoral enthusiasm, and Dáil reform, are essential ingredients for greater parliamentary participation in the EPC procedures. At present, the plague of personalism prevents TDs becoming actively involved in EPC issues, had they the aptitude or ability to do so. An inadequate committee system fails to compensate for this lack of individual initiative. The Parliamentary Committee on the Secondary Legislation of the European Communities, established in July 1973, is empowered to examine only Community legislation. It has no competence even to discuss EPC, because that development is outside the Treaty framework. An all-embracing joint-committee on European affairs, and a logical parent body for the orphan Committee on the Secondary Legislation of the European Communities, has yet to be established, despite widespread support for its existence.

In addition to strengthening the role of the Dáil, the Labour Party has proposed giving the European Parliament (EP) 'greater influence and control' over EPC.[59] Such a suggestion seems sensible, but its implementation is far from desirable. The EP does indeed want more

58. 'Developments in the European Communities', 20th Report, July 1982, pp. 79-80.
59. The Labour Party, 'European Political Cooperation', Policy Paper No. 6 (Dublin, undated), p. 15.

involvement in EPC, but for all the wrong reasons. Already, on the basis of a statement in the Luxembourg Report that 'In order to give a democratic character to (political cooperation), it will be necessary to associate public opinion and its representatives with it', the directly elected EP participates in the process to a limited extent.[60] Liaison with the President-in-Office of the Foreign Ministers meeting in EPC takes the form of four annual colloquies with the Political Affairs Committee, answers to questions on political cooperation, the annual report on EPC, and the Presidency speeches at the beginning and end of its term of office, which now usually include political cooperation subjects. Moreover, after each European Council, the President-in-Office makes a statement in Parliament, a precedent having been set by Mrs Thatcher in December 1981.

The EP is nevertheless dissatisfied with the quality and quantity of such contacts. Existing procedures are considered inadequate. The annual report by the President-in-Office is oral, not written, thus giving Parliament little opportunity to study it in advance. Mr Michael O'Kennedy, who delivered the first Presidential Report on EPC to a directly elected Parliament, was criticized by numerous MEPs for a 'superficial', 'disappointing' and 'trite' presentation. National, or, perhaps in this case, party political, blood being thicker than Community water, only Paddy Lalor jumped to his colleague's defence. The value of the quarterly EP-EPC colloquies has also been called into question. According to one MEP, they are, in effect, 'only diplomatic lunches rather than meetings between government representatives and members of parliament'.[61]

EUROPEAN PARLIAMENT TO MILITARIZE THE EEC?

The EP craves a greater role in EPC for two related reasons. The first is institutional. The EP will understandably seize any opportunity to extend its limited power. As the legislative branch of an embryonic European Union, the Parliament is particularly anxious to assert its position *vis à vis* the Council of Ministers. Especially in the developing field of political cooperation, Parliament is unlikely to allow the Council complete independence of action. Just as it is determined to consolidate its institutional authority, the EP hopes to extend the competence of the Community in every possible direction. The area of foreign policy and security coordination is clearly of paramount importance. The full potential of European integration, and of the EP within that process, will only be realized when a common foreign policy, and a common security policy, are endorsed.

60. *Selected Documents*, p. 149.
61. EP Debates, 24 October 1979.

Hence the series of resolutions adopted by the EP advocating Community involvement in armaments procurement, defence, security and foreign affairs. One of the earliest was the Pleven Report of December 1961, the latest was the Klepsch Report on EPC and NATO, easily adopted, despite Irish opposition, on 11 April 1984.[62] Since the 1979 direct elections, Parliamentary pressure on the Commission and Council to move more openly and quickly into the military and defence sectors has become acute. A centre-right coalition of three parties, the Christian Democrats, European Democrats, and Liberals and Democrats, now commands a majority on the floor, and in the specialist committees, of the Parliament.[63] Drawing on the 1979 result as evidence of legitmacy, this bloc, with Conservative support, is spearheading the campaign to militarize the EEC.

Parliament therefore seems a natural ally for the Foreign Ministers in their efforts to extend EPC. As Neils Haggerup explained in a debate on EPC in October 1979, 'Parliament would like to be in a position to keep an eye on what is being done in . . . political cooperation . . . not . . . to impede the fruitful development of this cooperation in any way . . . (but to facilitate) the development of an increasingly *European* foreign policy'.[64] The Foreign Ministers find Parliamentary support extremely useful. Although it is popular to deride debates and resolutions of the EP for being too far removed from reality, they provide an impressive body of literature, and an extensive collection of statements, for advocates of greater Community involvement in political and security cooperation to draw on. 'Not only will I submit your resolutions to my colleagues on the Council', M. Cheysson, incoming President-in-Office told the EP in January 1984, 'but I will make a special point of drawing the attention of my external affairs colleagues to them in the course of political cooperation meetings . . . I have asked for the same procedure to be followed at the monthly meetings of the Political Directors'.[65]

Yet the Foreign Ministers deny Parliament a greater role in the formal EPC procedure because they, like the Parliament, are anxious to strengthen their own institutional position. Competition between the executive and legislative branches of government is a feature of all political systems. In addition, foreign policy is traditionally the exclusive preserve of the executive. The twin imperatives of secrecy

62. The Pleven Report is in *Selected Documents*, pp. 116-118. For the Klepsch Report, see *The Irish Times*, 12 April 1984.
63. See 'The Impact of the EP on Community Policies', EP Research and Documentation Papers, No. 5, January 1984, p. 44.
64. EP Debates, 24 October 1979.
65. 'Impact of the EP', *op. cit.*, p. 174.

and swiftness of action make parliamentary involvement undesirable. Such is the case with EPC. The London Report of October 1981 noted that 'The success of the process of political cooperation depends to a large degree on its confidentiality; certain particularly delicate matters need to be handled in a way which guarantees that the required level of confidentiality is maintained'.[66] Widening the circle of EPC cognoscenti to include a gaggle of garrulous Euro-Parliamentarians therefore seems unlikely.

Although Parliament's formal involvement in EPC is limited, its input into Community moves in the direction of a new defence and security system is considerable. Given the strength of the centre-right in Strasbourg, this tendency is difficult to check. What can Ireland's 15 MEPs do? Even if equally committed to Irish neutrality, which is doubtful, their influence in Parliament is minimal. With few friends or allies of Irish neutrality in the House, they cannot assert their position. As it is, the majority of MEPs, Irish included, have no idea what Irish neutrality means. Those who made an effort to examine the issue are none the wiser. Colm Boland of *The Irish Times*, in his 'European Diary' of 16 April 1984, claimed that members of the Parliament's Political Affairs Committee, having met a number of Irish politicians from all parties, were told 'that Irish neutrality, meaning a refusal to join NATO, is all to do with partition and the presence of British forces in Ireland. They say they cannot get anyone to come up with anything more substantial than that'.[67]

IRISH MEPS UNWILLING TO LOBBY FOR NEUTRALITY?

The first task of Irish MEPs should be to educate themselves, so that they can educate their colleagues, about Irish neutrality. But Ireland's MEPs do not operate together in Strasbourg. They sit with larger party groups, according to their own political affiliation. With the gradual increase in rigid bloc voting, particularly on sensitive political and security cooperation issues, Irish MEPs must toe the Euro-party line. This is especially worrisome in the case of Fine Gael politicians, who are members of the Christian Democrat group. The Christian Democrats, more than most, want the Community to assume a definite military identity as an equal partner with the US in the Atlantic Alliance.[68]

With Irish MEPs either unwilling or unable to lobby support for Irish neutrality in the European Parliament, pressure groups have a

66. *Selected Documents*, p. 541.
67. *The Irish Times*, 16 April 1984.
68. See: *Europe: The Challenge. The Principles, Achievements and Objectives of The EPP Group from 1979 to 1984* (Strasbourg, 1984), pp. 11-13, 18-23.

decisive role to play. An indication of the growing influence and importance of the EP is the extent to which MEPs are contacted by pressure groups. Many groups with an interest in Community developments are represented in Strasbourg, and at meetings of EP committees in Brussels.[69] Interest groups supporting Irish neutrality have not generally been active in this way. A useful opportunity to lobby the Parliament's Committee on Political Affairs was available during Ireland's Presidency of the Council of Ministers. Colloquies on EPC, between the President-in-Office and the Political Affairs Committee, were then held in Ireland. Perhaps Irish interest groups could use these occasions to explain to befuddled Euro-Parliamentarians what Irish neutrality really means.

Irish neutrality, to quote the title of a recent series on the subject, is at a crossroads. The crossroads has been reached because growing support for the principle of neutrality is at variance with the present practice of the policy. Participation in EPC has been a decisive factor in bringing this situation about. The purpose of EPC is to ctonribute to full European Union. Once that goal is achieved, Irish neutrality will cease to exist. In the meantime, EPC makes a policy of neutrality difficult to sustain. At the CDE in Stockholm, part of the CSCE process, Ireland operates with the EEC group. Given the extent of East-West polarization, the EEC group is effectively a subgroup of NATO. Our rightful place is surely with the NNA nations.

Recent efforts to extend EPC into overt military and defence cooperation are more disturbing. Their failure is cold comfort for Ireland. Far from satisfying the Seven, the revival of WEU will emphasize the superiority of the EEC as a platform on which to build a new European security system. On this occasion, pressure on Ireland to participate in such efforts was not strong. Greece and Denmark deflected the worst of it. Next time, particularly if we stand alone, we cannot expect to escape so lightly.

Early in 1983, at a conference in the National Institute for Higher Education, Limerick, Professor David Coombs concluded his assessment of Ireland in EPC with the observation that '. . . neither the demands of political cooperation nor the definition of neutrality have become so precise as to conflict with each other'.[70] Much has happened in the interim. Even more will happen in the coming months, particularly with Italy in the presidency of the Council of Ministers. One year hence, with EPC and neutrality on a collision course, the inevitable conflict might well have occurred.

69. 'Impact of the EP', pp. 55-56.
70. David Coombs: 'Ireland's membership of the European Community: Strange Paradox or Mere Expedience?', Conference Paper presented at the NIHE, Limerick, 5 May 1983, p. 20.

10   *Irish Neutrality and the European Community**

Patrick Keatinge

INTRODUCTION

Some years ago, following governmental agreement on the terms of Ireland's accession to the European Community, there occurred a prolonged and often intensive public debate leading to the referendum on May 1972. Both supporters and opponents of membership agreed on one thing, that they were arguing about a major turning point in Irish public life. The debate was of course mainly in terms of what seemed to be quantifiable hopes and fears for economic issues, but less tangible aspects of the country's role in international affairs were also raised, the most persistent theme being that of neutrality.

During the past twelve months this question has again become a matter of central concern in Irish foreign policy, with more parliamentary attention devoted to it than during the previous eight years put together. A full-scale debate on neutrality took place in the Dáil on 11 March 1981, the particular question of its compatibility with EC membership arose in a controversial way in the Dáil from 20 to 22 October, and the whole question was again covered in an important debate in the Senate on 2 December. The reason for this heightened interest is illustrated in the comment of one speaker on the last occasion: 'there is a general unease about the present position, the possibility that EEC membership and membership of what is called European defence are brought together'. Senator Catherine McGuinness went on to refer to various rumours and statements which 'all leave the feeling that the policy of neutrality is being progressively and quietly abandoned. This is all the more dangerous because there is nothing explicit about it'.[1]

The main purpose of this paper is to try to see in what respects and

*This is a revised version of a paper given at the conference on 'The Defence of Neutrality in the Nuclear Age' at the Irish School of Ecumenics, Dublin, 6 February 1982.

1. Seanad Debates, Vol. 96, col. 1116 (2 December 1981).

to what extent these fears are justified. In an attempt to focus more closely on what is an extremely ambiguous and speculative subject, two connected but rather different questions are examined. Does the mere fact of EC membership, with its ultimate goal of 'European Union', rule out effective neutral status for a member-state? And, even if we leave ultimate goals to one side, does the actual experience of membership involve political pressures, working through established channels of influence, which tend to weaken or inhibit Irish neutrality?

NEUTRAL STATUS AND EUROPEAN UNION

Both these questions beg many others, especially the first one, where we are dealing with two concepts, 'European Union' and neutral status, which are hedged around by a forest of qualifications. By 'European Union' we refer to the very generally stated goal, included in basic documents on the European Community, such as the preamble to the Treaties, in the form of an aspiration and not as a specific treaty obligation. It is variously seen as taking the form of a federal 'United States of Europe' or something less, of an ill-defined nature. It was the mere possibility that it take the form of a *sovereign* and comprehensively supranational political entity which, among other considerations, scared off other potential neutral applicants for membership, such as Sweden. But if Swedish neutral status were to be so critically affected why not that of Ireland? There is, it appears, neutrality . . . and neutrality.

The significance of these national variations in the theory and practice of neutrality did not for various reasons emerge very clearly during the referendum debate in 1972, and this is, perhaps, partly responsible for some of the confusion surrounding the subject now. It is worthwhile, therefore, to see just how this country's neutral status compares with that of other neutral states in the west European region — Switzerland, Sweden, Austria and Finland.

These four states have a broadly similar approach which both they and others refer to as Permanent Neutrality.[2] In legal terms there may be variations in the ways in which the position is expressed. Switzerland and Austria have clearcut obligations in international treaties and in constitutional form, but for Sweden and Finland neutrality is derived more from principles of foreign policy than from treaty obligations. This is true also of Irish neutrality. While some recent government statements have referred to Articles 1 and 29 of

2. See Hanspeter Neuhold: 'Permanent Neutrality in Contemporary International Relations: a Comparative Perspective', *Irish Studies in International Affairs*, No. 3 (forthcoming).

the Constitution, these are rather general and permissive statements of the sovereign independence of the state and its predilection for an international code of good behaviour, respectively. There is no explicit commitment to neutrality here, though these articles do indeed indicate the sorts of principles upon which Irish neutrality is based.

Care must be taken in introducing the term 'principle' to any discussion of Irish neutrality. All too often it is the occasion for heated debate as to whether neutrality is 'principled' or 'pragmatic', in which these terms are used in quite different senses and with consequences which, to my mind, obscure rather than enlighten our understanding of neutrality.[4] If we mean by principle a basic rule of conduct we can see that Irish neutrality is based on two sorts of principle. The first sort derives from the fact of statehood — the self-regarding principles of sovereignty, independence and self-preservation ('Article 1 principles'). The second sort of principle pertains to the whole world in which we live and derives from notions of order and justice at that level ('Article 29 principles'). The precise mix of these two sorts of principle in Irish policy is infinitely debatable, and the implementation of the principles is of course pragmatic, in that prevailing circumstances make their presence felt in varying degrees. This is equally true of the Permanent Neutrals: witness Sweden's 'certain consideration' for each side, at different times, during the Second World War, or Finland's muted response to the Soviet invasion of Afghanistan, or Switzerland's abstention from the UN General Assembly, the main forum of international opinion. Permanent Neutrality may lead to a variety of political effects, and Ireland is not so very different from the Permanent Neutrals in this respect. Indeed, none of the five countries can be described as 'ideologically neutral', for all five are capitalist societies with a fundamental orientation towards the values of 'the west'.

The Permanent Neutrals do not see their status as depending solely on legal criteria or stated principles. Another critical prerequisite lies in their defence policies, for Permanent Neutrality involves the obligation to provide a credible defence posture against potential invaders. They are required to pursue the strategy of 'the entrance and occupation price'. Again, in practice we find variations. The richer Permanent Neutrals (Switzerland, Sweden) have significantly higher levels of defence expenditure than the poorer (Austria, Finland). Even for them the ability to identify and provide the appropriate defence policy is always problematical, though at least the problems are given a public airing. A recent Irish Minister for Defence, Sylvester Barrett, has claimed that defence against external aggression is 'the primary role' of the Defence Forces,[3] but neither he nor any of his pre-

3. Dáil Debates, Vol. 327, col. 1432 (11 March 1981).

decessors or successors since 1945 has given any comprehensive and detailed public statement about what that role entails. Indeed, even more recently a former Chief of Staff is reported as saying that the country's defence has for long been inadequate.[4] There is at least a question mark over the defence of Irish neutrality, in the purely military sense.

But where Irish neutrality diverges most clearly from Permanent Neutrality implies a relatively low degree of economic integration with other states, both in respect of the institutional arrangement employed to manage economic relationships and in the actual substance of those relationships. To the extent that the institutions of economic management are even only formally supranational they may well be regarded as being incompatible with Permanent Neutrality. In practice supranational decision-making, implying majority rule, may be frequently breached by national vetoes and in a sense rendered redundant by the ever-present possibility of a national veto; nevertheless, if supranational economic management is the formal and idealized mode of decision-making — and 'European Union' is a manifestation of this — then Permanent Neutrality is out.

Such, at any rate, was the Austrian view. The requirement that economic integration, in substance, be relatively low is less clear-cut, and Austria with her striking economic dependence on the European Community's leading national economy, the Federal Republic of Germany, illustrates yet another of the dilemmas that neutral status entails.

With respect to either of these aspects of economic integration Ireland fails to meet the requirements of Permanent Neutrality. Membership of the European Community is the most visible manifestation of this, but it is open to question whether at any time since the Second World War Irish governments' implementation of neutrality amounted to a serious effort to meet the difficult conditions outlined above.

This is not to say, of course, that if we do not merit the adjective, 'Permanent', we necessarily forfeit the noun, 'Neutrality'. It does mean, however, that to the extent that Permanent Neutrality is seen by others as the orthodox (or possibly even the ideal) form of neutrality, there is something inherently unique and equivocal in Irish neutrality. If we are not all that often called upon to explain its mysteries (either to others or to ourselves), it is partly because the concept which at first sight seems to oppose it most directly, 'European Union', is itself unique and equivocal.

At the time of Ireland's initial application to join the EEC in 1961 the conventional wisdom was that the Six (or 'Six-plus', but never

4. See the interview with Lietutenant-General Carl O'Sullivan in *The Irish Times*, 2 February 1982.

'Six-minus') were en route, in a measured and controlled way, to becoming a single political entity, probably in the form of a federal union. The ethos of committed 'Europeans' abounded with images of 'a nation writ large' or, more controversially, a new European super-power; the official terminology referred to 'European Union'. The logic of such an assumption quite plainly implies that 'full political union', as the then Taoiseach, Mr. Haughey, referred to it in March 1981, means the end of Irish neutrality for the very good reason that it means the end of Ireland as a sovereign entity in matters of inter-national relations. Anything less can hardly be described as 'full', though there is a coy shade of the conditional in Mr Haughey's recog-nition of this logic.[5]

Of course the conventional wisdom about European integration was not the same in March 1981 as it was twenty years earlier. Even ten years ago, at the time of accession, the interpretation was less forthright. A typical academic view then was that the European Com-munity was not moving towards centralized federal authority and was not moving towards significant economic homogeneity. 'Beyond the nation-state, but not very far beyond' was the verdict.[6] Ten years later the most optimistic observer would see political integration as marking time. The attempts to regain momentum — the Paris Summit of 1972, the Tindemans Report of 1976, the Three Wise Men Report of 1979 — increasingly bore the imprint of a dutiful ritual, paying lip-service to a concept whose further elaboration would prove divisive. It remains to be seen whether the Genscher-Colombo proposals have more significant consequences.

Some integration theorists used to argue that the essential dynamic of integration lay in the prevalence of inter-locking crises demanding collective solutions. In a sense they are right; our experience of mem-bership is not lacking crises, the only trouble being that the significant responses are by no means predominantly collective. There is no longer even the degree of consensus concerning economic mechanisms which existed among the member-states at the time of the first enlargement, and policies, both national and international, take the form of short-term holding operations. In this context it is

5. The key statement was as follows: 'In the event . . . of the European States being organized into a full political union, we would accept the obligations, even if these included defence'. (Dáil Debates, Vol. 327, col. 1396). In opposition, Mr Haughey later suggested that it would be possible to impose specific pre-conditions for raising the question of defence, viz. the achievement of full economic and monetary union and Irish *per capita* income 'at least 80 per cent of the Community average and rising' (Dáil Debates, Vol. 331, col. 922, 2 December 1981). Whether this situation is supposed to occur before, with, or after 'full political union' is not clear; con-sequently, it is difficult to be sure what Mr Haughey is saying.
6. Donald J. Puchala: 'Of blind men, elephants and international integration', *Journal of Common Market Studies*, Vol. 10, No. 3, 1972.

now the conventional wisdom that 'European Union' will not arise 'in the foreseeable future', if at all. Hence, largely by default, the continued continuation of Irish neutrality.

A residual anxiety deserves some consideration. If 'European Union' proper is indeed an exceedingly remote possibility, could not its existence as an aspiration, however feeble, in certain circumstances prove to compromise neutral status? In other words, does 'European Union' pose, as it were, a sort of intermediate threat as well as an ultimate one? A potential or actual belligerent might use it as a justification for not treating Ireland as a neutral, on the grounds that it implies an unacceptable degree of solidarity with members of a military alliance. Such an argument could conceivably be deployed in a serious military crisis, but whether it would be a determining factor in putting impossible pressures on Irish neutrality is doubtful. Past experience shows that in serious military crises intervention against neutrals, no matter how permanent, tends to be based on serious military considerations. The rule book goes out of the window; the essential threat to neutrality in such a case lies in the strategic interests of other countries rather than in diffuse political ideals.

THE IMPLEMENTATION OF NEUTRALITY AND EUROPEAN POLITICAL CO-OPERATION

Any discussion of the impact on neutrality of such general and hypothetical notions as 'European Union' is itself bound to be general and hypothetical. The current debate in this country has not of course remained at this level of abstraction, for it reflects many fears about short-term pressures arising in the international system at large, as well as the effects of these on our closest diplomatic partners in the European Community. (It also reflects a much more specific set of considerations arising in the context of Anglo-Irish relations, and the way in which this impinges on the broader European pressures will be considered briefly below).

It is important to remember that when neutrality was last a serious issue, in 1972, it was seen against a background of heightened expectation about international relations in general. That very year saw the apotheosis of superpower détente in the agreements signed by Nixon and Brezhnev in Moscow, and even the recent free-for-all between international currencies was not necessarily to be seen as a permanent and diseased condition in international economic relations. Of course both superpowers did still use or encourage the use of force outside their borders, and even non-aligned states did not always shrink from this traditional instrument of foreign policy. But expectations about détente made it possible to present these acts as exceptions to the rule, and decidedly un-European at that.

Now this optimism has dissipated. There is widespread uncertainty not merely about the intentions of others but of the 'rules of the game' themselves. There is no single source of these uncertainties, but rather a gloomy list. Initially, the failure to manage the international economy effectively was joined by disillusionment with the ambiguities of détente; the pace quickened late in 1979 with dissent over the nature and mechanisms of military deterrence, uncertainties about leadership changes in both superpowers, and unexpected manifestations of violence in Iran, Afghanistan and now Poland. It may be exaggerated to claim this to be the return of the Cold War, but it does mark the return to fashion of the imagery and attitudes of 'power politics'.

This deteriorating international climate is in itself a general threat to neutrality, of no matter what variety. It encourages non-neutral governments to reconsider strategic assumptions, including perhaps those assumptions which in happier times allowed them to accept this or that case of neutrality. It tends to restrict the mediatory roles which neutral states can play and on which, in part, they may justify their neutral status to others.

If in these circumstances a neutral state, like Ireland, has close and varied ties with one set of potential belligerents the credibility of its stance may suffer, and there may even be pressures to 'take sides'. In trying to see whether these types of pressures are in fact already operating in our case let us look at the Community's political system with two questions in mind. First, through what channels might pressures against Irish neutrality be exerted, and is there in fact evidence of significant pressure coming through these channels? Second, what views among our partners would encourage them to impose pressures on Irish neutrality, and is there in fact evidence of the evolution of such views?

The most important channel of multi-lateral influence to consider is the process of European Political Co-operation (EPC).[7] This is a process of regular and frequent consultations between specialist officials of the member-states' foreign ministries, topped at the political level by ministerial meetings and feeding into the heads of governments' European Council. The primary purposes of the process are, first, to consult and inform other member-states on foreign policy matters, and, second, to arrive at common positions where possible. The process is essentially confidential, but general reports of its deliberations are made public after ministerial or head of government meetings, and these are considered in the European Parliament and, with varying degrees of attention, in national parliaments.

7. The fullest account is Philippe de Schoutheete, *La Coopération Politique Européene*, Fernand Nathan, Brussels and Paris, 1980.

Before examining Ireland's experience in this diplomatic coalition it is necessary to refer to some general characteristics of EPC, which have a significant bearing on her position as the only neutral country in the group. First, the process is one seeking political consensus and not legally binding obligations. Second, while ostensibly it deals with foreign policy in general, in practice the term 'foreign policy' is employed in a deliberately restrictive way. It excludes foreign policy matters arising primarily between member-states, thereby, incidentally, excluding one of Ireland's major foreign policy problems, Anglo-Irish relations. It also excludes what is often seen as a sort of Siamese twin of foreign policy, namely, defence policy. This particular exclusion is critical for the maintenance of what credibility Irish neutrality enjoys. It is not the case, however, that the exclusion of military matters has arisen merely to accommodate Ireland; for the other member-states it derives principally from their position within NATO. The separation between EPC and NATO has been important for reluctant or dissident NATO members, such as France or Greece, as well as for committed NATO members, anxious lest a European defence identity weaken the American commitment to defend western Europe. As a consequence, once foreign policy issues concerned with the general goal of security touch on military matters the line is drawn between EPC and 'alliance' business. Finally, another general characteristic of EPC is that it operates as a distinct and well-organized diplomatic group or 'bloc' in most major international fora, such as the UN General Assembly or the Conference on Security and Co-operation in Europe (CSCE). Attempts by member-states to participate fully in alternative groups would not generally be regarded as compatible with EPC membership. Thus in CSCE, for example, Ireland's membership of EPC precludes her from membership of the 'neutral and non-aligned' group to which the Permanent Neutrals belong. It would also preclude her from membership of the non-aligned bloc, which has been advocated in Labour Party policy. It does not, however, preclude her from co-operating with members of such a group.

Ireland's experience within European Political Co-operation has not, until quite recently, aroused much domestic interest or concern, and it is necessary therefore to summarize it briefly, and to assess (so far as is possible with regard to such a secretive procedure) to what extent it imposes constraints on national policies.[8] The many issues covered during the last nine years may be divided into five major categories. The first is that of East/West relations, first in more senses

---

8. See Padraic MacKernan: 'Ireland and European Political Cooperation', *Ireland Today: Bulletin of the Department of Foreign Affairs*, No. 984, January 1982, pp. 6-8; and Patrick Keatinge: 'Ireland' in C. Hill (ed.), *National Foreign Policies and Political Cooperation* (forthcoming).

than one, for it was in the original CSCE negotiations that EPC first
proved to be an effective diplomatic process; thus Ireland's first
serious direct involvement in East/West relations coincided with the
formative stages of political co-operation. At present the main
emphasis of Irish policy appears to be to maintain what is left of the
fabric of détente, and it is arguable that to date EPC as a whole is
operating in this sense.

Shortly after taking shape in CSCE political co-operation among
the Nine had to meet the challenge of the Community's 'southern
enlargement', as a means of supporting the emerging parliamentary
regimes in Greece, Spain and Portugal. Support for Portugal was
partly organized during Ireland's first Presidency of the Council of
Ministers in 1975, thereby affording Irish diplomacy a central
responsibility. Four years later the second Irish Presidency was
responsible for the Nine's consensus on the Middle East conflict
which stressed the need for a comprehensive settlement. The latter
emphasis, with its implications for a recognition of the Palestinian's
case, had for long been an objective promoted by Irish governments
in the face of the reluctance of many of their EPC partners.

A fourth set of issues is generally found under the heading
'decolonisation', and was during the seventies mainly concerned with
southern Africa. These issues are the purely 'political' aspects of the
broader question of policies towards the Third World in general.
These of course are not restricted to the political co-operation framework but are dealt with at the international level by the Lomé conventions or the mechanisms of the North-South dialogue as a whole.
A final set of issues arising under EPC concerns disarmament
matters, and on these there are marked divergences between member-
states. Both decolonization and disarmament are traditional concerns
in Irish foreign policy, on which fairly distinct positions were taken in
the United Nations context, and they therefore provide an indicator
of the extent of change in Irish policy since joining the European
Community.

At first sight the evidence seems to be rather paradoxical. It is
precisely on these two sets of issues that Irish governments have
borne the bulk of what domestic criticism they have received. Anti-
apartheid supporters have claimed that pronouncements on South
Africa have been muted since joining EPC, while similar charges of
neglect or evasion have been made during the last four years by the
growing disarmament lobby. But it is also with regard to decolonization and disarmament that we find the greatest extent of Irish diver-
gence from majority positions within EPC. Comparative studies of
voting behaviour in the UN General Assembly, where the EPC delegations make serious attempts to arrive at joint positions, show a
persistent trend in which Ireland belongs to what has been called a

'progressive minority' on Third World and disarmament matters. The most recent figures (for 1980) showed that out of 27 divided votes in which Ireland was in a minority of four or less, 19 votes were on these types of issue, 11 on decolonization and 8 on disarmament questions.

It is arguable that EPC membership may sometimes moderate the tone or manner of a member-state's policy position (e.g. on a UN vote abstention may be preferred to a clear yes or no), but the record to date does suggest considerable continuity with the main directions of Irish policy in the United Nations before 1973. And it must be remembered that even then Irish positions were hardly among the most consistently radical, particularly where approval for the use of revolutionary force was being sought. Taken together with continued participation in UN peacekeeping operations, it can be seen that the sorts of mediatory or bridge-building roles, which are sometimes seen as the basis of 'positive neutrality' are being maintained.

Two factors may have helped sustain this continuity. First is the fact that Ireland is rarely isolated among the Nine (now the Ten) on these issues, with Denmark, the Netherlands, sometimes Italy (and now probably Greece) tending towards the 'moralist' rather than the *realpolitik* end of the diplomatic spectrum. Second, as a consequence of the consultative process itself the relevant Irish officials are more numerous, more specialized and have access to more information than they had ten years ago. There is an inbuilt check to being swamped by the received opinions of a major great power, because they now have considerable access to the official mind of several great powers and several smaller powers.

Ireland's experience in European Political Co-operation does not therefore show evidence of sustained or concerted pressures on her freedom of action in general, or on her conception of neutrality in particular. However, a cloud has appeared on the horizon, in the form of what is represented as the latest attempt to renew the quest for 'European Union'. The 'European Act', proposed by the West German foreign minister with strong Italian support (the Genscher-Colombo proposals), was mooted early in 1981, appeared in draft form in November, and is currently 'on the table'. Its ostensible purpose is to provide a new sense of relevance and cohesion to the EC political system, both by rationalizing and legitimizing existing procedures and by expanding the scope of the Community's activities into the fields of cultural, legal and security co-operation.

This last suggestion has prompted discussion of what is meant by 'security'. Broad security matters have always been regarded as legitimate issues in EPC and in other fora. Neither Ireland (nor most other neutrals) have felt inhibited from taking positions on, say, confidence building measures in the CSCE or disarmament in the UN.

The line has been drawn, as we have seen, when the discussion of security impinges on the military measures to be taken to implement broad security goals: that is, defence policy, in its technical, military sense, whether it be collective or individual defence policy, has been taboo. 'Extending the scope of security co-operation' at least poses the question of whether this now conventional distinction is to be maintained.

Before examining Ireland's official response to this question, it is necessary to be aware of the way in which this issue became embroiled in domestic party politics during an election year, and to be aware that this was the first occasion on which EPC or neutrality became a contentious issue in nine years. This has been a source of ambiguity and confusion, to the extent that there have been advanced at least two different interpretations of what is going on.

The story started, not at the level of European politics, but in the context of Mr Haughey's Anglo-Irish policy. From his first Summit meeting with Mrs Thatcher (May 1980) there developed a ground-swell of rumour and kite-flying to the effect that neutrality was to be abandoned as a quid pro quo for Irish reunification; it was this which led to the Dáil debate in March 1981. At that stage the Anglo-Irish and European dimensions started to converge, but it is not clear precisely how. One view[9] points to a British preference for the defence aspect of 'the totality of relationships' being seen in a multilateral rather than bilateral setting; in response, it is argued, the Fianna Fáil government was prepared to reconsider the scope of security co-operation in the context of early EPC discussion of the Genscher-Colombo proposals in May. With the change of government, however, the Fianna Fáil foreign minister, Mr Brian Lenihan, accused his sucessor, Senator Jim Dooge, of failure to hold the line, claiming, inter alia, that the distinction between security and defence had become 'hollow'. In heated exchanges in the Dáil during three days in October the new Taoiseach, Dr Garret FitzGerald, in defending his government's position went so far as to argue that Irish credibility in maintaining the security/defence distinction had been seriously weakened by Mr Lenihan, with the inference that neutrality was threatened. An alternative interpretation[10] argues that the threats to neutrality suggested by both Mr Lenihan and Dr Fitzgerald were manifestations of the 'overkill' of parliamentary party politics, and indeed only a month after these exchanges in the Dáil, at a conference on EPC (organized by the National Committee for the Study of International Affairs of the Royal Irish Academy) neither Mr Lenihan nor Senator Dooge made any attempt to pursue the controversy. In any

9. See Bruce Arnold in *The Irish Independent*, 21 November 1981.
10. See the editorial in *The Irish Times*, 24 October 1981.

case, even before the row in the Dáil an important EPC statement on the scope of political co-operation had been agreed.

The London Report of 13 October 1981 is in fact where the official position rests at present. The relevant section reads as follows:

> As regards the scope of European Political Co-operation, and having regard to the different situations of the member-states, the Foreign Ministers agree to maintain the flexible and pragmatic approach which has made it possible to discuss in Political Co-operation certain important foreign policy questions bearing on the political aspects of security.[11]

The key phrase, from the Irish point of view, is 'political aspects of security', implying the exclusion of military or defence aspects — in short, the preservation of the status quo, given an added degree of legitimacy because it appears in written form for the first time. As the British Foreign Secretary, Lord Carrington, representing the Presidency, said at the press conference on 13 October:

> Obviously there is a particular interest on the part of the Irish government in this because they are not members of NATO, they are neutral and therefore they are very anxious to see that security is defined in a way which is acceptable to them and we have made it very clear that the sort of security aspects that we're talking about are political aspects and not defence aspects. It's got to be ad hoc more than anything else but it's certainly not going to impinge on defence or embarrass the Irish.[12]

The London Report also accepts the link between real progress in economic integration, through the framework of the EEC Treaties, and the extension of political co-operation, which has been one of the primary arguments deployed by the Irish government in its approach to the Genscher-Colombo proposals. Thus while the latter, in the form of the draft 'European Act', still contain certain ambiguous wording which might 'embarrass the Irish', the level of agreement in the London Report suggests the draft act will not escape amendment.[13]

The fate of the draft European Act will no doubt remain a matter

11. EPC London Report, 13 October 1981.
12. Verbatim report of Lord Carrington's press conference, 13 October 1981.
13. The preamble of the draft 'European Act' contains a general reference to the Atlantic Alliance, and hints (Part Two: Section 4(1)) that 'details' of security could be considered by a Council 'of different composition' than foreign ministers. Even if this does not mean defence ministers it does suggest a 'two-tier' procedure, and this would probably meet strong opposition as a matter of general principle.

of interest in coming months. But a brief reference must also be made to a separate channel of influence, operating through the orthodox mechanisms of the Treaties of Rome and Paris. The relationship between EC industrial policy and arms procurement has for some years now been raised in an intermittent dialogue between the EC Commission and the European Parliament and several expert studies have been undertaken. The significance of this dialogue may be assessed by referring to one of the most recent expert reports, the 'Greenwood Report', circulated to the Political Affairs Committee of the European Parliament in February 1981.[14] The rationale for co-operating on arms procurement is both military and economic; there are military advantages, such as standardization of weapons systems, and economic advantages arising out of economies of scale and reduced dependence on American sources. Nevertheless, the Greenwood Report argues that there is 'little support for vesting real authority in a supranational or intergovernmental agency to manage the demand side of the armaments market [and] little enthusiasm for the Commission, or any other agency, assuming a formal role in the management of the supply side of the military equipment market'.[15] The most that can be expected is common policy on 'high technology' in general, and a bureau for the exchange of information about defence needs and procurement possibilities.

This conclusion is if anything more modest than earlier suggestions made in the European Parliament *before* the '1979 crises' in East/West relations. The involvement of the EC Commission and the European Parliament demonstrates that channels of influence other than that of Political Co-operation could be used to raise the issue of Irish neutrality, even if only incidentally. But what forces within our partners' political systems would lead to the use of any of these channels in such a way as to impose a serious threat to the continuation of Ireland's position?

It might well be that if, for example, the electorates of the other nine member-states were asked their opinion of this issue, the majority, who support the general idea of collective defence, would condemn Ireland's refusal to bear the costs and risks of that defence. But they have never been asked that question, so we do not actually know what, if anything, they think. Nor is it likely that their governments will solicit their opinion of other countries' national policies. We do know, however, that the opinion of some individual political figures in the other nine countries is hostile to the continuation of Irish neutrality. For example, Mr Christopher Tugendhat, a British

14. *Report on a policy for promoting defence and technological cooperation among west European countries*, by David Greenwood, Centre for Defence Studies, Aberdeen.
15. *Ibid*., p. 30.

member of the EC Commission, has argued that neutrality should not
be permitted to stand in the way of links between the Commission
and NATO.[16] It is plausible to suggest that similar attitudes might be
found among many European politicians who support the concept of
collective defence, and within the transnational political groupings in
the European Parliament Irish politicians are indeed called on to
defend their case.[17] We do not, however, know either the extent or the
intensity of such attitudes.

None of these straws in the wind become significant diplomatic
pressure until two conditions exist. The first is that they are translated into clearly defined proposals at the *intergovernmental* level; the
second is that Ireland be *isolated* among the Ten on the broad
question of a west European as distinct from an Atlantic defence
system. At present neither of these conditions are fulfilled. The
Genscher-Colombo proposals with regard to security are by no
means clearly defined; the clearest intergovernmental statement to
date is the London Report, preserving the status quo. Our partners in
the Community do not seem to be closer than they were before the
'1979 crises' on fundamental questions concerning the Atlantic
Alliance. While their doubts about American leadership have become
more obvious, their reluctance to break the Atlantic defence connection and focus on a purely 'European defence arrangement is also
evident. The American administration, for its part, does not
encourage such an eventuality. At this stage, then, even a
deteriorating global situation has not resulted in coherent and critical
pressures on Ireland to abandon her neutrality in the context of
membership of the European Community.

The circumstances in which serious pressures *might* emerge are of
course a matter of speculation. Agreement on a west European
defence system could follow either an American withdrawal of the
nuclear commitment (based on isolationist disillusionment with
ungrateful allies) or the unilateral (or even agreed) creation of a
European nuclear free zone. Both these moves would imply a fundamental reconsideration of existing strategic doctrines and might well
lead to a measure of collective conventional defence. The question
would then arise how Ireland (and the other neutrals) woul fit into this
scheme of things; would Irish neutrality ironically succumb to the
creation of armed neutrality on a west European scale? Even here the
outcome would depend to a large degree on the extent of the
country's diplomatic isolation. It has been argued that if Ireland was
also isolated on another, and electorally sensitive, issue (such as
defence of the Common Agricultural Policy), then the loss of

16. *The Irish Times*, 15 May 1981.
17. For example, see *The Irish Times*, 24 October 1981 for a report of Richie
Ryan's speech to his Christian Democrat colleagues.

neutrality might be an acceptable price to pay in an eventual bargain. Quite so — but at this point it is as well to remember that we have mounted the ladder of speculation a good many rungs above the reality of early 1982.

CONCLUSION

The present weaknesses and strengths of Ireland's neutral stance may be summarized as follows:

A. Weaknesses
  (i) a deteriorating general climate and increasing uncertainties about East/West relations;
  (ii) the aspiration to 'European Union' precludes the status of Permanent Neutrality;
  (iii) close association with a group of non-neutral states contains the potential for pressures on Irish policy;
  (iv) doubts have been raised about the credibility of Ireland's external defence posture.

B. Strengths:
  (i) East/West deterioration has not got to the point either where consensus about purely European defence co-operation is emerging or where neutrals can no longer play mediatory roles;
  (ii) the commitment of the Irish government has been clearly restated, most recently by the Minister for Foreign Affairs, Senator Dooge. Not only is it 'not the intention of the Government to join any military pact', but there is a specific assurance that Ireland is not committed to go to the defence of one of our EC partners who comes under attack;[18]
  (iii) Irish neutrality is still formally accepted by the other member-states in European Political Co-operation;
  (iv) there are signs that neutrality has wide support within Ireland.

This latter point deserves some amplification. Before neutrality re-emerged as a parliamentary issue in March 1981 there had been no clear indication for years of what public attitudes were one way or the other. While the treatment of the matter in the Dáil demonstrated a good deal of petty partisan squabbling, much of this can be put down to the persistence of a horse-drawn parliamentary system. Running thoughout the contributions made on several occasions in both houses, and in the general election campaign in June 1981, was the theme of support for neutrality, with members of all parties (and

18. Seanad Debates, vol. 96, cols. 1134 and 1140 (2 December 1981).

none) committing themselves to the status quo. The exception of the few known critics of neutrality merely proves the rule. Moreover, many parliamentarians claimed that their constituents' attitudes were similar. If this is indeed the case, Irish governments will be in a stronger position to oppose any pressures that may arise in the future at the diplomatic level.

11 Postscript: The Case for Active Irish Neutrality

Bill McSweeney

The point was made at the end of the Introduction and in several papers which followed that a decision on the neutrality question is a moral obligation on each of us which cannot be left to politicians and civil servants to make on our behalf. Whether we decide to abandon neutrality, pay the costs and gain the benefits of joining a defence alliance, or to recreate neutrality on a different cost-benefit analysis, we must reckon above all on the implications of our decision for peace and security for ourselves and others. To ignore this aspect on spurious grounds of realism, impotence in international affairs, ignorance of the complexity of super-power rivalry, is to abandon an elementary human responsibility to be aware of the consequence of our actions.

But realism and impotence are not necessarily spurious. A foreign policy motivated by the desire for peace — indeed a policy motivated by any virtue whatever — sounds an alarming prospect to those whose understanding of history and politics has made them sceptical that anything but the promotion of self-interest is possible in international affairs. The very term 'peace', when it is not used rhetorically by politicians, conjures up an image of sentimentalism, utopianism, a desire to make the grand gesture which will set the world to rights. It suggests an attitude which is affronted by human vice but which fails to take account of the fact that vice is institutionalized in forms which are immune to conversion. It fails to recognize that the universal acceptance of vice and virtue as moral opposites, which is a condition of making such a gesture, evaporates when we try to define good and evil in any but the broadest metaphysical terms. One group's pursuit of 'social justice' is another's recipe for 'totalitarianism'; one society's 'violent aggression' is another's 'legitimate recovery of territory'.

Morality is a poor guide to the conduct of foreign policy. We should be neither horrified nor surprised when we observe nations behaving in terms of calculated self-interest whenever their own profit or security conflicts with the demands of justice or elementary con-

ceptions of human decency. The primacy of self-interest in international affairs does not arise because of human malevolence but
because of the fundamental conflict between the internal political
structure of nation-states and the structure of international politics
which is the arena of their foreign policy. If we are in fact frequently
horrified at the crudeness of power politics, it is because of the
ingenuity with which nations routinely manage the conflict between
their own and humanity's interest, and contrive to wrap their pursuit
of self-interest in an acceptable package of moral concern. Some
nations feel this compulsion to package foreign policy more than
others — for example, French politicians seem to find it easier than
American to present foreign policy in all its nakedness — but this
variation reflects cultural difference rather than ethical rank.

It it seems cyncial to counsel realism on these lines — to claim that
not only do nations in fact limit foreign policy to the boundaries of
self-interest but that this is a constraint which they cannot escape—then
perhaps cynicism is a necessary antidote to naivete. We are too easily
persuaded that the susceptibility of individuals to moral
pressure provides a model to predict and judge the behaviour of
states. But it is not a counsel of despair. It does not mean that
nations are so constrained as to exclude the possibility of acting for
the common good. What it does mean is that the ethical component
must be linked to conceptions of self-interest in a way which attaches
a political or economic benefit to the particular moral behaviour,
making it profitable, in some sense, to be good. This convergence of
interest and virtue may occur without much effort to create it, as in
the case of Ireland's trade interests with black Africa and corres-
ponding tendency to oppose apartheid in South Africa, or Britain's
guarantee to the Protestant majority in Northern Ireland and the
benefits for defence which accrue. Characteristically, the moralist
tends to dismiss the virtue in such cases on the spurious grounds that
virtue and self-interest are incompatible. But such uncontaminated
motives are seldom present in individual behaviour, much less in
international politics, and it is this illusion of pure goodness —
moralism — which drives realists to despair, encourages civil servants
to be secretive about the reality of foreign policy and undermines the
potential strength of movements of social reform which cannot tolerate
compromise.

A convergence of interest and virtue is a necessary condition for
the successful implementation of a foreign policy conceived as a
moral imperative. Where such convergence does not occur, it is the
duty of mass movements and public opinion to create it and to oppose
realism in its unacceptable form — often masquerading as *realpolitik*.
Although realism proper, in the discipline of international politics, is
only one among competing intellectual perspectives, emphasizing the

balance of power as the central factor in stability and change, in fact it is often advanced as a legitimation of existing relations, as a justification of the existing system, defining any attempt at reform or change as impossible or misguided. Moralism, therefore, is simply the other extreme of this kind of ideological realism, the one refusing to recognize the political limits of change, the other making the *status quo* absolute or limiting change to the politics of power.[1]

The Frank Aiken period of Irish UN diplomacy (1957-61) is often claimed by moralists as historical evidence of an ethical role in foreign policy. Ideological realists would see this as posturing, just as they judge all declarations of moral concern in international affairs as the public relations component of the power process which only the gullible take literally. As I argued in Chapter Eight, neither view is correct. It was not a strategy representing even a government consensus at home but a diplomatic exercise of a detached, free-floating kind which could have become effective if the political will was there, but which lost out to other interests and other policies. If there is a case to be made for active neutrality today, it is one which must learn from the fifties that ethical considerations, however attractive in themselves, are useless as a motive of foreign policy unless they are grounded sufficiently in self-interest to create the political will to sustain them. It is no good having the Skibereen Eagle keep an eye on the Tsar if the people and government are looking the other way. It is scarcely more meaningful to advocate that Ireland should maintain and strengthen its tradition of neutrality when the tradition to be maintained was merely a political instrument for most of its life, and when the strengthening demanded is located only at the expressive end of the chain of policy — that is, at the diplomatic end.

Diplomacy is the mouthpiece of society. To put it another way, it is the symbolic representation of a society's identity and policy in the international forum. It speaks the truth only when it expresses the nation's interests as these are understood and promoted by government and people. This not to say that symbols are unimportant — diplomacy can cause a war or end it, create a market or destroy it — but that their significance is always determined by the stance of the government. Just as Ireland's diplomacy changed after 1961 because it had a vital part to play in the new policy of the Lemass government, so, in the event of a commitment to active neutrality by the Irish people, our diplomats would have a key role in making it acceptable and effective.

In Chapter Eight I tried to establish that Irish foreign policy since 1961 has been methodically blurred to prevent public discussion of

1. For further discussion see Bill McSweeney: "Morality and Foreign Policy" in Dermot Keogh ed.: *Central America: Human Rights and US Foreign Policy*, Cork University Press, 1985 (forthcoming).

an essential feature — gradual persuasion into military alliance — and to afford maximum publicity to other selected features which, it is insinuated, are conditional upon the first. In this paper I shall argue the case for a new foreign policy which is morally tolerable, practically possible and, far from entailing the isolationism and deprivations which are threatened by governments, will expand and intensify Ireland's involvement in international affairs without any predictable ill-effects on the Irish economy. The need for making such a case is obvious, since almost all the literature on the subject either rejects neutrality — usually by implication — or advocates some form of a positive neutrality, but without saying what it would look like and how it would be accomplished apart from a change in diplomacy.

CHARACTERISTICS OF AN ACTIVE NEUTRALITY

Before setting out the main features of a new Irish neutrality, a few points should be made to emphasize the characteristics which distinguish active neutrality from common perceptions of Irish neutrality. It may be helpful, in the process, to say what this new policy is not. This will draw together some central aspects of neutrality which have been more generally discussed throughout the book but which, I hope, will bear repetition here.

Neutrality, as here understood, is not a fact, but an accomplishment. That is to say, it is more like child-rearing than childbirth, like trade rather than a trade agreement. This may seem obvious to some, but the static, objective idea of neutrality is very pervasive, indicated particularly by the weight given to the legal definition or the wartime function of neutrality. Even in the past, when neutrality was understood mostly as a wartime role, it was the planning, negotiation and management, rather than the legal conventions, which determined success. Of course, neutrality requires a declaratory base and the support of any agreements, laws or conventions which may strengthen it and sharpen its public image. But these are like the birth certificate or the trade agreement. What matters is what is accomplished afterwards. The term 'active' helps to underline this ongoing and self-dependent aspect of neutrality; it does not just refer to its moral or principled aspect but to its political character as a process and an achievement. It must grow and be creative if it is to survive.

Neutrality, secondly, does not mean withdrawal into isolation, removal from involvement with others who are not neutral. This interpretation is an understandable reaction to some of the more anti-British or anti-American sentiments which often accompany the interparty rituals in the Dáil. But it can also be a ploy to distort the term by suggesting that neutrality is incompatible with our ideological and cultural preference or any strong partiality in peacetime for one or other of the parties to a potential conflict. As ready discussed in Chapter One, the frequent use by government of the phrase 'we are not ideologically neutral', as a qualification of Irish neutrality, indicates either a culpable ignorance of the requirements of international law or a crude tactic to abandon neutrality by defining it beyond the bounds of possibility. Certainly the *weight* of ideological leaning towards one and against the other party is a factor, among many others, which needs to be considered in accomplishing a strong international posture, and clear public image. But this does not mean the *fact* of leaning one way or the other — how could any voluntary neutral do otherwise? To say Ireland is not ideologically neutral is to say nothing significant about the concept of neutrality — unless, of course, one specifies the respect in which we are not impartial. If we are talking about the Cold War, about Irish anti-Communism or partiality to the Western military alliance, then the phrase is clear: we are not neutral. Neutrality does not require a retreat from the international world, nor from that part of it with which we have a close affinity born of history, trade, culture and religion. What it does require is that we reconsider, in our own interests, how to construct an active involvement in the process of peacemaking which is consistent with retaining our positive ties with Europe and the West.

Neutrality, thirdly, is not primarily a wartime role. In the sense that its accomplishment demanded long planning and negotiation, it was always more than that. But there is a particular sense today in which active neutrality must be understood as essentially a peacetime policy, however much its ultimate reference is to war. In yesterday's world, reference to war was discreet and periodic — too frequent, certainly, but by no means constant; and declining rapidly after war, sometimes for lengthy periods, as in nineteenth century Europe. Today, war is a constant factor in the peacetime relations between the major powers and their allies. The Cold War seems permanent, not in intensity nor in the allegiance of its participants, but in the fact that a world seems inconceivable without the primacy of nuclear weapons and rival alliances in international affairs. We are always preparing for war and, therefore, for participation or nonparticipation in it. And the weapons of war, which the Cold War multiplies, are seen officially as the weapons of peace. Each alliance regards its arms build-up as a peacemaking process, but one which can easily fail to achieve its defined goal if the other side is allowed to take the initiative. Non-members of the alliances — the neutral or nonaligned — are forced to prepare for their appropriate role in the preparations for war which now seem to be a permanent, peacetime obligations.

There is another sense in which neutrality must inevitably be a peacetime activity. The war to which it refers will not last very long.

This war, at least, will be over by Christmas, but only because its consequences will be so horrendous as to make the two world wars together seem like skirmishes. If neutrality is to have the time and the opportunity to play a role, it must be in peacetime. Modern neutrality, like the nuclear weapons which help to define it, is a political instrument with reference to war which is designed only as a deterrent.

Neutrality is not non-alignment. The non-aligned movement is an alliance of nations, founded on the initiative of Yugoslavia, India and Egypt at the Belgrade Conference in 1961, which rejects alliance with the superpowers but is not particularly averse to war or to the possession of nuclear weapons. A vigorous anti-colonialism unites the movement and directs much of its combined voting policy, as do its Third World leanings. Since neither the peacetime policies nor the wartime role of non-aligned nations can be predicted from the fact of their membership, the attraction of the movement as a model of a new neutral status lies mainly in its title and in the fact of active engagement in the visible arenas of international diplomacy.

Finally, active neutrality is not primarily a moral response to the problem of war in the nuclear age. Virtue of that order is beyond the capacity of nations to practise. It is also the case that the successful management of neutrality requires a cold calculation of self-interest on the part of the neutral state and of the interests of other states, which must be used to advantage in constructing the political relationships necessary for the international and internal defence of neutrality. Such calculation probably precludes too great a preoccupation with the moralizing of active neutrality, even in those essential neutral activities which lend themselves most easily to virtuous interpretation, which are discussed below.

AREAS OF INSTITUTIONAL CHANGE

The discussion which follows lists four major institutional areas, the support of which would be required if a policy of active neutrality were to be declared and to have minimal chance of survival and success. Success here means, above all, internal support and consensus, born of public confidence in Irish foreign policy. It means, also, confidence in the international acceptability of the policy and the awareness of a tolerable balance of costs and benefits — made more tolerable by a sense of pride and prestige which even a sober marketing of the policy could achieve for a modest country, to which history, political marginality and an instinctive deference to the judgment of others have given more than enough to be modest about. One could expand the list with little difficulty. But the role to played in transforming foreign policy in Ireland by the institutions of diplomacy, military, culture and politics suggest that these at least are central and critical.

A. DIPLOMACY AND ACTIVE NEUTRALITY

It is in the international arena that foreign policy succeeds or fails, and the job of diplomacy must be to use the existing institutions and machinery to advance and protect neutrality. Obviously, the main institution is still the United Nations. Despite growing world-wide concern about its inability to act effectively, it is still all that we have by way of a world authority transcending the interests of nations and their powerful blocs. It is misused by its member-states, large and small, who treat its judgments and resolutions as opportunities to be exploited, its voting system as an occasion for displaying the right stance for the interest groups at home, conniving with other states to construct a voting record which will establish their 'independence'. Nonetheless, the UN is still the repository of values which all nations hold in common and, as such, it has a symbolic importance as a moral authority, with power to define and judge and pronounce which it is still costly to ignore.

As noted in the Introduction, neutrality in 1945 was widely understood in a way which seemed to make it incompatible with UN membership and which certainly relegated it to a position of low esteem and irrelevance in the functioning of the organization. This was mainly because the United Nations was then, and still is, the privileged forum of the victors of World War II which are now the five major nuclear powers. Yet there is a sense in which active neutrality represents an ideal of the United Nations, a foreign policy wholly in line with the aims of the Charter. The collective security, which was originally envisaged as an essential instrument of peace-making and peacekeeping so that the UN could fulfil its Charter resolution 'to unite our strength to maintain international peace and security', was not incompatible with neutrality, as it was earlier argued.[2] Certainly a narrow, isolationist neutrality excludes, by definition, the collective securing of peace by military force. But an active neutrality is incompatible only with the division into military blocs of the nations aspiring to international peace and security — blocs which today constitute the principal obstacle to the realization of the Charter aims. Active neutrality lacks the element of international organization which the UN provides. In other respects, it provides the commitment which the UN has failed to organize. This commitment to work for international peacemaking, for the genuine repudiation of nuclear weapons and for the construction of a credible domestic base in the interests of a nation's own and its neighbours'

2. See Introduction.

security — this, in theory, is what should make neutrality an attractive ideal for the United Nations and, therefore, the basis of a diplomatic effort to raise its status.

Ireland is not only neutral. It is also nuclear-free and the initiator of the Non-Proliferation Treaty. The setting-up of nuclear-free zones was a significant step in trying to prevent the proliferation of nuclear weapons particularly in countries where the threat of weapons might encourage the development of a nuclear capacity. While many agreements are under consideration by the UN and the regions involved, the only one in existence, affecting a densely-inhabited region, is the Treaty of Tlatelolco (1967), currently in force for twenty-two Latin American states. The object is to obtain the guarantee of the nuclear powers to keep their weapons out of the region, in return for the guarantee of the states in the region not to acquire them, and thus to create an area of collective security from weapons and threats of weapons. There are obvious problems with nuclear-free zones, as there are with all instruments of arms control. And there are enormous problems in creating such zones inside the territories of the superpower alliances. But the commitment of the UN to the extension of such zones as a major part of the peace-making process is unqualified. There is every hope, therefore, that imaginative diplomacy can forge the clear link between nuclear-free zones and neutrality — in other words, between the creation of *physical* areas of security aimed at preventing the proliferation of nuclear weapons and the creation of the *political conditions* actively to advance the cause of security and non-proliferation. If the Swedish proposal for a nuclear-free corridor in Europe across the East-West border is now widely discussed as a realistic possibility, with a chance of being implemented if conventional armaments can be included, then why not active neutrality as a means of strengthening security within the corridor or of supporting it from other parts of Europe? And Ireland, instead of submitting to the NATO link on offer from a Conservative government in Britain, could be a passive model, if not an active support, for the other voices in Britain which would welcome a nuclear-free zone for the British Isles.

Ireland's initiation of the Non-Proliferation Treaty during the Aiken period of UN diplomacy is a historical involvement with a major instrument of UN peacemaking which diplomacy could use creatively to strengthen security and neutrality as its instrument. The nuclear-free zone was intended to make proliferation less attractive and, therefore, to reinforce the Non-Proliferation Treaty. The threat of nuclear war today comes from the confrontation between the superpowers and the unpredictable risks of proliferation. But the superpower rivalry is, in effect, a kind of proliferation. If Europe could return to the mutual threat of weapons located only in the US

THE CASE FOR ACTIVE IRISH NEUTRALITY

and the USSR, the world might still not be safe but millions fewer people would be terrified of the danger. Now the superpowers have built arsenals for deployment in locations as extensive as their zones of influence. And now, too, the Euro-missiles — in themselves a vertical proliferation of weapons contrary to the obligations undertaken in the Non-Proliferation Treaty (NPT) — have spread horizontally to West Germany, Italy and Britain. What difference does it make to the spirit of greater security underlying the NPT that these Cruise and Pershings — and the Soviet misslies also when these are exported to the friendly countries — belong to the superpower and not to the host country? What has been proliferated, in the case of Euro-missiles, is a half-share in an effective decision to launch a nuclear missile, not technically a violation of the Treaty, but certainly a violation of its spirit. Active neutrality adds to the fact of being non-nuclear the additional fact of not being part of the confrontation between the superpowers and, therefore, a potential recipient of their nuclear weapons through the back-door of the Non-Proliferation Treaty.

In these three peacemaking instruments — active neutrality, nuclear-free zones and non-proliferation — Irish diplomacy has an already-existing basis in Ireland and in the security aims of the United Nations for raising the status and the international acceptability of neutrality. This must include working for a UN definition of neutrality which specifies indicators of active peacemaking involvement and of the nature of internal military defence which will distinguish active neutrality from the narrow isolationist policy which is not compatible with the United Nations. It should also seek, secondly, to have some emphasis placed on the appropriateness of the participation of neutral forces in the United Nations peacekeeping force. Ideally, the *reservation* of UN peacekeeping to nations which conform to a UN standard of active neutrality would be the kind of recognition which would compensate for neutrality's poor image in the past. Thirdly, diplomacy could canvass international opinion on the possibility of a Standing Conference of European Neutrals, or some such flexible consultation body. Clearly, the attraction of this depends on creating a better climate for neutrality than history offers. But whatever its title or precise nature, it seems essential that active neutrality should have a European focus in cooperation with other nations — which may not necessarily be neutral, may even be deviant bloc members — to further the aims of European security through nuclear-free zones and active foreign policies not predicated on worst-case predictions of NATO or the Soviet bloc.

These three possibilities of diplomacy, while they are mainly about talk and symbols, are nonetheless significant in preparing the necessary ground, flying the necessary kites for more concrete achievements. Some form of UN incentive to neutral and non-nuclear nations to construct the kind of defence capability necessary to win domestic support for active neutrality and to guarantee its non-aggressive nature for neighbouring territories, would strengthen the terms of nuclear-free zones agreements. One of the problems of the Palme proposal from Sweden is that Soviet enthusiasm for it, and American reluctance, arises from the fact that it leaves aggressive conventional forces in place. If the Palme proposal were for a weapons-free corridor or something close to that, it would be a step to neutralizing the most dangerous area in Europe.

It would surely be appropriate for a neutral Ireland actively to support the Swedish proposal and to co-operate with Sweden and other nations in extending this mechanism for peace to other areas of Europe? With moves afoot to give Europe greater independence from the United States within a European defence context — which will inevitably become a nuclear defence programme — and with Ireland co-operating to make this possible within the limits allowed by domestic sensitivities, it is worth considering an alternative kind of European independence which would retain a sufficient link with American nuclear forces to avoid the charge of naive unilateralism. This is the 'Swedenization' proposal put forward by Michael Howard — and the fact that it was suggested by a policy theorist untainted by the suspicion of pacifist sentimentalism lends it some kind of authority.[3] His argument is for replacing nuclear deterrence, which relies on missile deployments in Europe, with terri-torial defence in depth and ultimate reliance on the American nuclear guarantee, which would be no less trustworthy then than it is now. The idea is immensely attractive, since it offers a form of collective defence which protects European territories against aggression and at the same time protects Europe against fragmentation into rival armed units with all the historical memories of war to recover. Some steps in that direction would give Irish diplomacy a worthier objective than conforming unnecessarily to the demands of European Political Cooperation or contriving an independent image at the United Nations.

B. ACTIVE NEUTRALITY AND THE ROLE OF THE MILITARY

On the face of it, Ireland's army, and defence organizations generally, are an ideal institution to be transformed into the main defence agent of active neutrality. It is badly equipped by the standards of conven-tional armies, it has played its only active military role magnificently

3. Michael Howard: 'NATO and the Year of Europe' in *Survival* January/February 1974.

in the service of the United Nations, it has not other training or active links with other armies — none which are publicly acknowledged, that is — it has an exemplary record of submission to the political will and it is a traditional institution which does not suggest, on ideological grounds at least, an antipathy to neutrality. This public image, if it is correct, may not reflect reality in all respects. Poor equipment may not be an obstacle to re-equipping an army for the kind of defensive role required by active neutrality. But it is the kind of military deprivation which, together with decades of government policy to facilitate a new defence role in Europe, is likely to have stimulated pro-NATO thinking in the army rather than any alternatives. Increasingly, the leadership of the army is being taken over by officers who entered the service long after the early post-war years and even after the beginnings of the Irish orientation to Europe and the EEC. A role in NATO, or in some substitute in Europe or the British Isles, is naturally attractive to soldiers as a means of advancing careers, providing 'relevant' experience, better training and the possibility of action. At present, only the glamorous prospect of a United Nations posting offers some foreign experience as an escape from the routine of barracks activity which, by military definition, is inactivity. NATO is where the action is, where the military hardware is and, apart from the UN, where the glamour is. In addition to these understandable disincentives to neutrality, the Irish army has for long been recruited to anti-terrorist and general home security service which bear no relation to the military duties for which it was trained, or even to territorial defence for which it was not. Motivating men to be soldiers in the textbook tradition when a great deal of their activity consists in guarding the transfer of money to a village post-office or policing the back-roads of the border territory is as demoralizing for the Irish army as it is for the British in Northern Ireland — but at least the British soldiers have other prospects after their Ulster tour.

This makes it essential that military training should be consistent with the military goals of active neutrality. Territorial defence requires a different kind of soldier, with different attitudes and expectations, but not so different that it would be impossible to achieve with the present force. A strengthening of neutrality's claims to UN peacekeeping would be one of many factors contributing to the reorientation of the military perspective. The creation of new links with Swiss and Swedish training schools would afford some compensation for abandoning those informal arrangements with NATO countries which the army is understandably secretive about today.

Since no country in Europe today, least of all Ireland, needs to defend itself militarily against nuclear weapons,[4] the primary object of

4. Partly because there is no defence anyway and partly because the threats come from both blocs and cancel each other out. See Introduction.

territorial defence is to provide a deterrence adequate to the realistic assessment of external threat and the needs of internal confidence. It seems beyond question that Ireland can afford such defence in financial terms.[5] This would include the cost of adequate military and civil defence and the equipment appropriate to the new needs.

However, there may be other costs of a different nature which pose different problems for our willingness to pay them. Conscription, if it were required, would furnish a large part of Irish territorial defence needs, but it would create a political problem, similar to that in European NATO countries, which has made nuclear defence seem to be a cheaper alternative. While there are problems inseparable from conscription, the principal one of recruitment is not necessarily as problematic as it seems. Obligatory recruitment into a NATO army is ruled out by politicians because the popular support for the policy which requires the army is notably lacking in the age-group to be conscripted. This is not say that a different policy would eliminate popular resistance. But if it were seen to be necessary as an alternative to NATO and as a condition of a permanent active neutrality, it would hardly attract intolerable resistance. This is all the less likely if the cultural elements of active neutrality are also brought into line with the policy.

C. CULTURE AND ACTIVE NEUTRALITY

The term 'culture' stands for the social products which come to us as knowledge, opinion and values. It denotes particularly, for our present purpose, the institutions mainly responsible for producing those products in our society, for distinguishing truth from falsehood, creating the moods, temper and fashion which make some ideas questionable and others taken for granted, for managing the process by which moral and political values are selected, defined and ranked according to priorities dictated by a complex interaction of tradition, prejudice, interest and personality. (This elaborate way of describing the obvious is not intended to suggest an overwhelming or crass determinism, but merely to draw attention to a significant aspect of culture which is relevant here.)

One could easily expand the list of institutions engaged in the culture industry in Ireland, but for reasons of brevity I shall confine my comments to the main two: the Church and education. And, since the comments are general, I shall make the unecumenical decision to confine discussion of the Church to the largest, most visible and most

5. What is adequate is, of course, dependent on the particular needs of Ireland and on a political judgment of how much defence is required for public confidence. Some indication of the requirements of territorial defence for Britain may be seen in the Alternative Defence Commission's report discussed in Chapter Two.

influential of the denominations.

Recent events notwithstanding, the Church in Ireland is still a powerful force of moral persuasion and political influence. It is difficult to imagine any attempt to bring about cultural change which could withstand persistent resistance by the Church which, for all the factors which distinguish it from the dominant institution of the fifties, still retains a strong hold on the minds and affections of the people. Its potential is comparable to that of the media, but without the fragmentation and competiveness which blunts the media's impact.

There are many positive and negative features of Irish Catholicism which bear upon the issue of foreign policy and neutrality. Some recent recruitments to the episcopacy have brought with them the beginnings of a new openess and a new sense of mission relevant to public policy and international affairs. One does not have to agree with Bishop Eamonn Casey's raising the question of diplomatic links with the United States over the violence in Central America, with similar comments over the imprisonment of Fr Niall O'Brien in the Philippines, or with the episcopal delegation's oral evidence to the New Ireland Forum to recognize and welcome the shift in moral awareness which gives the political and the structural a significance previously reserved for the sexual and the interpersonal. (Indeed, one wishes a similar degree of openness was evident among the parish clergy and seminarians.) A second feature of a positive kind follows from this. The concern for social justice in the Third World and for peace in Northern Ireland has given the voice of the Catholic bishops a ring of prophecy very different from the hierarchical tones of the fifties. Another positive factor, less prophetic but relevant to the neutrality question, is the indentification of the Church with the symbols of Irishness, defined for over sixty years in opposition to economic values and 'materialism' — for reasons which have more to do with the spectre of foreign influence beloved of the guardians of nationalist culture than with theology.

On the negative side, one must rank first a theological tradition which Irish Catholicism shares with Protestantism and with Churches throughout Christendom but which Irish Catholics have a particular reluctance to question. This refers to biblically-justified elements of the Christian tradition which encourage the glorification of war, the definition of an enemy and the easy identification of a human enemy with moral evil, making it less uncomfortable to consider its eradication. The counter-images in the Bible are intended as a simple pedagogic device — light/dark, God/Satan, good/evil, for us/against us — but they are also powerful metaphors which can be conscripted to any ideological cause. The traditional stress on the primacy of the next world over this makes light of suffering and death if the cause is right; and this is reinforced by a conception of original sin which inclines humanity to evil and thereby justifies an exaggerated realism which sees war as an inevitable and justifiable product of sin and sees the violence of authority as the unavoidable response to the evil of humanity.[6] Finally, the emphasis on compliance with lawful authority, which ignores the general thrust of the Gospels and gives a distorted significance to certain texts — notably Romans 13:4; 'it is not for nothing that the authorities bear the sword' — is used, particularly in the Catholic and Lutheran traditions, not just to support public order positively and reasonably but to silence dissent and to legitimate compliance when the moral order is challenged by questionable acts of government.[7]

These are powerful images which distort the Bible and put the Gospels to the service of particular political and economic forms without any conscious effort on the part of Christians or their leaders. This is not to say that other forms are precisely what Christians must have — socialism instead of capitalism, active neutrality instead of NATO alliance. It is rather to suggest that Christianity is not about institutional forms old or new; it is about values, and the values of peace and justice may be better secured, or less obscured, by certain political changes. The job of a prophetic Church is, surely, to measure all political forms against the moral values relevant to the social order, as these are best understood. It is very difficult to see how these can exclude an overriding concern today with the problem of peace — not simply peace in the abstract, but positive peace*making* and reconciliation of enemies.

This leads to consideration of a consequence of the biblical counter-images and of nineteenth-century Catholicism which is the most serious obstacle to Catholic involvement in the peace question and without which Irish Catholics might well choose active neutrality as an expression of moral concern as readily as they chose a constitutional amendment on another matter. This is the question of anti-Communism. There is a certain human need for an enemy to which popular anti-Communism provides a response and which makes it an easy belief to serve the political purpose of any organized religion. Anti-Communism should not be confused with opposition to Communism. The degree to which the former is used indiscriminately, extensively, normatively, without openness to counterfactual evidence, allows us to distinguish it from the latter. Communism has

6. This Augustinian view is corrected in modern Catholic theology, which understands the effect of original sin more as a weakening of the will than a proclivity to evil. Karl Rahner ed.: *Encyclopedia of Theology*, Burns and Oates, London 1981, p. 1148 ff.

7. One could add to these images the tradition of the main Churches of supplying army-ranked and army-paid chaplains. This is not to make a point against armies but to question the need for *this* institutional link, which reinforces the warrior image of Christianity.

an all-purpose function as a label, used to condemn the entire range
of a nation's or a person's activities or belief. Or it can have a more
specific function as a label, already mentioned — like that which
served the social order in the Middle Ages by transforming innocent
women into witches, thereby making them worthier and easier targets
of violence; and that which serves one American's view of the social
order today by transforming millions of human beings into 'the focus
of evil', thus legitimizing the present Administration's demands for
bigger arsenals and more dangerous strategies of nuclear confrontation with the Soviet Union. The Kremlin has its own stock of
dehumanizing labels, but their anti-Americanism lacks the profound
religious resonance of Western imagery. 'American', like 'capitalist',
is ambiguous, suggesting glamour as well as evil. 'Imperialist' or
'fascist' are not flattering in the Russian vocabulary, but they are dull
and one-dimensional — too rational to compare with 'Communist'.
AntiCommunism is magic.

The Church's complicity in polarizing humanity between Communism and freedom, Communism and human rights, Communism
and Christian values, the common enemy and the West, is most
visible in the period since the nineteenth century, and owes much of
its force to the manner in which first anti-socialism, then anti-
Communism were woven into the fabric of popular piety. But
probably the origins go back much further. Unlike anti-Semitism,
which defined the Jews as enemies, anti-Communism was a useful
label for an already-existing enemy — the Eastern Church, which
merged in Western consciousness with the political enemy of
imperialist Russia. It is useful to remember that the opposition
between Catholicism and Communism is not an integral feature of
the belief-systems themselves, though it is deeply rooted in some
versions of them and would be difficult to extricate completely from
any. It results from the accident of a history which might have taken
a different path, a history of ambivalence, opposition and rapidly-
escalating conflict, leading inevitably to the re-writing of their
separate histories and the incorporation of counter-image elements
into their identities. The 'focus of evil' is a modern riposte to the
'opium of the people'.[8]

There are some realist arguments for keeping the military alliances
in place, discussed in the Introduction. But they in no way justify
their extension into anti-Communism or into Irish support for
NATO. There is historical evidence which can be used to support the
fear of the Soviet Union in parts of Europe, though it requires the

8. See Bill McSweeney: *Roman Catholicism: The Search for Relevance*,
Blackwell's, Oxford, 1980, chs. 2/3. Many Catholics probably still remember the
three Hail Marys at Mass which nourished the Satanic image of Communism within
a sacred context.

spectacles of an ideologue to read into it a case for such fear in Ireland — still more in the United States. But the Cold War in its present form is more than the product of reason. It is the institutionalization of hatred in moral terms, and the Western contribution to it comes mostly from the cult of anti-Communism. This is the real focus of evil, disguised as the strategy of containment, or as implacable political opposition, which supports that indefensible element of US foreign policy which still seeks to impose a Pax Americana through strategic superiority — or its alternative, Soviet economic collapse — despite all the evidence of post-war history that the search is vain and counterproductive.[9] The Catholic Church in Ireland has, in the past, unconsciously contributed to this hatred. If there are now increasing signs of a critical awareness in the Church of the moral dimension of international politics and foreign policy, this new witness to the Gospels cannot stop at the point where violence and injustice touch fellow-Catholics and fellow-Irish. It is for all Christians, not just the Catholic bishops, to be aware that not hating Communists is not enough; that reconciliation between divided communities requires imaginative, positive action; that cultural unilateralism — actively promoting reconciliation — is even safer than nuclear unilateralism which many Churches in NATO countries demand of their own governments; above all, that there is a link between the global hatred of the Cold War and the hatred on our streets and television screens between the Christians of Northern Ireland — if not in its cause, certainly in the solution being discussed. There are moral and political grounds, this book argues, why that solution should be rejected. There are no grounds whatever why that link should be ignored and the question of Irish neutrality dismissed as a politicians' problem, irrelevant to Christian concerns.

The day may come when the Catholic Church will give the nuclear issue the moral priority it warrants, like the question of abortion since the early fifties, or, in some canonical form, like heresy in the Middle Ages, or IRA membership in the thirties. It is worth considering the example of another Christian community: the Evangelical Protestant Churches in Germany. The Barmen Declaration of May 1934 was their attempt to give emphatic expression to their revulsion towards Nazism and its hatred of the Jews. They declared that it was a confessional matter — *status confessionis* — which excluded from fellowship with the Church public Christian support for the Nazi regime. Now the Reformed Alliance has given this priority to the peace issue in West Germany as Jürgen Moltmann notes in Chapter Seven. And the Federation of Evangelical Churches — mostly Lutheran — has

9. See Seweryn Bialer and Joan Afferica: 'Reagan and Russia' in *Foreign Affairs*, Winter, 1982/83; John Lewis Gaddis: *Strategies of Containment: A Critical Appraisal of Postwar National Security Policy*, OUP, New York, 1982.

given the same significance to the Christian obligation to work for reconciliation and peace between East and West. This is an alliance of Protestant Churches in East Germany, all of them citizens of a Communist state.

The second main institution of culture central to a domestic base for active neutrality is education. So much has been written and said of the impact of education on beliefs and values as factors in the Northern Ireland conflict — all the more powerful because they are held unconsciously, without awareness of their origin or their nature as artefacts or human constructs — that the case for its effectiveness can be assumed. The change of policy entailed in a government declaration of active neutrality would hardly be possible to achieve and sustain without the support of teachers. Their work in changing values from those which treat war as a remedy, nationalism as a virtue, violence as glamorous, to those which question these macho attitudes and make it acceptable to deride them and approve of less aggressive impulses in children is the long-term work of peace and non-violence. It is an urgent job for schools and schoolchildren because it was neglected by their parents and grandparents. This is the work being promoted by the Catholic and Protestant Churches in Ireland through the Irish Commission for Justice and Peace in Dublin and the Irish Council of Churches in Belfast, and already many schools throughout the country are using their curriculum to counter the positive images of violence to which Irish society is prone.

But there is also the need to inculcate in secondary schoolchildren a more critical attitude to society and government arising from a sense of moral concern that can no longer be taken for granted as part of the baggage of university students. Secondary children are not too young to learn about violence and poverty directly from its incidence all around them and from their reading about wealth and poverty in other parts of the world, which they can be helped to connect with their own lives. There is something wrong with schools whose secondary pupils see nothing problematic in snobbery, conspicuous consumption and the distribution of wealth.

A critical awareness of politics, with some sense of moral concern deriving from the simplest example of poverty, should in itself be a check to the automatic and instinctive nationalism in Ireland, which rises and falls with the fortunes of the main actors — the Northern Catholics, the IRA and the British Army — but which never disappears. It is always there in reserve, standing by, waiting to be called up. It would be good to feel that Irish nationalism could serve the needs of active neutrality, supplying the energy and commitment for territorial defence. Nationalism is about fighting for one's country; it resists foreign alliances. But active neutrality is not about fighting for one's country except as a last resort and it is *primarily* about foreign alliances and commitments which make the policy work to its benefit.

Nationalism is an unlikely recruit to active neutrality. If a peace programme did nothing else in schools but diminish its lure and unpack for children the complicated delusions and deceits which are its substance, it would merit all the effort of educators, Churches, media which could make it possible. Nationalism teaches people to kill and to hate with an enthusiasm which leaves no room for healing and reconciling and adding a crumb to the quality of life. It taps the most barbarous and primitive instincts to forge a superstitious attachment to symbols of cloth and abstractions like freedom. Nationalism is the meanest face of opportunist politics. It promises everything, but delivers nothing — not even to the nationalist, who is left to savour victory and cherish freedom in the same squalor from which he sought it. Yet we are hypnotized by its symbolism, happy to march to its tunes, applaud its Brit-bashing, venerate its grandfathers and turn a blind eye to its consequences. It has had more terrible effects in some other countries than in Ireland. But it has killed enough and maimed enough and crippled our political life for long enough for it to lose its magic and lie dormant for a while. Would anything happen to our world if teachers now whispered the truth to our children: there is nothing noble about dying for Ireland?

There is something of a new mood in Ireland today, encouraged by the peace groups, the Churches, the despair over Northern Ireland, the growing realization of the costs of unity in the harsh economic climate of the eighties, the awareness that it is the difference to people that matters in policy, not the difference to anthems or flags or memories or any of the squalid abstractions that make up the nationalist dream, the consciousness that it is a nobler ideal by far to heal our hatreds and reconcile our communites than to end partition — particularly if the price of unity is involvement in a more dangerous war and participation in a larger hatred. It needs information and education to understand the link between active peacemaking in Ireland and active neutrality in Europe, and educators have a role here, too, in making not only the political but the moral connection for the peace groups oriented separately towards the two issues — Irish and international.

The work of the Irish Commission for Justice and Peace is not the only resource for educators in Ireland. The past four years have brought a new concern for peace education all over the world and there is now something of an international publishing industry trying to match the demand from primary and secondary schools for imaginative learning aids and teaching materials which will shift the age-old emphasis of school textbooks from the acceptance of force-efficiency as the model of conflict resolution to the awareness of violence as a disease, not a remedy, and the search for political and non-violent alternatives.

D. POLITICS AND ACTIVE NEUTRALITY

Politics includes diplomacy and it is more than government. But because diplomacy has a specific and key role in foreign policy and in the creation and strengthening of an active neutrality, it has been dealt with separately. Here I shall look only at the role of government. It is for government, ultimately, to declare and sustain a policy of active neutrality and to create the conditions, in all areas under its control, to make that policy effective. Given a change in public consciousness through the agencies described in the previous section, and given the consequent electoral pressure on politicians and their parties, certain actions of government would be necessary to give the policy legal and political force.

A declaration of intent.

Foreign policy changes occur mostly without public declaration, usually without public awareness, often with great care taken to hide what is happening behind a screen of secrecy or disguise. Most changes in policy are really gradual shifts later defined as decisions for change. And some declared changes are not changes at all, but merely political attempts to hide continuity. The classic case of sudden policy change, formally declared, is war. The obvious reason for declaring the outbreak of war is the need to comply with international law on the matter. But there are usually less virtuous pressures at home — above all, the need to mobilize all the resources of the country to the war effort and away from the everyday competiveness and divisiveness and rumblings of revolt that characterize democracy, even at its best. War makes government easy because it makes foreign affairs dangerous and difficult.

It is this need for mobilizing resources that makes it necessary to propose some public declaration that policy is undergoing change. One can conceive of circumstances in which the intention to remain militarily neutral in war was withheld from the public until secrecy was no longer possible. It underlines the enormous difference between such a policy of *military* neutrality and *active* neutrality to make the point that publicity is of the essence. It should also be clear, for the same reason, that a declaration is only the ritual or symbolic part of active neutrality.

As with war, there would be no point in declaring such a policy change unless there was already the political will and minimal resources to see it through. The nature and importance of these resources, sketched out above, make it plain that declaring and doing are not the same thing as regards active neutrality, as they must be, inevitably, as regards war. A declaration of intent would be necessary and useful in order to strengthen the domestic base of neutrality and make a later formal declaration possible.

Ireland and the EEC.

As already discussed in Chapter Eight, all the overseas pressure on Ireland to abandon neutrality in favour of direct or indirect alliance with NATO comes from the EEC, through its political machinery, and from the British government, through its involvement in Northern Ireland. It will help if I summarize and extend this argument here since the proposals to be made are dependent on it.

There is no evidence that EPC — European Political Cooperation — is either a legal requirement of EEC participation or that it has become, in fact, an unavoidable condition of participation in the European Community. There is abundant evidence of some European pressure to make the link and to define the economic and political parts of the Community as inseparable. And there are strong indicators that this inseparability, with the consequence for Ireland of alliance with NATO in some form, has gained considerable additional force from the Irish side. This is not to say that there was great Irish anxiety, independent of Brussels and Strasburg, to join NATO. On the contrary, Irish officials and politicians have always been aware of the political difficulties of any attempt to abandon neutrality. But they have given little indication, on the other hand, that they would pay a high, or even a low, price to stay out of NATO. Stiff resistance to military alliance on principle was never on the agenda of the Department of Foreign Affairs.

This is patently clear from the records of official statements on the matter, which hint at the irresistible coming-together of EEC and EPC from the European side and the intolerable financial cost of opposing it from the Irish side. If this were, in fact, the case — rather than an Irish definition of it — then it would be perfectly simple to produce the evidence for all to see. This is precisely what the government has done, for example, as regards the Common Agricultural Policy, the reform of which was fiercely and publicly resisted by Ireland because it will damage our economy unless special exemptions are made. It would be silly for the government merely to hint at that damage since, if it occurs, they want everyone to be clear where the blame lies. Why, then, does the government not do the obvious thing and expose the NATO members of the EEC as the culprits making our neutrality impossible? The answer seems to be as follows.

The Irish government — which here means, primarily, the Department of Foreign Affairs — is committed to maximizing the economic benefits of the EEC. It is not committed in any way to neutrality, but is obliged by the political risks to avoid making that fact clear. It is under undefined pressure from NATO countries to play the game in European Political Cooperation (EPC) and this is transmitted through bureaucratic and interpersonal channels. It has estimated a weak or manageable domestic support for neutrality — in line with its own evaluation — and that this will continue if the issue is treated sensitively and equivocally until NATO members are no longer willing to keep up the pretence that EPC is just talk about 'security', but will press for formal military alliance. The Irish judgment then, is that deviance in the EEC is difficult and might be costly, but no one can say by how much. Until EPC is formalized, the safest stance is one of careful ambiguity which will avoid giving ammunition to the neutrality lobby; which will strengthen the business lobby against it; and which will keep NATO-members happy and willing to cooperate with Irish officials by providing the appropriate statements and evidence for the Irish to manage this sensitive issue.[10]

The whole Irish case, therefore, rests on the potential cost — in direct penalties or loss of bargaining power — of remaining neutral in a Community of NATO members. Since legal penalties cannot be imposed, then some unstated loss of bargaining power must be assumed. (This is what Padraic MacKernan means by the need for a 'credible' contribution to EPC, discussed in Chapter Eight.) But NATO has no need whatever of Southern Ireland while it has the North. Is it, therefore, partition which is the problem; is it Irish unity which is the goal of our EPC policy? (MacKernan, in the same paper, refers to a 'policy imperative' of 'the domestic political situation'.) This would suggest that we can expect strong EEC pressure on Britain to settle the Northern question along the lines proposed in 1980 by Charles Haughey. So Ireland is pressing the NATO members of the EEC to bring about Irish unity in return for an all-Ireland entry into military alliance, and to cooperate in presenting that fact to public opinion in Ireland as if it were the logic of EPC pushing our struggling civil servants into a dilemma from which there is no escape: military alliance or intolerable economic loss. So we are back to 1949, with neutrality for sale in return for unity, and the EEC playing America's role as the lever exerted on a reluctant Westminster. With Britain's strained relations with the EEC, a suspicious neutrality lobby in Dublin and a powerful Unionist lobby in Belfast, and with Europe uncertain about the nature of its defence alliance which Ireland would join if the price were right, it is not surprising that Irish officials have a delicate job managing the news.

If that is not the case — if Ireland, without reference to partition, is offering the *Republic* to the NATO countries in the context of EPC, in the vague hope of *increasing* bargaining power in the economic sphere, then there must be a serious question about the intellectual level of our representation in Europe. NATO has little need of any

10. The management of news of this kind is notoriously difficult to prove. But it would be unlikely that such cooperation from NATO members was not sought by a sophisticated civil service well versed in such matters and experienced in the construction of presentable voting statistics in the United Nations.

part of Ireland. Why should its EEC members pay for a second bit?

It seems clear, therefore, that Ireland is not being forced into the military alliance which is intended in EPC by anything or anyone else other than 'the domestic political situation', in MacKernan's phrase, and by the political judgment of Irish politicians and civil servants that neutrality is, or will be, dispensable. There are no faceless bureaucrats in Brussels threatening poverty if Ireland does not lend a hand in the defence of Europe, as Irish governments like to imply. The real threat comes from Ireland, from our friendly, local bureaucrats in Dublin and from the politicans whom they brief.[11]

Since the EEC is quite compatible with a neutrality policy — as the Irish government itself declared in support of entry in 1973 — we are not faced with a choice of joining NATO or leaving Europe, staying neutral or staying in the Common Market. But we are faced with a European situation which will present itself in that light, thanks to the lobbying abroad of Irish officials who need that picture drawn for domestic political purposes. And there is certainly a difficulty created by the level of present integration into Europe and the mere fact of NATO dominance in the Community. It is essential for a policy of active neutrality, therefore, that the anomalies be corrected, where possible, and steps be taken to withdraw from those aspects of EPC involvement which are incompatible with it. And it is also essential that the government take action on the direct threat to neutrality from Britain — which, of course, does not only come from Britain but which will be made to appear that way to save the blushes of the Irish government — and on other matters under its control. The following five-point programme for government would begin the process of restoring credibility to our political parties, would protect neutrality and would make active neutrality possible.

1. *Strengthening neutrality in the EEC.* What is required to achieve this is an explicit recognition of the acceptability within the EEC of Irish neutrality and non-membership of any military alliance. Ideally, this should be done within the EEC as a Community by defining Ireland's involvement as the participation of a neutral country — this is legally possible — and by a Community declaration that such neutrality is compatible with full participation in the Common Market. The claim that neutrality is already recognized by the EEC, making such a declaration unnecessary, is simply not true. There are statements by representatives to this effect, but these are private comments, footnotes to footnotes, inserted 'not to embarrass the

11. The emphasis throughout on Foreign Affairs does not mean that other departments — notably Agriculture and Finance — are not also centrally involved in Ireland's EEC role. But the spearhead of policy formation and implementation is the Department of Foreign Affairs.

Irish', as Lord Carrington pointedly, if unwittingly, put it. Failure to achieve a Community declaration would make it necessary to seek an official declaration from individual governments in the EEC. Failure to achieve either would probably have a very positive effect on public debate on the subject in Ireland.

Apart from clarifying the formal aspect of EEC membership, it would also be necessary to modify, if not withdraw from European Political Cooperation. A modification could take the form of a *clear* definition of security, as distinct from defence, and a bureaucratic procedure for keeping the two questions separate. Since this is highly unlikely, some other form of two-tier involvement in EPC would be necessary, perhaps on the lines of the two-tier NATO system which respects French interests. But given the nature of EPC development and the motives consistently expressed to justify it on the part of its NATO members, it is difficult to see how any aspect — including foreign-policy coordination — could be meaningfully made to coexist with a policy of active neutrality. The two-tier solution, therefore, must apply to membership of the Community, not of its EPC aspect. And this possibly means withdrawal from political cooperation, but not from the economic and cultural aspects of our European involvement within the Community.

2. *Neutrality and Anglo-Irish Relations.* There will not always be a Tory government in power in Britain, nor one made to Thatcher's measure, when it returns. In the interim, it would obviously be essential to press any claims for an Irish dimension in a solution to violence in the North by means other than a defence pact. It is also clear that active neutrality must be explained in terms of its relevance to the Protestant majority in the North — not only as a more attractive element in the policies of their Southern neighbour, but also in order to strengthen a case for *compatible* policies, even with partition. A nuclear-free zone for the territories, formalized according to United Nations conventions, would provide a more secure base for active neutrality in the South and a safer policy, without the historical overtones of neutrality, for the Northern community. Finally, it would important for the Irish government to work for explicit acceptance of Irish neutrality by the British Labour Party, without prejudice to their existing policy on Northern Ireland.

3. *Re-organization of Irish defence.* Like most other real factors, as distinct from symbolic, defence organization for active neutrality is an accomplishment. Its adequacy at any time is in large part determined by domestic and international opinion. It can be helped initially by restructuring the different sections of the Department of Defence according to the new needs of neutrality. Probably a new

title more appropriate to those needs, such as Department of Civil
and Territorial Defence, would also encourage public confidence and
involvement at an appropriate level.

4. *Recognition of Active Neutrality in Foreign Affairs.* There is
already in the Department of Foreign Affairs a creative and informed
section dealing imaginatively, within government budget constraints,
with development aid to Third World countries. This is an essential
part of a policy of active neutrality. There is another departmental
section responsible for disarmament which, for its size, makes a
valuable contribution to international negotiations on peace and
human rights which is internationally recognized, despite the fact that
its operations are severely restricted by the hidden agenda of the
Department as a whole. It would be a recognition of serious commitment to Irish neutrality if these two sections were to be linked
together under junior ministerial responsibility. There is ample scope
for such an initiative to be taken uncontroversially in the first place by
a major party in opposition, by creating a spokesperson on Disarmament and Development.

5. *Commission on Neutrality.* Because active neutrality, unlike conventional defence, relates to a wide range of activities and skills and
requires active public participation if it is to be politically acceptable
and effective at moderate cost, it would be desirable to break the
monopoly of expertise and policy-making presently vested in the
Department of Defence. A permanent Commission on Neutrality,
functioning like an American National Security Council — but with
very different attitudes and tasks — could be a powerful instrument of
information, expertise and public relations in maintaining a viable
policy and providing the imagination and improvization needed. Its
primary function would be to examine, advise on and monitor the
alternative defence needs of a neutral Ireland and the international
opportunities for peacemaking — as well as peacekeeping — which
active neutrality affords.

It goes without saying that if the Irish government were to commit
itself to active neutrality, it would find wide public support. It would
find, too, that something of the domestic benefits to government of a
declaration of war would be forthcoming, making a contrast to the
dangerous level of public disorder today and the low esteem in which
politicians are held, partly because of their apparent unconcern with
the values they profess and their constant readiness to dissemble and
equivocate whenever short-term gains are at risk. Active neutrality
could change more than foreign policy in Ireland if politicians can

seize the opportunity. It could legitimate authority and lift Irish morale far above the depressingly low level at present. It could make people a little less cynical, a little more ready to take pride in something we really stand for. Active neutrality could give us a role to play in international affairs as enriching as any, which other nations might emulate when they also see that, far from being an anachronism, it is more sensible and more rewarding than all the other options available in the modern conditions of the threat of nuclear war. With the will and the foresight and the courage of our political leaders, active neutrality could strengthen our commitment to the European Community, as this book makes clear, offering the service of neutrality to the peoples of Europe, instead of the begging-bowl in one hand and the weak compromise in the other, which has become the traditional posture of our officials in their negotiations with the representatives of the other states.